CHEVRONS

Illustrated History and

CHEVRONS

Catalog of U.S. Army Insignia

William K. Emerson
Lieutenant Colonel, U.S. Army

Smithsonian Institution Press
Washington, D.C.   1983

Library of Congress Cataloging in Publication Data

Emerson, William K., 1941–
Chevrons, illustrated history and catalog of U.S. Army insignia.

Includes index.
1. United States. Army— Insignia. I. Title.
UC533.E43 355.1'4
82-600002
ISBN 0-87474-412-1
AACR2

The paper in this book meets the guidelines for permanence and durability of the Committee on Production Guidelines for Book Longevity of the Council on Library Resources.

This book was designed by Carol Hare Beehler and edited by Ruth W. Spiegel.

TO MARCIE

A wife who has cheerfully moved all around the world with me for seventeen years.

CONTENTS

LIST OF TABLES

FOREWORD

Insignia—military, ecclesiastical, or civil—have, for thousands of years, served as outward manifestations of rank and function in hierarchical organizations or societies. Consequently the collection and study of insignia can greatly aid both historian and curator in describing or reconstructing organizations of the past.

In his history of the chevron in the United States Army, Colonel Emerson has described and analyzed the evolution and development of the insignia of enlisted ranks in the United States Army from its beginning in 1775 up to the present day. By doing so, he has given the scholar a research tool as useful for the study of the institutional history of the Army as the carbon-dating method is for archeology. For example, knowledge of the chevron's date of design and manufacture is a necessary element in fixing the dates of old pictures of soldiers in uniform.

When the War Department became the Department of the Army in 1947, over three hundred different chevrons had been authorized and since that time more than a score have been added. The author has succeeded in bringing order to this highly complex subject. Students of military history will long be in Colonel Emerson's debt for this achievement.

James L. Collins, Jr.
Brigadier General, United States Army
Chief of Military History, Department of the Army

PREFACE

This book started ten years ago as a short magazine article and got out of hand. Actually, as a collector and researcher of military insignia, with some unidentifiable urge to lay out information in a logical way, I wanted to describe the evolution of enlisted chevrons in a sequential order, noting the forms that might be systematically grouped together. As a military insignia collector for several years, I had picked up various chevrons and enlistment stripes, but found no one who could tell me much about them. I researched to satisfy my own curiosity and gathered fragmented notes about many old chevrons still readily available. As the notes grew, it became apparent a brief magazine article was insufficient—and even now this volume is far from an exhaustive history of Regular Army chevrons. Given all this information, it is logical to ask if a particular chevron is scarce or common. How scarce is a particular chevron? Is it rare? Worth money? If only twenty-five men ever wore it, it must be scarce! To too many people, the degree of rarity is an important consideration. But degrees of scarcity or relative values are not discussed in the book, although in some cases the number of men who wore a particular chevron is noted. In many instances, the number of people authorized to wear a chevron and the scarcity of the chevron are not in fact linked. Today a chevron three hundred men wore may be more scarce than a chevron only thirty men would have worn. Army supply activities long since completed dictate scarcity today.

While visiting one dealer I was shown a box of ten thousand chevrons, all of the same rank. He was slowly selling the chevrons at shows to collectors one at a time, and to other dealers in small lots. I took a sample with a note of the markings on the box that indicated the insignia were from a World War I contract, and commented it would be a long time before all ten thousand chevrons were sold. The fellow then showed me two more crates, each containing twenty thousand of the same chevrons! *He had enough to outfit the entire AEF in 1918 for that one rank.* The Army had several other grades with many more than fifty thousand men in World War I, yet chevrons for these more common grades are not as easily found today. The government has destroyed many chevrons, and in some cases, it purchased the correct number so that few were left as excess.

More interesting are the truly scarce chevrons. Research uncovered a chevron authorized for only one man; the Army made only three pairs. One pair was issued to the soldier. By discussing the chevron with the dealer from whom I had obtained mine, I was able to determine who owned two of the other three chevrons. The noting of such facts in the text would encourage reproduction of selected chevrons, however, and there is far too much of that activity today, with some people preying on the public and even on museums if the ruse can be made successful.

For over ninety years excess Civil War chevrons were available, but it was interest in the Civil War Centennial that caused Civil War buffs to buy up in two or three years the thousands of insignia surplus dealers had not been able to sell at virtually give-away prices in nearly a century. Enough on scarcity. Suffice it to say value does not run with the number of men authorized to wear a chevron.

For many collectors and historians, Mr. J. Duncan Campbell is a legend in his own time. A most generous and friendly man who began collecting as a youth in the later 1920s, he has wide knowledge of insignia; the various collections he has assembled are marvelous. Although I first met Duncan Campbell over twenty years ago, a most dramatic experience occurred in 1973. Duncan was gravely ill and not expected to live. Before his "last" trip to the hospital he asked his wonderful wife Peggy to box his chevron collection, with instructions that should he die the chevrons were to be given to me. Happily Duncan recovered. He sent me the chevrons, however, knowing I was researching this book and still active with my collection. Some pieces truly are unique, gathered over the years—and then given away! Such generosity is humbling. With people like Duncan in the world, the least I can do is share my knowledge with others. Duncan himself has generally disposed of his collections now and is not active, but he does do research and always has a tidbit of knowledge to share with researchers.

Dr. Opal Landrum, of the Army's Institute of Heraldry, and Mr. Donald Kloster of the Smithsonian Institution both encouraged me to complete this work, and both were most generous with their time. Without their assistance and encouragement, I would not have continued. Donald Kloster also had the foresight to encourage me to study service chevrons as well as rank chevrons, since the Army treated them in similar ways. I am in debt to both of these people. In addition, I want to thank the Division of Military History, Smithsonian Institution, for allowing many of its chevrons to be illustrated here. Without the use of this excellent chevron collection and the photographs, this book would have been far less complete.

As a professional army officer I and my family move every year or two; in 17 years of military service, we have been in the same house for two consecutive Christmases only once. This series of moves entailed obtaining new typists at each post. The number of people who assisted in the typing and gave helpful suggestions is too great to mention. Nonetheless, I would like to single out some of the generous people who helped with this book: Mrs. Myrna Carpenter of Ft. Knox; Shirley Rexroat of Stillwater, Oklahoma; Mrs. Ester Seminare of Ft. Belvoir, Virginia; and Mrs. Linda Dupke and Mrs. Karen Maas of the Detroit area. Mr. Howard Churchill of Manassas, Virginia, took most of the photos showing my collection, although Mr. David Waters of Muskogee, Oklahoma, also assisted by taking some pictures. Helpful suggestions as to content were given by Duncan Campbell, Don Houston, Bruce Bazelon, Leonard Ball, and Mrs. Muriel Cutter. Without the encouragement of those cited, and most of all my wife, I would not have been able to complete this work. I thank all who have helped me. There are no doubt errors and omissions. They are mine, and there would have been more were it not for the help of the people here acknowledged.

W. K. E.

PUBLISHER'S INTRODUCTION

This book is the first to describe, catalog, and provide an identification guide to chevrons worn by members of the United States Army throughout its history.

Description is based on visual recognition of chevron design and manufacture and on historical evidence. To organize the history of chevrons, service stripes, and to a lesser extent of uniforms and Army organization as it pertains to insignia authorization, the years from the American Revolution to the present have been divided into four major chronological periods: pre–1872, 1872–1902, 1902–1920, and post–1920. Chapters 2, 3, 5, and 7 tell the historical story for these four periods respectively. Sources are mainly official documents such as Army regulations, orders, annual reports, and other staff papers and are indicated in the text with superior note numbers of the style.[1] The notes themselves are located at the back of the book.

Cataloging is based on a single numbering system. Each catalog number identifies:

(i) Period of authorization or dates of use. The hundreds digit controls:

Chronological Period	Catalog No.
pre–1872	1–99
1872–1902	100–199
1902–1920	200–399
post–1920	400–499
Special chevrons, awards, and other insignia	500–

Not all numbers are currently in use. Newly identified or authorized chevrons can be assigned numbers within the appropriate hundred (and where necessary within the appropriate tens) without disturbing the entire system.

(ii) Chevron design. This is the distinctive configuration of bars, devices, and/or wreaths tied to a rank or grade title and sometimes a branch of service. In abstract, design is the symbol that distinguishes personnel of one rank from persons of all other ranks within a given period of United States Army history. In use, design tells who wore the chevron.

NOTE on the numbering system: So that all chevrons in use during the fourth period, 1920 to the present, can bear catalog numbers in the 400 series, certain numbers (403, 404, 405, and 406) have been assigned to chevrons that also appear in the 300 series:

Pre–1920	Post–1920
Lance Corporal, Catalog No. 314	Private First Class, Catalog No. 406
Corporal, Catalog No. 313	Corporal, Catalog No. 405
Sergeant, Catalog No. 312	Sergeant, Catalog No. 404
Sergeant First Class, Catalog No. 337	Staff Sergeant, Catalog No. 403

The post–1920 chevrons listed are identical to the corresponding pre–1920 chevrons except for the colors. Double numbering has been assigned in one other case only, and for a similar reason: the pioneer's chevron for the pre–1872 period is assigned Catalog No. 15, and the pioneer's chevron of the post–1920 period is assigned Catalog No. 151. Chevron Nos. 15 and 151 have identical designs.

Illustration is provided for each catalog number to assist identification. Line drawings of chevron design, photographs of actual chevrons, drawings and photographs of chevrons on a uniform, and historical photographs of soldiers wearing their chevrons are used.

In Chapters 2, 4, 6, and 8, illustrations are presented throughout the text. Chapters 4, 6, and 8 are composed of illustrations with expanded captions functioning as text.

In Chapter 7, catalog information is summarized in tables containing illustrations. This use of tables was devised for the post–1920 period because after World War I chevrons came and went in similar-looking groups. Table 2-2 is used to summarize catalog information for the pre–1872 period.

Illustration and table numbering is of the style Figure 1-1, Table 1-1, to indicate chapter of occurrence. Appendix tables are numbered 9A-1 to 9A-5.

The first four illustrations in Chapter 1 are basic to the system, as follows:
Figure 1-1 is typical of the pre–1872 period.
Figure 1-2 is typical of the 1872–1902 period.
Figure 1-3 is typical of the 1902–1920 period.
Figure 1-4 is typical of the post–1920 period.

Color is acknowledged as a special and complex problem in chevron identification. This is true for branch color or color otherwise specified in regulations, and for arbitrary color variations of the backing cloth or background due to material and style of manufacture used.

To allow completeness and specificity of chevron identification, two systematic indicators are used in addition to the catalog numbering system. These two indicators are branch designation and manufacturing code.

Branch designation. For pre–World War I chevrons, designation of branch of service is necessary owing to the Army's practice of giving an arm, service, or department its own distinctive one or two colors. These colors underwent change historically, evolving as did the Army.

Manufacturing code. This letter system was devised to amplify description and provide general keys for ready recognition of chevron types with respect to color, materials, and style of manufacture. A letter is used to indicate the type and color of material used for the design, device, and/or background, the cut of the cloth, and the appliqué or stitching method.

Manufacturing codes are listed by chronological periods in Chapters 2, 3, 5, 7, and 8, respectively. Table 9A-1 summarizes the code in its entirety.

Code letters may be repeated when a manufacturing style is applicable to more than one rank. A group of chevrons produced by the same manufacturing process and worn during the same period constitutes a set; the same manufacturing code is applicable to all chevrons in a given set.

NOTE: During both world wars, the War Department compounded the chevron color and material problem by procuring chevrons not of the specified materials and colors, and then issuing these nonstandard insignia to the troops. For this reason, it is impossible to place an accurate identification code on all chevrons made. An attempt has been made to apply manufacturing codes in the case of World War I chevrons; each code identifies one type of material or manufacturing technique generally used at the time. World War II is more difficult in this respect. It is believed that use of codes for this period may cause confusion, as certain chevrons may not fit into any code designation. For this reason, no code letters have been used in the text covering the fourth chronological period, post–1920. Table 9A-1 nevertheless includes probable code letters for chevrons of this period. This listing allows extension of the manufacturing code system to identify chevrons of current manufacture.

Identification Guide: Use of the Catalog Numbers and Manufacturing Code Letters

This book is designed for use by the passerby, the devotee, the museum curator, and the chevron specialist alike. The use of numbers and letters is especially important in cataloging museum or private holdings with a minimum of written labeling, computer terms, or property card space.

To identify a Regular Army rank chevron, the illustrations in this book are the primary aids. The searcher follows this route:

First. Identify during which of the four chronological periods the particular chevron was made. This is most easily done by looking at Figures 1-1 through 1-4, each representative of a period of chevron use:

Figure 1-1   pre–1872
Figure 1-2   1872–1902
Figure 1-3   1902–1920
Figure 1-4   post–1920

19

Second. To match the chevron to its catalog number, consult the illustrations in the following locations:

Pre–1872	Table 2-2
1872–1902	Chapter 4 entire
1902–1920	Chapter 6 entire
post–1920	Tables 7-2, 7-3, 7-4, 7-6, 7-7, 7-8, 7-9, and 7-11

Third. Go to Table 9A-1 to identify the manufacturing code letter and thus determine color, material, and style of manufacture with greatest specificity.

Two examples of use of the identification guide follow:
Catalog No. *126, f, artillery* would identify an artillery drum major's chevron on khaki cloth. The catalog number, in this case *126*, indicates who wore the chevron—a drum major—and the *f* shows the chevron was made for the khaki uniform with the bars of the chevron formed using chain stitching, while "artillery" indicates that the chevron is red with black stitching.

Catalog No. *326, r* would identify a World War I chauffeur's chevron on olive drab wool. The catalog number again shows the design and who wore the insignia, while the *r* translates to the background material of olive drab wool and a design of similar material.

Appendixes

Appendix 1 is composed of tables:
Table 9A-1 is a summary of manufacturing code letters.
Tables 9A-2 through 9A-5 are alphabetical listings by rank title of the catalog numbers for each of the four chronological periods. For example, if a searcher starts with a reference to a color sergeant in the early 1900s, Table 9A-4 will show that the catalog number is 309.

Appendix 2 provides additional information on the 1920 conversion of enlisted grades, a systematic revision not well understood by many people. Prior to 1920, Congress dictated the pay of each and every rank, i.e., each and every job. In 1920 Congress simply fixed seven pay grades and the Army distributed the jobs among these seven grades. To trace a soldier and his chevron through the 1920 conversion, first determine what job (rank title) he had before 1920; this rank identifies his chevron, as illustrated in Chapter 6. Appendix 2 lists the post–1920 *grade* equivalents of the pre-conversion *jobs*. Through the illustrated tables in Chapter 7 the particular chevron that matches the grade and branch can then be identified.

Appendix 3 provides verbatim copy of the F. S. Johnston patent, dated 21 January 1873, for the revolutionized manufacture of chevrons. The invention and patenting of this process was the event that in fact opened the way for the second major period in chevron history.

Terms and Usage	_For terms used in the cataloging system_, consistency as a general rule has been established:
catalog number	the number assigned in this book to each distinctive chevron
design	the configuration of bars, devices, and/or wreaths authorized to represent a rank
device	an emblematic figure, such as a hatchet, circle, flag, horsehead, star, or crescent, used in a design
background	backing material or supporting fabric to which the design is applied in making a chevron
material	fabric and thread of various content and color (mainly khaki, dark blue, olive drab, white, and green for background; branch color or other for design)
branch color	the distinctive one or two colors assigned by the Army historically to an arm, service, or department
manufacture	method of fabrication by which the design is applied to the background
manufacturing code	the letter assigned in this book to each distinctive manufacturing process, technique, or style. Included are type of material used for design and/or background, color, cut, binding, size, shape, appliqué or stitching method, and position intended in wear. Thus, any given catalog number can have one or more manufacturing codes depending on the uniform for which the chevron was intended.

NOTE: Because of the great variety of materials and manufacturing techniques introduced after World War I, and the wide range of hues that came into general but unauthorized use in the making of chevrons, manufacturing codes have not been applied in the text for the post–1920 period. Probable codes for this period have been included, however, in Table 9A-1.

For historical terms that changed, developed, and evolved, consistency defers to historical appropriateness, and as far as possible the term in use during each chronological period is preferred:

enlistment stripe/service stripe/service chevrons:

Service stripe is preferred.

arm/service/department:

Arms are the fighting units or portions of the Army that engage in combat, such as the infantry and the cavalry. Services and departments are portions of the Army that support and give assistance to the arms, as for example the Medical Department and the Quartermaster Corps. The exact titles of services and departments changed every few years; corps also is a term in constant use. As far as possible, historical accuracy governs the use of these terms in the text.

title/grade/rank:

rank is most commonly preferred, but all three terms are used. As to the specific ranks, writers tend to capitalize the corps titles and often the rank titles as well. For substantive and also orthographic purposes, distinction ought be made between the rank of Sergeant of the Ordnance Corps and the rank of ordnance sergeant. For greatest simplicity, however, and a measure of consistency, the ranks in this text are lower cased and unit titles are capitalized; in tabular material, ranks and unit titles both are capitalized.

Dimensions

All measurements refer to the horizontal distance from edge to edge of a chevron. Illustrations are not to scale.

COLOR PLATES

Color Plate 1

1. A Civil War artillery sergeant's chevron from the National Collection of the Smithsonian Institution. By War Department policy, company NCOs (first sergeants and below) wore chevrons made from worsted binding.

2. A Civil War infantry quartermaster sergeant's chevron. Officially the senior NCOs assigned to regimental headquarters used chevrons made from silk lace, as pictured here.

3. Hospital stewards wore this type of "half chevron" from 1851 until 1887. The chevron came in matched pairs so the lower end would be forward on the soldier's arm.

4. The Army introduced chevrons made with heavy chain stitching in 1872 and at the same time Corps of Engineers colors changed to red with white trim. The combination of manufacturing techniques and the color change is shown in this 1872–1902 Corps of Engineers first sergeant's chevron.

5. Soldiers wore light blue overcoats in the late nineteenth century. To allow greater visibility on overcoats, from 1876 until 1900 infantrymen wore dark blue, nearly black, chevrons of this type on overcoats.

6. The Quartermaster General introduced gold lace chevrons in 1884 for men to wear on dress uniforms. The branch color—yellow for cavalry in this case—formed the background, while the bars and some distinctive devices were composed from the gold. Shown is a cavalry saddler sergeant's chevron, used until the Spanish-American War.

7. A chevron for an ordnance sergeant, 1901–1902. The Ordnance Department used this color until 1902.

8. A Corps of Engineers lance corporal's chevron used on the dress uniform, 1892–1902.

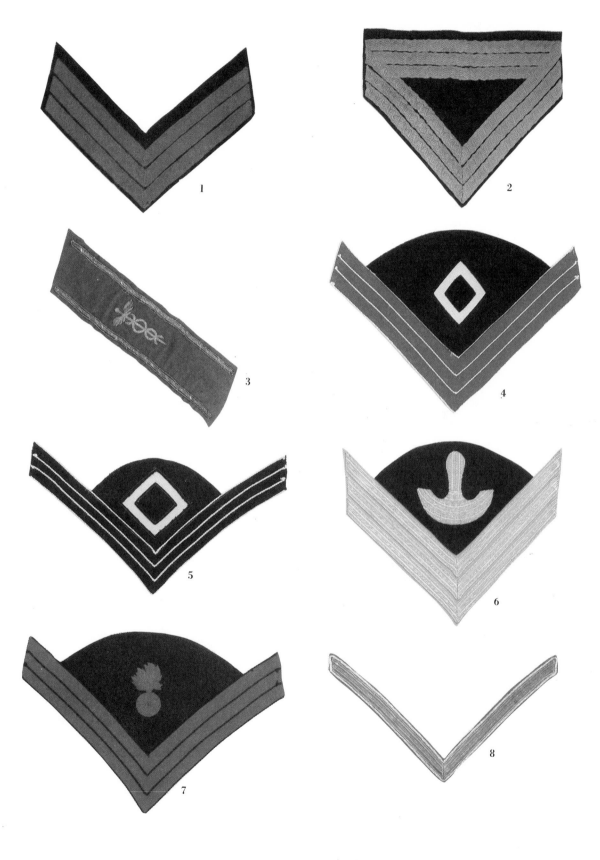

Color Plate 2

1. Coast Artillery Corps troops wore special brown chevrons that matched their work uniforms in the early twentieth century. This chevron has a gunner's device, shown by the red shell, added to a sergeant's chevron.

2. Signal Corps and artillery blue denim work uniforms carried matching denim chevrons shortly before World War I. Heavy stitching outlined bars and designs as in this Signal Corps corporal's chevron from about 1914.

3. Quartermaster Corps cooks and bakers wore buff embroidered chevrons on white cotton. Shown is a chevron for a sergeant serving as a cook, about 1916.

4. Coast Artillery Corps rating for a gun pointer.

5. This chevron is for a Coast Artillery Corps master gunner to wear on khaki uniforms, and was made about 1904. This was the first chevron to use a wreath.

6. First class gunner rating, used by men of the Army Service School Detachment.

7. This chevron is for a Corps of Engineers master engineer senior grade. The chevron is typical of the privately manufactured cotton chevrons of 1918.

8. Enlisted band leaders of 1918–1920 wore chevrons of a star, lyre, and wreath. The long shape, pointed top, and light color of embroidery on this chevron indicate it was made in Europe for United States forces during World War I.

9. This ordnance sergeant's chevron is typical of those insignia made in the United States during World War I for wear on the cotton uniform.

10. This privately manufactured wool chevron for World War I use was intended for Transportation Corps sergeants.

11. In January 1920, the Secretary of War approved several chevrons that, because of subsequent events, soldiers never wore. Shown is the insignia for a master engineer junior grade. Other chevrons in the set come with stars and with other center devices. This chevron represents the first attempt to bring color back to chevrons after World War I.

1

2

3

4

5

6

7

8

9

10

11

Color Plate 3

1. Signal Corps troops began to wear black chevrons with gold lace in 1891. This black, used behind the gold lace bars and arc, is different from the dark blue used as background for the crossed flags and torch. Gold lace chevrons often had hand-embroidered center devices, although the Signal Corps device is the most striking.

2. The Spanish-American War caused the Quartermaster Corps to introduce khaki uniforms and chevrons with khaki backgrounds. The chevron is for a post commissary sergeant as shown both by the design and by the cadet gray color.

3. Service stripes *(top to bottom):*
   a. Cavalry service-in-war for dress uniform, using the pre–1887 light yellow.
   b. Cavalry service-in-war for dress uniform, using the post–1887 medium yellow.
   c. Signal Corps service-in-war for dress uniform, 1884–1889.
   d. War service in artillery, current Hospital Corps Service, 1896–1902.
   e. Infantry war service, 1872–1884.
   f. Artillery war service, 1902–1910.
   g. Artillery peace service, 1902–1910.

4. A privately made hospital steward's chevron, 1901–1902, for the dark blue shirt.

5. In 1903 and 1904 the Quartermaster General's Department made chevrons with background colors to match all four uniforms then prescribed. This insignia was for a post quartermaster sergeant to wear on the khaki coat.

6. This 1903–1904 chevron was for a sergeant first class, Signal Corps, to wear on an olive drab wool coat.

7. The War Department authorized all troops to wear branch-colored chevrons on white coats during 1903 and 1904. The chevron shown is for an Ordnance Corps lance corporal.

8. Between 1905 and 1911 all branches wore khaki chevrons with khaki designs on the summer coats. Some center devices and all wreaths were hand embroidered, as was done with this chevron for an electrician sergeant first class.

9. Shown here is a chevron for engineers, Coast Artillery Corps, about 1910.

10. Shown here is a chevron for a private first class, Medical Corps. The round background indicates the insignia was made after 1908, while the use of colors shows it was made for dress uniforms before World War I.

11. In late 1916 and early 1917 the drum major was also the first sergeant of the regimental headquarters company and wore this design of chevron. The particular chevron is for an infantry first sergeant (drum major) dress uniform.

12. Shown is a corporal's chevron, United States Military Academy Army Service Detachment, 1909–World War I.

13. Shown here is a chevron for dress uniform, 1926–World War II. The gray bars with yellow piping indicate that this chevron was for a Finance Department sergeant.

Color Plate 4

1. This 1920–1942 first sergeant's chevron is typical of the official rank insignia made before 1939, with the design cut out of olive drab cloth and sewn onto a navy blue background.

2. The War Department did not authorize specialist or branch devices in post–1920 chevrons (those with olive drab designs on navy blue backing), but many units allowed men to wear them nevertheless, as was the case with this sergeant's chevron for a man assigned to a tank unit.

3. A staff sergeant's World War II rayon woven chevron.

4. This sergeant's chevron shows embroidery commonly used in the 1920s and early 1930s. The War Department authorized neither the tan design nor the Signal Corps device.

5. A typical unauthorized specialist chevron used between 1920 and 1942. These came on khaki backgrounds (shown) and on navy blue backgrounds, and both with specialty marks (Air Corps shown) and without specialty marks.

6. Shown here is a technician fifth grade's wool chevron introduced at the close of World War II for Women's Army Corps beige dresses.

7. Women began wearing these taupe and goldenlite 2-inch-wide chevrons at the time of the Korean War.

8. Women have been wearing white chevrons with gold designs on optional white uniforms since 1951. Shown is a chevron for a sergeant first class from the Korean War era.

9. A noncombat corporal's chevron of the type worn between 1948 and 1951.

10. Combat troops wore blue designs on gold, like this first sergeant's chevron, for three years, starting in 1948. The particular chevron shown was made in Germany for United States forces.

11. Men and women alike wore 2-inch-wide specialist insignia in the 1950s. This is a chevron for a specialist E-8.

12. A staff sergeant chevron for men's dress blue uniforms of the 1970s is shown here.

13. This is a typical Vietnamese-made chevron, used when men wore subdued cloth chevrons on fatigue clothing, about 1967.

CHAPTER 1

The Story of Chevrons, Uniforms, and Service Stripes

Chevron History: An Overview

If generals provide the brain power of the army and enlisted personnel function as the muscle needed to carry out decisions, then surely the noncommissioned officer is the backbone. It is the NCO who links policy decisions from the top level with their ultimate execution at the lowest levels. He transforms objectives into actions. He has served proudly and effectively throughout the history of the United States Army, and his distinctive rank insignia—the chevron—is as well known to the average American as is the general's star.

Americans often see chevrons in historical photographs, and many people relish actual photographs of army troops in the field. Civil War soldiers in casual repose or row upon row of an entire World War I regiment ready for parade are exactly captured by the camera. Determined officers, in the center, stare through time and are flanked by their key subordinates—various sergeants and corporals. One may recognize many enlisted ranks immediately: the first sergeant with a diamond in addition to other marks on his coat sleeve, the "buck sergeant" with three cloth V-shaped bars, and the corporal with two bars. The movement of time was halted when the camera winked at the assembled sergeants and the men. Forever frozen, the moment is presented to us, never to be changed.

When we study the picture, other sergeants may be identified—sergeants because they have the chevrons of a sergeant, but not a "regular" sergeant as is clear from the other markings seen with the stripes. These are devices which may be as diversified as hatchets, a circle, flags, or a horsehead. Some viewers quickly scan the photographs and pass on to other interests, but certain observers may be roused to ask, "What rank is that?" or "When was that chevron used?" The answers, one hopes, are to be found in this book.

The American noncommissioned officer rank insignia has evolved over the past one hundred and fifty years from a hodgepodge of sashes, epaulets, cockades, and other displays to today's limited set of standardized, stylized chevrons. During this evolutionary period, however, chevrons were available in a variety of sizes, shapes, styles, and colors.

This book is designed to acquaint the reader, be he passerby or devotee, with the history of United States Army chevrons from the earliest days until the present. The subject is complex and confusing, even to the scholar; the old War Department had authorized well over three hundred different chevrons before yielding to the Department of the Army in 1947, and more than twenty chevron designs have been authorized since then. Colonel Robert E. Wyllie, Chief of the War Department section charged with designing new chevrons in 1920, explained that there were so many chevrons in use that even he could not recognize them all.

The history of United States chevrons may be usefully divided into four chronological periods: pre–1872, 1872–1902,

1902–1920, and post–1920. This book presents a chevron catalog system based upon these four periods. Despite the inherent difficulty in dividing any evolutionary process into discrete segments, this division into chronological periods is based on historical criteria and is therefore able to bring satisfactory organizational results.

Various writers have cataloged military medals, buttons, ribbons, and other insignia but chevrons, owing to their many variables, cannot easily be identified and cataloged—and in fact never have been cataloged before. There are complexities on all fronts. The Army often used one basic design for several different titles of ranks or grades, and changes were made in the backing upon which a given design was fabricated. A chevron design may have been shrunk, enlarged, inverted, or otherwise modified; the rank title, meanwhile, may also have changed. Basic designs changed title, titles switched from one design to another, and in terms of use, designs came and went and then came back again. To provide a permanent, standard, and common means of reference, each distinctive chevron design has been given a catalog number; this is the heart of the present work.

Chevrons of the Pre–1872 Period

Chevrons used before 1872 are described in Chapter 2 and are assigned catalog numbers below 100.

Figure 1-1. A first sergeant stands with his buddy at leisure during their Civil War enlistment. The chevrons shown in this photograph are typical of those in use during the first period of chevron history, pre–1872. Usually the chevron background was not so noticeably different from the coat as appears in this example.

Some United States enlisted rank chevrons were introduced shortly after the War of 1812. The exact shape and size of the insignia from these early years cannot always be precisely listed. *In 1829, chevrons were withdrawn, but were reintroduced four years later in new form.* Since 1833, chevrons have been used continuously for one branch or another of the United States Army. Before the 1850s, chevrons were made by sewing strips of cloth directly to coat sleeves. Starting about 1851, chevrons were generally made by sewing stripes onto a piece of backing material which was subsequently applied to the coat.

Chevrons of the 1872–1902 Period

Chevrons made from 1872 through 1902 are listed in Chapter 4 and are assigned catalog numbers in the 100s.

In 1872, the Army adopted chevrons made by a new manufacturing process. This new manufacturing technique, patented by F. S. Johnston, completely changed the way the United States Army made chevrons, and the patent is included as Appendix 3 so readers may see in the original the change that started the second of the four periods of chevron history. The heavy chain stitching used to make the 1872–1902 chevrons makes them visually different from all other chevrons. The three V's of a sergeant's chevron, for example, were made from a single piece of material, and each bar was outlined by the new heavy stitching.

Shortly after 1872, the War Department published Quartermaster Clothing and Equipage Specifications. These specifications established standard manufacturing criteria. In addition, the War Department began to improve military record keeping at that time, so that there is a sizeable increase of information available to historians. Thus, 1872 is a suitable date for ending the first period of chevron history, in terms not only of manufacture but also of documentation standards.

At the end of the nineteenth century, the Army made a major effort to upgrade NCO prestige. The attempt caused a trend toward more specialty ranks and contributed to a proliferation of NCO grades. Color sergeants, signal sergeants, and even lance acting hospital stewards, to name a few, were given their own distinctive grades and chevron designs. Before this time the rank system was unsophisticated, but to stimulate the desire for men to specialize, the Army adopted more and more distinctive chevrons. Thus, the third period of chevron history began—and the chevron came to represent not only a soldier's rank but also his job.

Chevrons of the 1902–1920 Period

Chevrons made from 1902 through 1920 are listed in Chapter 6 and are assigned catalog numbers 200 through 399.

Because of the great variety of chevrons introduced in this period, this run of catalog numbers is further subdivided into

Figure 1-2. The soldier in this photograph is wearing chevrons typical of the second period of chevron history, 1872–1902.

Figure 1-3. This 1910 photograph shows First Sergeant Amos Hay, Company F, 30th Infantry Regiment (at the Flushing Barracks, New York City), wearing a uniform and chevrons typical of those in use during the third period of chevron history, 1902–1920.

groups of ten and twenty. Large *V-shaped* chevrons began—at the end of 1902—to be replaced by small *inverted V* chevrons of the size and shape worn today.

The proliferation of special-use distinctive chevrons began during the Spanish-American War and continued beyond World War I. As an example of this growth, by 1919 the Medical Department alone had seven different chevrons that no other branch used. The design and manufacture of chevrons for many special enlisted grades was complicated by expansion of the Army for World War I. Another factor was the creation of new specialists and the associated need for new rank insignia. The overwhelming problems of pay, grade titles, and allowances—with duplication of authorizing legislation—caused Congress in 1920 to consolidate all ranks into seven pay grades.

Chevrons of the Post–1920 Period

Chevrons made from 1920 on are listed in Chapter 7 and are assigned catalog numbers in the 400s.

Fashions changed, and the Army responded by replacing the high-collar coat with a lapel coat shortly after World War I. This change generally coincides with the beginning of the fourth and final period in the history of chevrons. The general cut of the coat and the chevron designs remain basically unchanged today.

This fourth period, which began in 1920, resulted from the congressional decision to simplify the enlisted ranks structure to seven basic pay grades. As went the structure, so went the chevrons. This resulting simplifcation of ranks was accom-

Figure 1-4. This January 1942 photograph of First Sergeant Corbett Meeks, 38th Infantry Regiment (at Fort Sam Houston, Texas) shows special chevrons typical of those in use between the two world wars, the early part of the fourth period of chevron history, post–1920. On the lower left sleeve Sergeant Meeks wears service chevrons indicating his many years in the army.

panied by a changeover in chevron rationale in 1920 to the basic concept used by the United States Army today: a chevron represents a pay grade, not a job.

Prior to 1920 Congress had created each rank within the Army in such a way as to give each job a distinctive title and pay, and the Army then would issue a unique chevron for each rank. The 1920 congressional overhaul of this cumbersome system created seven pay grades.

Correlated Uniform Regulations

It is enlightening to inspect the uniforms on which chevrons were worn. Conveniently, chevron changeover dates approximate uniform changeover dates. Until recently, governing regulations were seldom clear since the sole suppliers of enlisted uniforms were the Army Quartermaster offices. If a change were to be made, it was accomplished before the supply depot issued the items. Consequently, documented information on what soldiers actually wore during much of the nineteenth century is now difficult to obtain and in fact supply records and War Department interoffice memos are often more informative than the brief regulations.

Nineteenth-century uniforms can generally be classified as intended for dress or for field wear. Uniforms other than those intended for dress or field wear were in fact used by the Army, but on these garments there were no chevrons. Canvas stable clothing and white uniforms used by mess hall waiters and for summer undress wear are two examples of special uniforms authorized late in the last century that are in neither the dress nor the field uniform category. They are not, however, pertinent to an examination of chevrons as no rank insignia was worn on them. Dress type uniforms were actually at times classified as "full dress" and at other times simply as "dress" depending on additions to the over-all uniform.

Field uniforms of the nineteenth century varied a great deal. Generally, the term "fatigue uniform" referred to a uniform worn in the field, or worn during special duties (such as stable duty). At times, specially designed uniforms were worn for field use. Examples of this are the fatigue coats prescribed during the Mexican War, the undress five-button blue coat used during most of the post–Civil War Indian campaigns, and khaki uniforms of the Spanish-American War. Drab uniforms became dominant in the early twentieth century, when soldiers wore the dress blue uniform only once or twice a year. This increasing use of field uniforms was finally completed in World War I when all Army members wore only the field uniform, regardless of occasion. Although General Pershing's uniform was not identical to that of doughboy in the trench, the basic color and cut were the same. During World War II, special twill fatigue uniforms were introduced for field use; this relegated the khaki and olive drab uniforms to the undress role, although the same chevrons were worn on all uniforms. In 1956, green uniforms were introduced. Jungle fatigues came into use during the Vietnam War. Naturally, chevrons changed directly as a result of these and other uniform changes.

Service Stripes

Service chevrons, commonly called "hash marks" or service stripes, were established by George Washington to show completion of three years' service, but after the Revolution they fell into disuse. Reinstituted in 1832, they have been authorized in one form or another ever since. These service chevrons in some instances showed the branch of the enlistment and the distinction between peacetime and wartime service. Originally, men wore service chevrons on both sleeves of various uniforms, but during the 1890s soldiers wore service chevrons only on dress uniforms. Today service chevrons have evolved into a simple embroidered stripe worn on the left sleeve of the uniform coat.

Special Chevrons, Awards, and Insignia

Special chevrons and miscellaneous insignia are listed in Chapter 8 and are assigned catalog numbers in the 500s and 600s, subdivided as necessary.

Many miscellaneous insignia look like and are often confused with chevrons. Further compounding the problem of chevron identification is the fact that supply personnel in the Quartermaster General's Department classed many assorted insignia as chevrons. It is convenient to follow this precedent now; therefore, miscellaneous insignia that are closely related to chevrons have been included in Chapter 8.

Chevron Identification: Complexities of Color, Period, and Style

To extend this brief overview of chevrons in the United States Army, it must be noted that many factors influence the authorization of a particular chevron at any given time. These factors include Army organization, public sentiment, mood of Congress, the introduction of new uniforms, and the quantity of outdated chevrons on hand following a changeover. Although the United States Army changed chevron designs in an evolutionary manner, and did not comply with any long-term master scheme, it will be seen that there *was* an over-all logic for any given period of time.

Army regulations call for many twentieth-century chevrons and all nineteenth-century chevrons to be made in a different color for each branch of service. Complete identification, therefore, depends on branch color as well as design. To further complicate the identification problem, different chevrons of similar basic design and color appeared on many authorized uniforms simultaneously. In 1903, for example, a

34

Figure 1-5. A diagonal service stripe on the lower sleeve was first authorized during the Revolution to show a completed enlistment. This 1895 ordnance sergeant's six stripes on the lower sleeve indicate he has served six enlistments. Colors behind the gilt lace indicate the branches of war service or peacetime enlistments.

sergeant might have worn four different chevrons: the first type on his white summer coat, the second on his khaki coat, the third on his olive drab winter uniform, and the fourth on his dress blue uniform. Yet the chevrons he wore were all of similar design and color, differing only in the background material upon which the chevron had been made. Two years later a sergeant could have worn four types of chevrons, three of which differed from those of 1903; these many chevrons can then be distinguished by the style of manufacture or by the size.

During and after World War I, however, branch colors on chevrons disappeared. Now the distinguishing features become the kinds of material used in fabricating the design as well as the color variations and materials used for the backing cloth or background. World War I also saw the start of a new phenomenon: *private* manufacturers made a great many chevrons, and soldiers often wore these rather than chevrons issued by the government. Through this practice, chevrons of unauthorized design and manufacturing style came into wide use. While distinctive chevron designs may be classified and cataloged, the great variety of materials and color shades are never ending. Today one may find a World War I "olive drab" chevron that was in practice made in a bewildering number of hues—from light tan to bright green to chocolate brown. During World War II the same difficulty arose; moreover, during both wars the War Department itself compounded the problem by procuring chevrons not of the specified materials and colors, and then issuing these insignia to the troops.

Chevron identification information is drawn heavily from official documents, but it must be remembered that even though a precise date can be assigned to the introduction of a chevron by extracting information from orders, regulations, or staff papers, *in practice* dates of usage may not have even been within a year or two of the official time period. The United States Army, like many organizations, suffered from delays; when a new chevron was introduced, this delay might be caused by several factors. Distribution of the new general order or circular was required. Quartermasters then had to submit requests to depots, which oftentimes did not have the device in stock. Initial production of some chevrons occurred at least six months after the initial authorization. Finally, if designs or colors changed, the earlier chevron continued to be issued until all of the older stocks were depleted. As a result, many chevrons had a long wear-out period, and the collector or researcher has a difficult time fixing an introduction date for a particular chevron. In some cases official records show when a particular item was first made or worn, but in other cases it is doubtful whether the initial date of use was even within a year of authorization.

Chevron Illustration: Line Drawings and the Likenesses of History

In this book, line drawings of individual designs are supplied both in the text and in tables; so also are drawings of chevrons on distinctive uniforms. Historical photographs, however, have been the preferred choice of medium, and an effort has been made to use photographs not widely published or, in some instances, never previously published. Many of these photographs have been cropped and enlarged to illustrate a particular chevron as actually worn by an individual soldier. In these photographs we may see what was in fact *used*, a far more satisfactory effort than simply studying sterile regulations. Seated in front of a studio backdrop or outside in the sun, the soldiers of yesteryear offer us a chance to notice their uniforms, inspect their chevrons, and let their story fasten on our imagination.

CHAPTER 2

Evolution of Early Chevrons, Uniforms, and Service Stripes / Catalog of Pre—1872 Chevrons: The First Period

European Precedents and Early American Designs 1815—1832

Like many components of United States history, chevrons have their origins in early use by the French and British, the major powers during the formative years of the thirteen colonies' confederation. The French appear to have introduced "lace" on the sleeve as a means of showing rank, a specialty, or previous service.

Until the eighteenth century, uniforms from one country's various regiments and arms were as diversified as the uniforms of entire armies are today. The history of particular seventeenth- and eighteenth-century French and British insignia is found not on the national level, but considerably lower—at the regiment. (For example, within a few French units the use of lace applied to cuffs as a means of distinguishing rank appears to start in the late seventeenth century, although details are vague. The first firm date is in 1766.) French gunners attached to various colonial units were authorized to wear distinguishing chevrons on the coat sleeves above the elbow. Chevron colors varied with the legion to which the gunners were attached, starting with the initial use of white chevrons on the left sleeve for men attached to the Legion de Saint-Dominique (present-day Haiti). By 1772 several French units had the gunners wearing chevrons of blue, red, green, yellow, and white.[1] [Notes are located in the Notes and Abbreviations section at the back of the book.]

The home French army adopted chevrons for time in service in 1771, and the colonial troops initiated wearing of the devices in 1775. An Order of the King, dated 8 August 1775, prescribed for all noncommissioned officers, soldiers, and drummers who reenlisted a reward of cash or land, and a "distinctive mark" on the left arm, "a chevron of wool ribbon" that was the color of the facings of the uniform. The basis for the general French scheme of wearing lace on the cuff to indicate rank, and lace above the elbow to show length of service or specialty, was established in the 1760s and 1770s.[2]

British origins of chevrons are murky, owing to the lack of complete records. It is clear, however, that a few British units introduced chevrons in 1777, and that most British units transitioned to rank chevrons at the start of the nineteenth century. In 1802 the British line infantry and line cavalry adopted the chevrons scheme still essentially in use: two and three V-shaped bars worn point down, midway between the shoulder and elbow. During the next few years other British units adopted similar chevrons, with the single V-shaped bar coming into use in 1815.[3]

In 1815 General Winfield Scott exchanged correspondence with various United States War Department officials concerning the possibility that rank on the new uniforms with wings could be shown by "angles" on the sleeve. One letter concerning sample coats directed artillery sergeants "to wear three chevrons on the left arm, the Corporals two on the right (thus VV—)."[4] This even ties in with the British practice of some chevrons worn on one sleeve.

It might be assumed that the General Winfield Scott letters established the first chevrons in the United States Army. The Army would not have had to amend regulations to show this addition, since all enlisted uniforms were supplied by the Commissary General of Purchases; the new chevrons could have simply been added to noncommissioned officers' coats as the Army issued the uniforms.

The British had introduced more chevrons in 1815 and 1816; in the United States, West Point cadets initially wore chevrons in 1817. Even though cadet uniforms varied considerably from those of the Army, this introduction of a new insignia at West Point may have been influenced by the introduction of chevrons into the Regular Army. Military Academy officials changed cadet rank devices in 1830 to chevrons similar to the chevrons formally adopted by the Army in 1821.[5] Since the 1830 change in cadet chevrons followed the Army's change, it is not too unreasonable to assume the same thing had occurred in the case of the 1817 introduction of cadet chevrons, although there is no solid evidence.

In 1815 the War Department published *Rules and Regulations for the Field Exercise and Maneuvers of Infantry.* Singled out for special note were two companies in each regiment that were designated as light infantry companies. "Wings" or devices that extended outward from the shoulder seams of the uniform distinguished members of these special units. Prior to the introduction of wings, epaulets generally designated various NCO grades. Epaulets consisted of a cloth strap that extended from mid-shoulder to the shoulder end, terminating in a slightly larger flat cloth oval. The entire device was often reinforced inside by tin or pasteboard. Fringe decorated the edge of the flat oval end. Epaulet fringe size and over-all design distinguished the various enlisted grades.[6]

Epaulet

In contrast to this practice, the 1815 wings were not intended to indicate rank, but actually only decorated the uniform. Since soldiers could not wear both wings and epaulets, another device had to be found to show enlisted ranks. Perhaps the Army found the answer to the problem by introducing chevrons.

On 27 March 1821, the War Department issued a general order containing the first firm reference to the fact that United States soldiers were wearing chevrons:

> *The uniform of the General Staff will remain as at present established [with epaulets as rank insignia]. Officers of Regiments and Corps on duty will wear the uniform of the rank and file of their corps differing only in the quality of the materials with gold or silver wings and lace in lieu of worsted and cotton with chevrons of distinction, viz., Colonel, three on each arm, Lieutenant Colonel two, Majors one, Captains one on the right arm, and Subalterns, one on the left. . . .*[7]

Figure 2-1. Lieutenant Pierce Mason Butler, United States Infantry, is shown wearing, below his elbow, the chevrons prescribed for a subaltern in 1821. A similar scheme was introduced for West Point cadets in 1830, and is still employed today. Lieutenant Butler has wings rather than epaulets on his shoulders.

Shortly afterwards, in July 1821, the War Department published uniform regulations calling for captains to wear chevrons on each arm below the elbow, and for subalterns (equivalent to today's lieutenants) one on each arm below the elbow. "An arc of gold or silver fringe" designated adjutants.[8] In 1829 Army officials began to phase out these officer chevrons, and epaulets again became the insignia of rank.[9]

Despite this 10-year use of chevrons by some officers, most people usually think of enlisted grades when chevrons are mentioned. Since the March 1821 order stated that lace would be worn in lieu of worsted and cotton chevrons of the rank and file, this also implies that at least some enlisted men already wore chevrons. There is no additional evidence on enlisted chevrons, except that the July 1821 regulations call for sergeants major and quartermaster sergeants to wear a single chevron of worsted braid on each arm above the elbow, while sergeants and senior musicians were to wear the same insignia below the elbow, and corporals the chevrons only on the right arm above the elbow.

Since there is no widely published set of regulations before 1821, and since from 1821 to 1825 all NCOs wore the same

Figure 2-2. Catalog No. 1: This drawing shows an 1821 enlisted chevron on the appropriate uniform.

Uniforms and Chevrons 1833–1847

Metal Scale

chevron design, the 1821 enlisted chevrons are all cataloged here as Catalog No. 1. The color of these chevrons was to be the same as the coat trim and varied according to branch. A person might suppose that the 1821 system, or some semblance of it, may have been used after General Scott and others wrote in 1815 of their desire to institute chevrons.

Enlisted chevrons were made of worsted cloth in branch colors. Infantry was prescribed to wear white, artillery yellow, and riflemen black. The War Department did not specify the size and shape of the chevrons other than they be worn point up[10] (inverted V). NCOs wore these rank insignia until 1825 when the chevrons were modified to Catalog No. 2: sergeants major, quartermaster sergeants, and principal musicians would "wear a chevron of worsted braid on each arm above the elbow, with an arc of fringe . . . [connecting] the extreme points of the diverging lines of the chevron." Sergeants had a plain chevron of worsted braid on each arm above the elbow and corporals one on each arm below the elbow. Colors remained the same during the change of these chevrons, as did the brief description, "the angle of the chevrons to point upwards"[11] (inverted V). The Commissary General of Purchases, Callender Irvine, withdrew these chevrons in 1829 and 1830.[12]

Congress authorized the Regiment of Dragoons (now the 1st Cavalry Regiment) in the spring of 1833, and in May the War Department prescribed the men's uniforms, including both dress coats and fatigue jackets. Troops wore metal scales on the shoulders, precluding the use of epaulets as was then prescribed for other soldiers; chevrons therefore became the means of noting enlisted dragoon ranks. The forty sergeants wore "chevrons of three bars, points toward the cuff [V shape] on each sleeve, above the elbow." Corporals were similarly adorned but with only two bars. These were the only two chevron designs worn; the noncommissioned staff and first sergeants followed the tradition of sashes and aiguillettes as distinguishing devices. The War Department established yellow as the color for dragoon coat trim and chevrons. And in the fashion of the time, the ½-inch-wide yellow "worsted binding" was sewn directly on the sleeves of the jackets of sergeants and corporals to make their bars, a practice that continued into the 1850s.[13]

In 1845, the Horse Artillery (Light Company C, 3rd Artillery, also known as Ringgold's Battery) was issued dragoon-type uniforms, and these artillery sergeants and corporals began to wear red chevrons sewn onto both the dress coat and the jacket just like the dragoons. [Many historians regard the terms Horse Artillery and Light Artillery at this time as interchangeable; however, files of the Quartermaster General's Office indicate only the Horse Artillery (Company C, 3rd Artillery) was authorized uniforms in the dragoon style but with red trim. Official

Left:
Figure 2-3. Dragoon Sergeant's coat, 1833. When the Army formed the Regiment of Dragoons in 1833, it provided that two and three bars of yellow lace were to be sewn directly onto the coat sleeves midway between the elbow and shoulder—and by this provision reintroduced chevrons (withdrawn since 1829) for Regular Army use. Lace for the sergeant's chevrons added four and one half cents to the coat costs, while a pair of corporal's chevrons increased the cost of the coat three cents. The sergeant's chevron is Catalog No. 3; the corporal's chevron is Catalog No. 4

Right:
Figure 2-4. First sergeant's chevron, Regiment of Mounted Riflemen, 1851. This chevron was made of green worsted binding sewn directly to the coat sleeve.

letters recently located by Donald Kloster of the Smithsonian Institution show that some War Department officials inadvertently issued the Horse Artillery uniforms to Light Artillery units, since the distinction between the two types of mounted artillery was not fully understood. In various letters the intent of the distinction was brought to the attention of all those concerned and the Horse Artillery uniforms were withdrawn from those Light Artillery units affected.[14]]

Far beyond the Mississippi River, the West called to settlers, and the country needed more soldiers to protect the westward-bound Americans. After allowing a second dragoon regiment, Congress authorized the Regiment of Mounted Riflemen (now the 3rd Cavalry) in 1846. Men in this unique unit wore uniforms similar to the dragoons.[15] Sergeants wore chevrons of three and two bars respectively, point down (V shape), above the elbow. Initially the Quartermaster General issued fatigue uniforms to the Regiment of Mounted Riflemen, but it was not until 1851 that the dress uniforms—with green chevrons for the NCOs—were issued to the regiment, thus introducing chevrons similar to those of the dragoons except for the color.[16]

The Army grew during the Mexican War with the introduction of the first company of engineer troops on 15 May 1846. War Department suppliers selected yellow trim for the enlisted uniforms, the same as used by dragoons and others, but since the engineer uniforms were cut differently, yellow trim for more than one branch caused no confusion.[17]

Uniforms and Chevrons 1847–1860

When the War Department published a new Army regulation in 1847, epaulets and other items continued to show a man's rank for dress uniforms, but for the first time since 1829, fatigue dress chevrons were prescribed for all branches.[18] Some historians believe that chevrons were in wide use before 1847, but the

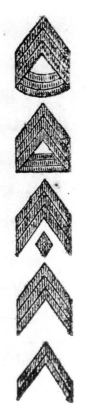

Figure 2-5. The chevrons shown here are taken from the 1847 Regulations. From top to bottom: catalog numbers for these "point up" (inverted V) chevrons are Catalog No. 5, sergeant major; Catalog No. 6, quartermaster sergeant; Catalog No. 7, first sergeant; Catalog No. 8, sergeant; Catalog No. 9, corporal.

evidence is not clear. Sketches and paintings made of infantrymen and artillerymen before 1847 do not show chevrons, although many drawings and paintings made after 1847 clearly show rank chevrons, even for events depicting pre–1847 activities. While this is not conclusive evidence, it does support the belief that the infantry and artillery did not use chevrons between 1830 and 1847.

The 1847 fatigue uniform chevrons are significant in two major aspects. The first is that not for the last time there was a change in the way chevrons pointed. From 1821 through 1829 chevrons had pointed upward (inverted V); the new 1833 dragoon chevrons pointed down (V shape). The War Department change of 1847 caused the ranks to reverse once more and point skyward.

The second significant aspect was introduction of the basic design concept used then for chevrons throughout the remainder of the nineteenth century—namely, sergeants wore three V-shaped bars, with special grades of sergeants wearing additions to the three bars. At this time, first sergeants added a diamond, sergeants major added an arc of three bars, and quartermaster sergeants added a tie of three horizontal bars. As Congress created additional ranks, the Army responded by adding other devices above the sergeant's chevrons as a means of denoting special grades.

Although the Regular Army was now larger than at any previous time, when the 1847 fatigue chevrons were introduced the military was still rather small by today's standards. People often overlook how few men actually wore these early chevrons. The strengths of the various branches is shown in Table 2-1.[19] From this it can be seen that *only about one thousand men in the Regular Army wore chevrons.*

In 1851, new Army regulations instituted several chevron changes. Dragoon trim was switched from yellow to orange. Infantry chevrons changed from white to "light blue or saxony blue." Crimson, which today might be described as light maroon or wine color, became the color for ordnance sergeants and a star was added to their chevrons to further distinguish

TABLE 2-1

Authorized Strengths of Soldiers Who Wore Chevrons in 1849[a]

Type of Unit	Number and Size Unit	Number of Men Authorized Per Unit[b]				
		Sgt.Maj.	QM Sgt.	1/Sgt.[c]	Sgt.	Cpl.
Dragoons	2 Regiments	1	1	10	40	40
Mounted Riflemen	1 Regiment	1	1	10	40	40
Artillery	4 Regiments	1	1	12	48	48
Infantry	8 Regiments	1	1	10	40	40
Engineers	1 Company	0	0	1	10	10

[a] Annual Report of the Adjutant General, 1849.[19]

[b] Also authorized were various chief and principal musicians, chief trumpeters, and 53 ordnance sergeants, all of whom had no special chevrons.

[c] First sergeants were not authorized as a separate grade and were drawn from sergeants.

44

Figure 2-6. This light blue chevron ("point downward") of an infantry first sergeant as used from 1851 through 1872 is Catalog No. 10. "Worsted binding" was used to make chevrons of first sergeants and lower ranks from the Civil War until 1872.

Figure 2-7. This quartermaster sergeant is wearing chevrons (cataloged as No. 11) adopted in 1851. From 1847 until 1851 a similar design, Catalog No. 6, had been authorized—with point up—on the fatigue uniform.

Figure 2-8. Made of crimson silk lace, this type of ordnance sergeant's chevron was issued by the Army from 1851 until 1872. Noncommissioned officers above the first sergeant grade had silk lace chevrons.

these NCOs.[20] Chevrons, just changed to "point up" in 1847, were reversed again when the 1851 Uniform Board simply recorded that by a vote of five to four "the chevrons indicating rank shall be the same form as at present, but that the points shall be downward (V shape) instead of up."[21] The prescribed material for chevrons also changed, with the senior NCOs not assigned to companies (the noncommissioned staff) now wearing bars of silk binding, while company NCOs continued to wear chevrons of worsted binding.[22]

General Order No. 53, published in the fall of 1851, created two more chevrons (i.e, for hospital stewards and pioneers) and marked the first time the War Department authorized insignia for enlisted men who were not NCOs. The Uniform Board which met earlier in the year had overlooked hospital stewards and pioneers. In a special meeting, members quickly acted and

45

the board recommended a unique chevron for hospital stewards. The design incorporated a yellow caduceus two inches long on a "half chevron of emerald green cloth," with ⅛-inch green edges, separated from the rest of the chevron by ⅛-inch yellow stripes.

In creating the unique hospital steward's chevrons, the Uniform Board considered a statement by Joseph Eaton, an Assistant Surgeon from 1821 until his death in 1861,[23] that while the hospital steward enlisted as a private, "the regulations place him in a respectable and responsible situation. . . . and they give him the pay and rations of a Sergeant. . . ."[24] Perhaps the idea that the hospital steward was a cross between a private and a sergeant caused the special design. General Order No. 2, 1857, changed the hospital steward's chevrons from green to buff. The cause for this revision in colors is unknown, but by 1861, the Uniform Regulations again specified green for hospital steward's chevrons.[25]

The Uniform Board in 1851 also created the pioneer's chevrons, which the minutes describe as "two crossed hatchets to be cut from cloth of the color of the collar of the coat . . . [with] the head of the hatchet upwards, its edges outward, of the following dimensions: Handle, 2½-inches long—¼ to ⅓ inches wide. Hatchets, 2 inches long—1 inch wide at edge. . . . " Board members originally visualized a rather detailed insignia, in contrast to the simple device produced. The recommended design is shown in Figure 2-10, along with the adopted insignia.[26]

About this same period, seamstresses for the first time made chevrons by sewing lace onto a background and then sewing the entire insignia onto the coat. The earlier practice of sewing the lace directly onto the coat sleeves continued until the 1870s for some units, particularly for Civil War volunteer units with unusual uniforms.

The first two cavalry regiments (now the 4th and 5th Cavalry) were formed by the Army, as authorized by Act of Congress, 3

Figure 2-9. This typical hospital steward's chevron showing the caduceus is in the National Collection of the Smithsonian Institution.

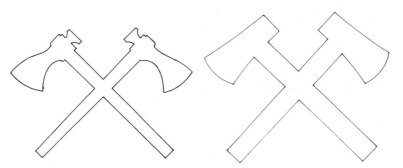

Figure 2-10. The pioneer insignia was adopted in 1851. The drawing on the left shows the officially proposed insignia; the drawing on the right shows what was actually manufactured (Catalog No. 15).

Figure 2-11. Hospital stewards, Petersburg, Virginia, 1864.

March 1855, and yellow was selected as the color for this new branch. Congress authorized one sergeant major and one quartermaster sergeant for each regiment, along with forty sergeants and forty corporals, with some of the sergeants acting as first sergeants.[27]

Uniforms and Chevrons of the Civil War Period to 1872

On 3 August 1861, Congress consolidated dragoons, mounted riflemen, and the cavalry into one branch and renumbered the resulting regiments. Yellow became the color of this consolidated cavalry branch. Owing to this change, regulations officially discontinued orange (for dragoons) and green (for mounted riflemen), while yellow chevrons came into wider use.[28] However, the practice of continued wear of the older uniforms and accouterments—and the great desire of the old dragoon troopers to keep their orange—resulted in some members of the 2nd Dragoons wearing their orange chevrons well

47

into 1863.[29] Certainly, the 1st Dragoons and the Regiment of Mounted Riflemen also kept their distinctive chevrons well past the summer of 1861.

During the Civil War, Regular Army chevrons remained the same as before the war. Ordnance sergeants, sergeants major, and quartermaster sergeants had chevrons made from ½-inch-wide silk binding; first sergeants, sergeants, and corporals had their insignia of rank made of worsted binding. The crossed axes of the pioneer were made from facing cloth, while the hospital steward's half chevrons were made from either wool or silk.

The Ordnance Department had only ordnance sergeants and privates early in the Civil War, and these men were scattered at the many posts throughout the United States. With the rapid expansion of the Army during the Civil War, however, a need arose for more ordnance soldiers. Because of this need, the War Department authorized sergeants and corporals of ordnance, with crimson chevrons of three and two bars, respectively.[30]

Today, the similar titles of "ordnance sergeant" and "sergeants of ordnance" for two different grades and insignia may be confusing, but in the nineteenth century there was no difficulty distinguishing between the two. Ordnance sergeants, members of the noncommissioned staff, wore sergeant's chevrons with a star in the angle. The term "ordnance" referred to the man's specialty or position, just as the term "quartermaster" in quartermaster sergeant does. Sergeants of ordnance were of the same rank as sergeants of the other branches such as infantry and cavalry, the title literally meaning "sergeant of the Ordnance Corps." Because of the significant differences in pay, position, and insignia, ordnance sergeants and sergeants of ordnance should be clearly distinguished.

The Army formed engineer regiments and battalions during the Civil War. Since yellow was then the color for the Engineers Corps, yellow silk chevrons were prescribed for engineer sergeants major and quartermaster sergeants even though men in these two senior positions actually wore the same rank insignia used by cavalry personnel.[31]

On 22 July 1864, Major William Nicodemus, the Army's Chief Signal Officer, wrote Secretary of War Stanton requesting that an order be published establishing cavalry uniforms as the Signal Corps uniform. Nicodemus wanted standard cavalry chevrons along with a special crossed flags device for the signal rank insignia: "*Sergeants* will wear chevrons of the same color as Cavalry with the designation of the Corps placed in the angle of the chevrons upon the left sleeve. *Privates* will wear the designation of the Corps in the same position on the sleeve as the chevrons of the Sergeants."[32] The Secretary of War approved the request, except that privates were authorized to wear the signal device on the left sleeve only. Captain Joseph Spencer of the Washington Signal Office ordered from Mr. Charles De Frondat of Boston on 20 August 1864 forty-five dozen sleeve badges.

Figure 2-12. This Civil War sergeant wears a nonregulation chevron. A single large star was worn by ordnance sergeants, but the significance of the two small stars is unknown.

Spencer described these as

crossed signal flags, on dark blue cloth, to be embroidered in silk; color of flags, one red with white centre, and one white with red centre; size of flag three-fourth (¾) of an inch square, centre one-fourth (¼) of an inch square, length of staff three (3) inches. To be finished in a substantial and workmanlike manner, and not to exceed, in cost, three dollars per dozen.

The badges were distributed in the fall of 1864 and more were ordered.

Beginning in 1868, "qualified men" wore the signal flags on both sleeves and "unqualified men" wore the flags on only one sleeve, although regulations specified that all NCOs and privates would wear the flags in pairs.[33] Yellow cavalry chevrons continued to be worn until orange became the signal branch color in 1872.

During the Civil War, most volunteer units adopted chevrons of the Regular Army. Some senior NCOs not authorized by federal regulations to wear distinctive chevrons nevertheless wore special insignia, the most common of which was a sergeant's chevron with a single horizontal bar added for use by company quartermaster sergeants. Other unauthorized ranks included drum majors, regimental commissary sergeants, battalion sergeants major, principal musicians, battalion commissary sergeants, and saddler sergeants. Many volunteer units that used Regular Army uniforms had a drum major who usually wore a special chevron. Generally, the Civil War bandleader's chevrons had a small star in the center and one to three bars or arcs in addition to the three V's of a sergeant. It is impossible to catalog these many nonstandard chevrons as their use varied from regiment to regiment. The use of these unauthorized chevron designs by state units, including volunteers, may have resulted in adoption by the United States Army of chevrons for company quartermaster sergeants, regimental hospital stewards, and regimental commissary sergeants shortly after the Civil War.

Figure 2-13. This is a typical example of a nonstandard Civil War chevron. The photographer touched up some tintype details, including the chevron, evidently for clarity.

Specifying "three bars, and a tie of one bar, in worsted," General Order No. 100, 1866, created a company quartermaster sergeant's chevrons, of the same design used by many volunteer units during the Civil War. Although the establishing order specified worsted binding, many chevrons were actually of silk binding made by removing the lower two bars from regimental quartermaster sergeant's chevrons.[34]

The next spring the Army authorized two more chevrons for the shrinking army. Regimental commissary sergeants wore sergeant's chevrons made of silk with "an angular tie (vertex pointing upwards)" of three bars. The Quartermaster General's Department made at least three-hundred pairs for the infantry,

Figure 2-14. The short-lived rank of regimental commissary sergeant had this chevron from 1867 until 1870 (Catalog No. 18).

Figure 2-15. Regimental hospital stewards wore chevrons of this design shortly after the Civil War.

cavalry, and artillery, and one-hundred and fifty pairs went to New Orleans.[35]

With the regimental commissary sergeant's rank insignia, the Army established chevrons for regimental hospital stewards, the device consisting of a sergeant's chevron and "an oval with a 'caduceus' embroidered in dark blue silk in the centre of the oval." Standard sergeant's chevrons were worn, and the caduceus was issued separately.[36] In the summer of 1870, after just three years, Congress abolished the grades of regimental commissary sergeant and regimental hospital stewards, although some NCOs in these grades continued to wear their distinctive chevrons for the next few years.[37]

Table 2-2 summarizes catalog numbers assigned to pre–1872 chevrons. Tables 2-3 and 2-4 summarize information on the manufacture of chevrons in this period.

General Montgomery C. Meigs, who served as Quartermaster General from 1861 until 1882, wrote in his 1871 *Annual Report* that a uniform change for the Army had been ordered. The subsequent change, which was initiated the next year, included a different manufacturing process for rank chevrons, and thus ushered in the second period in enlisted rank history.

Service Stripes: Revolutionary War Period

The Honorable Brigadier General Paterson [John Paterson, Brigadier General, Continental Army][38] . . . expressed "his wish that some honorary mark of distinction should be worn by each noncommissioned officer or private in his brigade who has served in the Army of the United States, a certain length of time; . . . Each noncommissioned officer and private who has served four years in any continental regiment shall be entitled to wear one stripe of white tape on the left sleeve of his regimental coat . . . [the stripe] shall extend from seam to seam on the upper part of the sleeve three inches from the parallel with the shoulder seam so that the tape may form a herringbone figure."[39] Dated 17 June 1782, this brigade order, issued at West Point, established the first service stripe. The Revolutionary War had dragged on for several years without hope of quick victory. Army leaders looked favorably on any device, however small, that might improve the morale and entice men to enlist or reenlist. To ensure only men who actually had four years of unblemished service would receive this "mark of distinction," only the colonel or the regimental commander could authorize issue of the insignia.

George Washington evidently thought the service stripe an admirable device, as Washington's headquarters issued the fol-

TABLE 2-2
Catalog Numbers for Pre–1872 Chevrons

Design	Catalog Number	Dates of Authorization	Rank
	1	1821–1825	Sergeant Major and Quartermaster Sergeant (worn above elbow); Sergeant and Senior Musician (worn below elbow); Corporal (worn above the elbow, right arm only)
		1825–1830	Sergeant (above elbow); Corporal (below elbow)
	2	1825–1830	Sergeant Major, Quartermaster Sergeant, and Principal Musician
	3	1833–1851 1851–1872	Sergeant (dragoon uniforms only) Sergeant
	4	1833–1851 1851–1872	Corporal (dragoon uniforms only) Corporal
	5	1847–1851	Sergeant Major (fatigue uniform)
	6	1847–1851	Quartermaster Sergeant (fatigue uniform)
	7	1847–1851	First Sergeant (fatigue uniform)
	8	1847–1851	Sergeant (fatigue uniform)
	9	1847–1851	Corporal (fatigue uniform)
	10	1851–1872	Sergeant Major
	11	1851–1872	Quartermaster Sergeant
	12	1851–1872	First Sergeant
	13	1851–1872	Ordnance Sergeant
	14	1851–1872	Hospital Steward[a]
	15	1851–1899	Pioneer
	16	1864–1891	Signal Service
	17	1866–1872	Company Quartermaster Sergeant
	18	1867–1870	Regimental Commissary Sergeant
	19	1867–1870	Regimental Hospital Steward

[a] Hand-embroidered silk edges. Cotton chain-stitched edges and hand-embroidered gold thread edges are of post–1872 manufacture.

TABLE 2-3
Manufacturing Code Letters for Pre–1872 Chevrons

Design Color	Dates of Authorization	Remarks	Code Letter
Branch color	1821–1850[a]	See Table 2-4 for colors authorized and exact dates. Chevron bars or design sewn directly to coat sleeve	a
Branch color	1850[a]–1872	See Table 2-4 for colors authorized and exact dates. Worsted binding sewn onto wool background	b
Branch color	1850[a]–1872	See Table 2-4 for colors authorized and exact dates. Silk lace sewn onto wool background	c

[a] Exact date of transition during the 1850s is not known.

TABLE 2-4
Colors of Pre–1872 Chevrons

Color	Branch	Dates of Authorization
Gold	Non-Infantry Officers	1821–1830
Silver	Infantry officers	1821–1830
White	Infantry	1821–1830; 1847–1851
Yellow	Artillery	1821–1830
Yellow	Dragoons	1833–1851
	Engineers	1847–1872
	Cavalry	1855–continued past 1872
Black	Riflemen	1821–1830
Red	Horse Artillery	1845–1847
	Artillery	1847–continued past 1872
Green	Mounted Rifles	1851–1861
Light blue	Infantry	1851–continued past 1872
Crimson	Ordnance	1851–continued past 1872
Green and yellow	Hospital Stewards	1851–1857; 1861–continued past 1872
Buff and yellow[a]	Hospital Stewards	1857–1861
Orange	Dragoons	1851–1861

[a] Unknown if worn. Green and yellow chevrons perhaps used the entire time.

lowing order of 7 August 1782:

> *Honorary badges of distinction are to be conferred on the veteran noncommissioned officers and soldiers of the Army who have served more than three years with bravery, fidelity, and good conduct; for this purpose a narrow piece of white cloth of an angular form is to be fixed on the left arm on the uniform coat.*
>
> *Noncommissioned officers and soldiers who have served with equal reputation more than six years are to be distinguished by two pieces of cloth set on parallel to each other in a similar form.*
>
> *Should any who are not entitled to the honors have the insolence to assume the badges of them, they shall be severely punished. On the other hand, it is expected these gallant men who are thus distinguished, will on all occasions be treated with particular confidence and consideration.*

Four days later, Washington amended the order to read that service had to be continuous, and also stipulated if a man had been punished during an enlistment, he could not wear the badge unless he redeemed himself "by some very brilliant requirement, or by serving with reputation after his disgrace. . . . " In a major change, the men were to wear the chevron in the color of the facings of the Corps and not in white

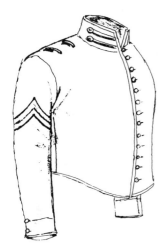

Figure 2-16. Service stripes, 1832–1851. The coat in this drawing bears two service stripes on the sleeve, each showing five years of completed service. For all but dragoons, rank was shown—up until the Mexican War—by epaulets and other insignia, except on fatigue uniforms.

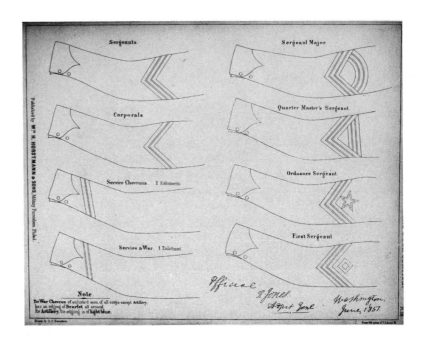

Figure 2-17. Diagonal service stripes were adopted in 1851. This page of drawings is from illustrated Uniform Regulations published by William Horstmann & Sons, makers of military uniforms.

Figure 2-18. Infantry war service and enlistment stripe, 1851–1879. The center is light blue, showing completion of an infantry enlistment, with the red edging indicating war service.

as originally specified. This system continued until the end of the Revolution when it fell into disuse. The coincidence is strikingly similar, however, to the earlier experience óf French gunner's chevrons: a white inverted V worn above the elbow, and later replaced by a similar design but in colors matching uniform facings.

After Washington's order all members of the Army were eligible for a three-year service stripe, and General Paterson soon rescinded his original order that had established the brigade service insignia. The service "badge of distinction" is often confused with the "badge of distinction" that is considered the forerunner of the Purple Heart since on a man's official record there would be an annotation that he had received a "badge of distinction." Because orders used the same terms, the two different awards are often not fully distinguished by the casual observer. Care must be taken when examining old records indicating award of a "badge of distinction."

Service Stripes 1832–1872

With the new uniform of 1832 came the first service stripes since the Revolutionary War. Enlisted men who had faithfully served five years wore an inverted V chevron on their dress coat sleeves above the elbow, an extra stripe being added for each additional five years' service. Men who fought in a war had each side of the service chevron trimmed in red, a practice that lasted forty-five more years.[40] Rank chevrons introduced for the fatigue uniforms in 1847 would have carried two inverted V's to represent a corporal, but the similar insignia on the dress uniform would have indicated ten years service.[41] A compromise between the older system of using chevrons to show service and the newer system for enlisted rank insignia was attempted in February 1850. The Adjutant General ordered rank chevrons be worn on the right sleeve of the frock coat and jackets, and service chevrons on the left sleeve. A new Secretary of War soon suspended this order, however, and the system was never used.[42]

During the following year, 1851, the Army adapted rank chevrons for dress uniforms, thereby forcing the enlistment chevrons to be worn elsewhere. The Uniform Board selected a ½-inch-wide "diagonal half chevron," in branch color, extending across the sleeve from seam to seam, with the front of the stripe nearer to and a ½-inch above the cuff point. An ⅛-inch red border on each side of the enlistment stripe indicated wartime service, except for artillerymen whose war stripes were trimmed in light blue.[43] These or similar color schemes continued until 1879 when the Army introduced a more complex system.

CHAPTER 3

History of Chevron, Uniform, and Service Stripe Development 1872–1902: The Second Period

In 1872, the Quartermaster General's Department introduced a new type of chevron that lasted thirty years. Simultaneously with the chevron changes of 1872 and 1902 came new styles of uniforms, or more accurately, the reverse is true—with the new uniforms came new chevrons, including in 1884 revised dress chevrons and uniforms. The Army changed considerably during the thirty years soldiers wore the 1872-pattern chevrons: many new ranks were established, new schools and promotion standards for several NCO ranks were instituted, additional branches were formed, several new uniforms were introduced, and, fortunately for the historian, more comprehensive records were entered and retained.

By 1872, the wartorn nation was returning to normal. The nation was expanding westward, pulling occupation troops out of the South. The Army again oriented its efforts toward the frontier and control of the Indians. The infantry, which had expanded to forty-five regiments during the Civil War, shrank to twenty-five regiments. These and other factors are part of the full understanding of the ranks introduced from 1872 to 1902.

From the Revolutionary War through the Civil War, the Army consisted almost exclusively of infantry, artillery, and horse units. In 1872, only 875 of all enlisted men in the Army were not sergeants, corporals, privates, musicians, or recruits. The few exceptions were distributed among eleven grades, of which seven had distinctive chevrons. By 1902, there were NCOs of twenty different grades who had distinctive chevrons.

The changes in grade structure and the proliferation of ranks during the last thirty years of the nineteenth century represented a major change in the Army. The expanding technology created a need for specialists. Army leaders felt that these specialists, already given higher pay than sergeants of the line, also needed insignia to distinguish them from the "ordinary" soldiers. Additionally, enlargement of the Army, and of the United States itself, created a need for NCOs who could stay and serve at major posts, regardless of any troop movement at that post. The year 1872 marks the beginning of an orderly expansion of the enlisted rank insignia.

New Designs in Uniforms

The Army adopted a new field uniform in 1872.[1] Although this new design lasted only two or three years, the coat introduced in 1858 and used during the Civil War was discarded. The new campaign coat introduced in 1872 is shown in Figure 3-1, and is easily distinguished by the four pleats and the nine-button front. In 1875 a simple five-button coat with a falling collar (Figure 3-2) replaced the 1872 coat.[2] Familiar to many students of military history, the five-button coat lasted until 1902.

Dress uniform coats, as well as field uniforms worn during the Civil War, were replaced in 1872 by a high-collar coat with the branch color facings on the front of the collar, on the cuffs,

Figure 3-1. These Indian guards at Fort Marion, Florida, wear the Army coat introduced in 1872.

Figure 3-2. This five-button coat is typical of those worn in the Indian campaigns from 1875 through 1902.

58

Figure 3-3. This sergeant and his friend wear a common variety of the khaki coat that was initially introduced in 1898.

and on the shoulder straps.[3] This design changed in the mid 1880s so the colored facings went completely around the collar, and trimming in the branch color was added to the coattails.[4] Although a new dress uniform made its debut in 1902, the 1885 coat continued to be worn—especially by various coast artillery units—until 1912 when the last units received as replacements these new dress uniforms.[5] Table 3-3 in this chapter shows dates of wear for the various chevrons and uniforms introduced between 1872 and 1902.

Authorized in the 1880s and 1890s were various new types of summer, winter, and fatigue uniforms, including canvas work coats and buffalo fur winter coats; however, soldiers did not wear chevrons on these uniforms. Men began to wear a summer khaki uniform, first introduced in 1898 (Figure 3-3), with 1872-design chevrons. Although the khaki coat had several variations, the basic cut remained the same throughout its use.[6] The 1898 chevrons differed from other chevrons by being made of cotton with the background for specialty devices made of khaki. In 1900, the Quartermaster General issued double the number of khaki chevrons as compared with the blue, denoting the popularity of the khaki uniform.[7]

After 1872, uniform regulations might require one thing and the clothing specifications another. Official correspondence and records often indicated still a third thing was actually done. The officers in the Philadelphia and Jeffersonville,

Figure 3-4. This hospital steward wears the style of dress coat and gold lace chevrons introduced in 1885.

Figure 3-5. Men wore overcoat chevrons below the elbow because of the cape. Infantry soldiers adopted dark blue chevrons for the coat since the coat itself was light blue and similar in color to chevrons worn on other garments.

Indiana, depots did not always supply all chevrons prescribed and, at times, issued unauthorized chevrons. In 1882, the Quartermaster General required the storekeeper at Philadelphia to send several pairs of each chevron being issued so that proper illustrations could be made. During an exchange of correspondence on this subject, Captain William Gill of the Schuylkill Arsenal mentioned most casually that the regulations should be updated, since the depot had been issuing farrier chevrons, while the regulations had no provision for the insignia.[8]

With the exception of the overcoat, men wore chevrons on all uniforms point down (V shape) midway between the elbow and shoulder. Overcoat chevrons were worn two inches above the cuff so that the rank could easily be seen despite the cape. Figure 3-5 shows an infantry sergeant wearing the dark blue infantry overcoat chevrons in this manner. The 1902 regulations called for the newly introduced small chevrons to be worn point up (inverted V); however, it took several years to manufacture the 1902 chevrons in the quantity needed to supply the entire Army. In this interim period, the 1872-pattern chevrons were worn point up. Figure 3-6 shows some engineer troops in November 1903. One of the men complying with the regulations wears the chevrons point up, while the other NCO is still wearing the chevrons point down as previously required.

Figure 3-6. In this 1903 photograph, members of the Corps of Engineers wear a variety of 1872 and 1902 chevrons. Soldier 1 wears his 1872 chevrons point up, as required by 1902 regulations, while soldier 2 wears his point down. Soldier 3 wears a 1902 private first class chevron.

Chevron Types: Cloth, Gilt, Shirt, Khaki

Chevrons worn on coats in this period are classed as one of four types: cloth, gilt, khaki, and shirt. "Cloth chevrons" is a misnomer since all chevrons are of cloth, but in the 1880s the term came to mean chevrons worn on the blue campaign or field coats and overcoats. Cloth chevrons were worn on all but fatigue uniforms until 1884, and on the blue campaign coats and overcoats from 1884 to 1902. The name "cloth chevrons" was instituted in 1884 when dress coat chevrons with gold lace V bars came into being, and a way was needed to distinguish the two types of rank insignia. (Prior to 1884, all chevrons were made of cloth, and the term "chevrons" had been sufficient. When gilt chevrons came into being, they were called "gold lace chevrons." To avoid confusion at this point, cloth chevrons had thenceforth to be referred to as "cloth chevrons" since the one-word generic was no longer sufficient.) Khaki chevrons are similar to cloth chevrons except that cotton or light wool was used in construction, and inserts carrying specialty devices were made on khaki cotton. Shirt chevrons, the last of the four basic types, were introduced in the Spanish-American War and are smaller than the other three types.[9]

Cloth Chevrons

In 1872, Mr. F. S. Johnston of Philadelphia had an idea that changed the design of Army chevrons for the next thirty years, and like the best of ideas, it was simple. The Johnston system of manufacturing reduced the cutting and sewing required to make a chevron. Instead of making each bar from a piece of cloth and

61

Figure 3-7. Four basic types of chevrons were authorized from 1872 through 1902. Cloth chevrons, manufacturing code d (top left) were first worn in 1872. Gold lace chevrons, code g (top right) were introduced in 1884 for the dress uniform. Khaki chevrons, code h (lower left) came during the Spanish-American War and were the same size and in the same branch colors as cloth chevrons. The smaller cloth chevrons, code i (lower right) were authorized in 1900, introduced in 1901, and were the basis for the new chevrons in late 1902. All chevrons shown are for a color sergeant.

then sewing the bars one by one to backing material, Johnston cut the over-all shape of the chevrons from one or two pieces of cloth. The bars were then outlined directly on the material with a special heavy chain stitching. Johnston patented the revolutionary idea on 21 January 1873 (*see* Appendix 3). The arms of the chevrons were slightly curved, each one "to be the arc of a circle about 25 inches in diameter" and "6 to 7 inches long." Each bar of the arm was to be a ½-inch wide, with the two arms meeting at "an angle . . . about 96 degrees; distance between extreme outer ends about 9 inches." The bars and devices on these cloth insignia were in colors distinctive of each branch. Inserts in the angle, bearing the distinguishing marks for NCOs not of the line, were of cloth on dark blue wool. The patent explicitly described the advantage of the new system: "Instead of employing braid . . . [this system must] use cloth which is cut to form the basis of the design required [and use stitching] . . . for the purpose of indicating a division line" (Appendix 3 reproduces the Johnston patent text, from which this is excerpted).

Gilt Chevrons
A change in dress uniforms occurred in 1885. The chevrons used on the new coat were introduced a year earlier. Gilt lace formed the bars and most of the center designs were of cloth background made in the branch color. Seamstresses used gold thread to hand-embroider those few devices that could not be made from the gold lace. The Philadelphia Depot had initial samples made in January 1884 and formally adopted the concept the following September.[10]

In 1886, each NCO was entitled to three gilt chevrons and six cloth chevrons per five-year enlistment. However, members of the Quartermaster General's Office found many of the men taking the gold lace and melting it for the silver and gold content. Before this practice was discovered in 1886, nearly 25,000 pairs of service stripes had been issued.[11] The following year, after closer accountability was initiated, the Chief of the Clothing Bureau wrote, "The demand for service chevrons has since been considerably diminished." The bureau issued only 3,971 pairs in 1888.[12]

Shirt Chevrons

The hot climates encountered during the Spanish-American War required soldiers to go without their coats; therefore, the War Department authorized chevrons to be sewn on shirt sleeves in July 1898.[13] Since the large cloth coat chevrons did not fit well on the shirt sleeves, troops in Cuba and the Philippines made small chevrons locally. Officers sent various samples to the Quartermaster General, urging the Quartermaster to adopt small shirt chevrons.[14]

Figure 3-8. Unofficial small shirt chevrons, such as this 5½-inch-wide chevron made for an infantry color sergeant, were used from 1900 until 1902 on shirts (for warm climates).

Of the several alternatives available, the two most obvious were simply to make a smaller chevron of the same style and design as then worn, or to return to the pre–1872 practice of cutting out individual bars and sewing them onto backing cloth. Some manufacturers made and sold small chevrons of the first type (Figure 3-8) briefly at the turn of the century. Specification No. 567 described the first *official* small chevrons in February 1902, although the Secretary of War had authorized smaller chevrons in July 1900. The chevrons were made by cutting out the bars and design from branch-colored facing cloth and sewing the pieces to a dark blue wool backing. Even though these 1902 shirt chevrons differed considerably from the large standard-issue chevrons, Quartermaster staff officers decided the regulations did not have to be changed because the basic designs and colors remained intact.[15]

Figure 3-9. Men began to use small shirt chevrons during the Spanish-American War. The corporal's chevron shown here for comparison is the standard Army-issue cloth chevron, while the sergeant's chevron (shown above the other) was made for the shirt. Many unofficial chevrons are even smaller than the shirt chevron pictured.

For several years Francis Bannerman and Sons, a large surplus store in New York City, sold some of these small 1900–1902 shirt chevrons, and dealers and collectors bought all of them, usually without knowing the purpose of the small chevrons. These 1900–1902 chevrons are identical to the chevrons adopted for blue uniforms after 1902, except that the center devices were placed so they would be upright when the chevron points were down (V shape). Today they are forgotten by most researchers and collectors, and are mentioned only in Specification No. 567 and in some correspondence.[16]

Khaki Chevrons

Khaki chevrons were introduced in 1898 and replaced in 1902. The same size and design as cloth chevrons, they differed in that they were usually made from cotton cloth or occasionally a

Figure 3-10. Small chevrons like those shown here were worn on shirts, 1899, in Cuba.

light coarse wool. Khaki chevrons with devices in the angle had
the background material in light khaki. The bars, chain stitching, and devices were of the same colors as the cloth chevrons.

Signal Corps Chevrons 1889–1891
General Order No. 18, 16 February 1889, established a special
uniform for Signal Corps enlisted men. Called for were sergeant's and corporal's "black silk braid" chevrons. There is
contradictory evidence as to what was actually worn between
1889 and 1891. Quartermaster Department specifications on
chevrons issued in June 1889 fail to mention special black braid
chevrons. Secretary of War reports show no issue of the chevrons, although the Secretary's 1889 *Annual Report* does show
special listings for black silk braid Signal Corps chevrons: 86
cents for sergeant's chevrons and 68 cents for corporal's chevrons. Even so, on page 40 of the 30 September 1889 *Report of the
Chief Signal Officer* the following statement is found:

> *The attention of the Secretary of War is called to the fact
> that Congress for a number of years has failed to make
> provisions for the uniform of the enlisted men of the Signal
> Corps, and an estimate for this purpose is again submitted.
> The uniform adopted is quiet and unobtrusive, so that its
> wearer is not prominent through gaudy and showy trap-
> pings.*

In 1890 Signal Corps corporals either were transferred to the newly formed Weather Bureau or were promoted to the new grade of Signal Corps sergeant second class.

Specialist Ranks

Chevrons which today might be considered specialist ratings began with the pioneer's crossed hatchets. By 1899, four other grades used special devices for chevrons. Specialists wore these insignia only on campaign uniforms; consequently, the Regular Army did not use the devices in gold lace. For cloth and khaki chevrons, the background material was approximately 5½ inches by 9 inches, but soldiers often trimmed the extra cloth to a smaller rectangle (or to the shape of a barrel) before sewing it onto a uniform.[17] Specialists' small shirt chevrons made before 1902 are identical to the standard-size post–1902 chevrons. Consequently, stocks of these insignia made *before the 1902 chevron change* were issued and worn after 1902. In essence, the various 1902 shirt specialist's chevrons, like NCO shirt chevrons, cannot be distinguished from post–1902 standard blue chevrons.

Other Insignia

A gunner's insignia was introduced in 1896. Not to be confused with a metal gunner's badge, which was worn like a medal, the gunner's insignia was worn on the right sleeve of the uniform coat as a mark to distinguish the wearer as a gunnery expert (*see further* below, in Chapter 8, the section on Artillery Sleeve Insignia). The simple device of a red projective initiated an entire new field of artillery specialist's ratings, which expanded rapidly after 1902.

Chevron Identification

The primary interest of collectors, dealers, curators, and researchers is to identify specific chevrons. To accomplish the identification, it is necessary to determine not only the period during which the chevron was worn and the specific title, but also the colors, design, and shape of the chevron. Table 3-2 lists manufacturing code letters identifying the various types of chevrons made in the period from 1872 through 1902.

Color

In 1872, as before, each branch wore chevrons of distinctive colors. Color changes can be used to determine when branches used certain chevrons. Table 3-1 shows the various colors and materials, including gilt, authorized for the 1872-pattern chevrons.

While yellow has been the cavalry color since 1861, the cavalry changed facing in 1872 to a lighter yellow. The new color was about the shade of a lemon. Many officers complained about this color since it faded badly after very little use and the trim looked almost white. In 1887, the Quartermaster General decided to switch to a deeper yellow to alleviate the problem. These darker yellow facings resisted fading better, and even after considerable fading, the color came to be about the shade of the lighter, pre–1887 yellow. This change was not specified in regulations or specifications, but was achieved simply by correspondence between the Quartermaster General's Office and the Purchasing Office in Philadelphia. After darker material for uniform trim and chevrons had been purchased, the helmet cords and other colored accessories were redyed to match the chevrons and uniforms and uniform facings.[18] This 1887 darker cavalry yellow has continued in use through today.

In 1872, men of the signal service wore the short cavalry shell jacket with orange facings. Sergeants and corporals had orange chevrons with black chain stitching. Signal service men wore a separate insignia of two crossed flags immediately above these chevrons.[19] When black chevrons replaced the orange in 1889, this separate chevron continued to be worn.[20] The burning torch was added above the black signal chevron in 1891, and the signal insignia was made an integral part of the chevron.[21] Orange returned in 1902 as the Signal Corps color, although the flags and torch continued as part of the Signal Corps chevrons.[22]

Regulations of 1872 describe infantry trim as "sky blue." In 1876, infantry overcoat chevrons were changed to dark blue with white chain stitching, while the light blue chevrons remained on other uniforms.[23] Troops complained that the light blue faded badly, and in 1884, white chevrons replaced those of sky blue.[24] The dark blue 1876 overcoat chevrons continued to be worn until 1900, when all infantry chevrons were changed to white.[25] Light blue was reintroduced in 1898 for infantry use on the khaki uniform. Despite Quartermaster optimism, the blue faded badly and in 1899 white became standard for use on khaki uniforms also.[26]

Engineers adopted red facing with white trim in 1872. When the Army adopted gilt dress chevrons, a method was devised to distinguish between the engineer and the artillery chevrons. Artillery dress chevrons had gold lace sewn onto red facing cloth; engineer dress chevrons were identical save for addition of white chain stitching around the edges of the gold lace.

Through this 30-year period Ordnance Corps NCOs wore wine-colored chevrons described as "crimson." Sergeants and corporals of the Ordnance Corps wore conventional crimson chevrons, while men of another rank, ordnance sergeants, wore crimson chevrons with an inverted star in the center.

Circular 10, 15 August 1890, established Indian Scout uni-

Figure 3-11. A Signal Corps corporal's chevron. Gold lace on orange wool was worn by signal corporals on dress uniforms from 1884 to 1889 until replaced by the unique black lace chevrons. Crossed signal flags alone were added above Signal Corps chevrons until 1891, when a torch was added to the flags. The red and white squares of the flags were edged in bullion, and the tips of the 3-inch "spears" were made of the same gold wire.

forms. White chevrons with red stitching were adopted on the recommendation of First Lieutenant E. W. Casey, the Scout Troop Commander at Fort Keogh, Montana.[27] The dress stripes consisted of white facing cloth with red chain stitching on each side of the gold lace. It is known that Indian Scouts wore cloth chevrons, but it is open to conjecture whether or not the Scouts actually wore the colorful dress chevrons. The Philadelphia Depot, however, did make and issue both the wool and the gilt Indian Scout chevrons through 1902.[28]

NCOs of the Army Service Detachment at West Point wore buff chevrons the last two years of the large chevron period (1900–1902). These were the same color as those worn by post quartermaster sergeants, but men of the Army Service Detachment wore chevrons of standard design, while post quartermaster sergeants had a crossed key and pen in the upper angle.[29]

Shape

Shape may also be a key in determining the period of use and in identifying the wearer of the chevron. Throughout the 30-year span of the large chain-stitched chevrons, some designs were continuously in use. To an extent, chevrons can be dated by shape and color. Some early chevrons have center devices which were made on larger backgrounds than were used later. An example is shown in Figure 3-13. Even though the original 1873 patent shows the more common arc-shaped background, some samples using this older background were sealed as official.[30] (On the application of waxed seals to indicate that a chevron sample was the official standard, *see further* below in the section on Chevron Procurement.)

At least one manufacturer made elongated chevrons. These were probably worn by military school cadets or by regimental bands. One interesting picture of elongated chevrons, taken in 1885, shows the West Point drum major (Figure 3-14). No official samples of this design are known, few of the actual chevrons now exist, and photographs rarely show men wearing them.

Design

Designs and designations of chevrons changed, and this often causes uncertainty today. In some instances more than one rank used a particular design. When a rank is identified by name or design, it is essential the time of use be specified. In 1883, the Quartermaster General created chevrons with a circle for color sergeants, the men who carry the national and regimental colors. During the same time, ordnance sergeants wore a chevron containing a star, point down. In 1900, the circle was discarded, and the sergeant's chevron with the inverted star was adapted by color sergeants. The ordnance sergeants then began to wear the flaming bomb above their chevrons.[31] If only the designation "color sergeant" is used, the chevron design is unknown. "Color

Figure 3-12. Indian Scouts wore white chevrons with red stitching. Chevrons of this type are seen in this late-nineteenth-century photograph of two Scouts.

Figure 3-13. An early 1872-pattern chevron. Between 1872 and 1878, some NCO chevrons were made with center devices applied on a background that completely filled the angle between the bars.

Figure 3-14. Drum Major, United States Military Academy Band, 1885. The drum major is wearing cloth principal musician's chevrons. For the dress uniform, cloth chevrons of this type were replaced by those of gold lace, starting in 1884. The chevrons later were specified to have the bell of the bugle face forward, but at this time chevrons were commonly worn either way. This is one of the few photographs that show chevrons of the elongated pattern. The braid on the chest of the coat was worn by all musicians.

sergeant 1883–1900," or "color sergeant 1900–1902" clears up the confusion.

The Hospital Corps changed chevrons several times between 1872 and 1902. The 1851 hospital steward's diagonal-pattern chevron continued in use through 1872; it is one of the few chevrons that did not change with the post–Civil War uniforms. When the War Department introduced gilt chevrons in 1885, the hospital steward's chevron design remained the same as it had been except that gold thread replaced the yellow thread.

Two years later, 1887, the Army determined acting hospital stewards needed a distinctive chevron. This caused two chevrons of more standard design to come into use, one for hospital stewards and one for acting hospital stewards. The cloth chevrons were three green V's with white stitching and a red Geneva cross. Identical designs were used for gilt chevrons, with the crosses of red cloth.[32]

When post personnel formed for a parade, the medical members not on duty at the hospital were at the parade to give

TABLE 3-1
Colors of 1872-Pattern Chevrons

Chevron Color	Stitching (Wool or Khaki Chevrons)	Branch	Dates of Authorization	Additional Data: Chevrons Made		
				Wool	Khaki	Gilt
Light blue	Black	Infantry	1872–1884	X		
Light blue	Black	Infantry	1898–1899		X	
White	Black	Infantry	1884–1902	X	X	X
Dark blue	White	Infantry[a]	1876–1900	X		
Red	Black	Artillery	1872–1902	X	X	X
Light yellow	Black	Cavalry	1872–1887	X		X
Medium yellow	Black	Cavalry	1887–1902	X	X	X
Red	White	Engineers	1872–1902	X	X	X
Green	Yellow	Hospital Corps[b]	1872–1887	X[c]		X
Green	White	Hospital Corps	1887–1902	X	X	X[d]
Crimson	Black	Ordnance	1872–1902	X	X	X
Buff	Black	USMA Detachment	1900–1902	X	X	X
Buff	Black	Post Quartermaster Sergeant	1884–1902	X	X	X
Orange	Black	Signal Corps	1872–1889	X		X
Black	White	Signal Corps[e]	1891–1902	X	X	X
Gray	Black	Commissary Sergeant	1873–1902	X	X	X
White	Red	Indian Scouts	1890–1902	X	X	X

[a] Overcoat only.

[b] Diagonal type only.

[c] Can be distinguished from pre–1872 chevrons by chain stitching on edges. Pre–1872 edges are sewn with yellow conventional stitching.

[d] Only chevrons with red crosses were made in gilt; the type with green and white crosses were not made in gilt.

[e] Militia type black silk lace chevrons evidently authorized from 1889 until 1891.

TABLE 3-2
Manufacturing Code Letters for 1872–1902 Chevrons

Background Material	Design Material and Color	Dates of Authorization	Remarks	Code Letter
Branch-colored wool	Formed by chain stitching	1872–1902	Any background material containing an insert is of blue wool with the insert top forming a quarter circle	d
Dark blue wool	Branch-colored wool	1872–1902	Specialty chevrons 8 to 10 inches wide and 5 to 6 inches high are included, as are devices worn by Hospital Corps privates and Signal Corps personnel	d*
Branch-colored wool	Formed by chain stitching	1872–1880a	Blue wool insert top is slightly convex and extends across entire chevron top, as shown in Figure 3-13	e
Branch-colored wool	Formed by chain stitching	1880s–1890sb	Elongated design; see Figure 3-14	f
Branch-colored wool	Made from gold lace	1884–1902	Phased out from 1902 through 1911, especially by the Coast Artillery Corps	g
Cotton or light wool, branch colored	Formed by chain stitching	1898–1902	Inserts, if part of chevron, are of khaki	h
Khaki cotton	Branch-colored cotton	1898–1902	Specialty chevrons, 8 to 10 inches by 5 to 6 inches, or on squares about 3½ inches on a side	h
Dark blue wool	Branch colors	1902–1903	About 3⅛ inches wide. Only chevrons in pre–1902 colors or with inserts that dictate the chevrons should point down are included	i
Varies	Branch colors	1898–1905	Unofficial type small shirt chevrons made for wear on blue shirts; see Figures 3-8 and 3-9.	j

a Official chevrons should be type d, but the Army is known to have issued some of this type, dates not known.

b Not authorized. General dates of use are shown.

* The same code letter is applied to chevrons produced by the same manufacturing process and in use at the same time. Such chevrons are said to constitute a set.

TABLE 3-3
Dates of Wear for Chevrons Introduced 1872–1902

Uniform	YEARS OF USE						
	1872	1884	1898	1902	1905	1911	
Dress Uniform	type *e* / type *d*		type *g*			+	(Coast Artillery only)
Undress Uniform & Overcoat	type *e* type *d*						
Khaki Uniform			type *h*	*			
Shirt			types *d, h,* and *j*	x type *i*			

+ Coast Artillery only.

* Philippines only.

x Shirt chevrons (type *i*) introduced in February 1902. These are basically the same chevron as prescribed for wear on the dress coats in August 1902 (type *k*).

Figure 3-15. In February 1901, this design replaced the red cross worn above the chevrons of Hospital Corps personnel. The insignia was "a modified Maltese Cross 2 inches wide and 2 inches high, of green cloth having a white border." This drawing is from the 1901 Annual Report *of the Quartermaster General.*

aid to those who might need medical assistance. Because of this, the one or two Hospital Corps members at parades wore white medical uniforms. When the Quartermaster General realized that Hospital Corps members did not use their dress uniforms, authorization for these uniforms was rescinded and additional white uniforms were issued in their place, causing the hospital Corps gilt chevrons to be discontinued.[33]

In the late nineteenth and early twentieth centuries, medical officers wore a Maltese cross on their collar. The Surgeon General saw no reason why officers and soldiers of the same branch should wear different insignia, and accordingly, in 1901 the white-edged green Maltese cross was replaced by the red Geneva cross, thus introducing another set of chevrons.[34]

Chevron Procurement

The Quartermaster Depot at Philadelphia made all chevrons, although a regiment might order from Jeffersonville, Indiana, or some other depot. Employment priority at the Philadelphia Depot went to widows and others who had suffered a loss in the Civil War. By the turn of the century, the depot let contracts to some firms such as Horstmann's to make chevrons, but that did not become a common practice until the Spanish-American War created an unprecedented demand for all types of military supplies.

Samples

Once the Quartermaster General's Office adopted a chevron as standard, several insignia had wax seals added and these became "sealed samples." These samples are the ones often cited

Figure 3-16. Shown here is a sealed sample of a saddler sergeant's chevron from the National Collection of the Smithsonian Institution. A wax seal was applied to a few samples of each type of chevron to make a particular design "official." Subsequent chevrons were to conform to the sealed pattern. The history of this particular piece is not known although it evidently was made between 1873 and 1875. Later Quartermaster General samples are known to have a different seal. This sample may have been a state sample.

in regulations where rather than describing the insignia in detail, the authorization simply describes as "according to pattern" or "according to sealed samples."

Specifications

The Quartermaster General's Department adopted a system of published specifications in 1876. These specifications described *in detail* designs and dimensions so a manufacturer could make the item suitable for Army use. An unnumbered specification published June 1876 initially prescribed the colors and quality of facing cloth. In turn, Specification No. 12, March 1879, described the cut and design of the chevrons which were to be made from the standard facing cloth described in the June 1876 specifications. As new chevron designs and materials came into use, specifications were replaced by new specifications, a system that has continued in use today with only some modification.

Army Organization

Knowledge of Army organization aids in understanding how various enlisted men come together to form an Army. A few bits of information may help in examining NCO insignia.

First sergeants, sergeants, and corporals served primarily in line companies, with lance corporals added in 1890. Other NCOs served as members of the regimental or battalion noncommissioned staff, including sergeants major, regimental quartermaster sergeants, regimental commissary sergeants, and color sergeants. Hospital stewards, ordnance sergeants, and post commissary sergeants constituted the post noncommissioned staff. When the Artillery Corps reorganized in 1901, regimental staffs were eliminated, and artillery district staffs formed.

Throughout the nineteenth century and the early twentieth century, Congress authorized ranks by branch. Decisions by the Quartermaster General and Secretary of War dictated which of these men wore chevrons. As Congress created additional grades, pay and clothing allowances were equated to previous grades. Some 1901 examples point up this practice. Artillery sergeants major senior grade received the clothing allowances of infantry regimental sergeants major. Chief musicians (except artillery) had the allowances of regimental quartermaster sergeants. The chief musicians of artillery received the same allowances as sergeants major senior grade. Thus, artillery chief musicians were equated to infantry regimental sergeants major, but Army regulations and Congress stated the monetary allowances in the above manner.[35] As long as the Army had only a few ranks, this system was workable, but as Congress created more ranks, the reference to other grades became unwieldy.

Relatively small and unsophisticated in 1872, the Army consisted of ten cavalry regiments, five artillery regiments, twenty-five infantry regiments, and one engineer battalion. Total enlisted strength outside these units was 650 men.[36] There were few rules for appointing various NCOs. Military schools for training enlisted men in military subjects had not yet been founded. By 1902, the Army had grown to fifteen cavalry regiments, thirty infantry regiments, the equivalent of thirteen artillery regiments, twelve companies of engineers, and 810 Signal Corps men, in addition to 2,877 other enlisted personnel.[37] Army-wide schools had been established to train electrician sergeants, farriers and blacksmiths, and Signal Corps members. Additionally the War Department required a minimum level of training before promotion to hospital steward, post quartermaster sergeant, and some other ranks.[38] The military was becoming more complex, and enlisted ranks reflected the trend.

One outgrowth of the Spanish-American War was a major reorganization of the Artillery Corps. Initially, the artillery organized into light and heavy batteries, mounted and dismounted units respectively, with little regard to battery type. The poor coastal defenses of Cuba and the Philippines showed Congress and the Secretary of War how vulnerable the United States was to sea attack. Actual facilities had been undergoing planned changes for several years, but more than brick, mortar and steel needed rework. Accordingly, in 1901 artillery regiments disbanded and formed numbered companies and batteries. From 1901 through 1907, the Artillery Corps consisted of 126 coast artillery companies and 30 field artillery batteries.[39] This reorganization caused a major chevron change insofar as the artillery is concerned, as many chevrons were retitled and some disappeared.

State Militia

Most state organizations wore chevrons of the same design and color as the Regular Army. When the infantry discontinued use of the dark blue overcoat chevrons, the Quartermaster issued these, as well as old medical chevrons, to some state militias.[40] Most states did not have all of the ranks used by the federal government, but the New York militia had all federal ranks, and others. Ranks peculiar to New York include battalion quartermaster sergeants and battalion commissary sergeants who wore rank insignia similar to those of comparable regimental NCOs, the only difference being the use of two horizontal bars. Mounted guidon sergeants of the New York Guard had a guidon above the chevron, while veterinary sergeants had the Old English letters "VS" in a chevron otherwise worn by regimental sergeants major.[41]

In the 1880s and 1890s some state units and other organizations such as veterans' groups wore cloth chevrons made with the bars and designs cut out and sewn onto a backing as had been the style before 1872. In addition to the older manufacturing process, the cut of these non-Regular Army chevrons makes them easily distinguishable. Several manufacturers made two basic types of chevrons. One type had straight bars, while the other had bars with a more pronounced curve than the standard issue chevrons. The bars themselves could be either of standard lace, or stuffed so as to be raised, giving a three-dimensional effect. Usually the background color or the color of the bars worn by these state and other units was not the same as that worn by United States troops. Today many of these various chevrons are misidentified as Civil War chevrons. They are clearly distinguishable, however, since the quality of the materials is usually better than most Civil War chevrons, and the colors are usually not regulation.

Veteran groups and militia organizations also wore various gold lace chevrons made in the same two basic designs. Contemporary catalogs show the great selections available in color and design for any unit desiring to use chevrons not issued by the War Department. The gold lace used for these nongovernment insignia often was of a lower quality than the issue gold lace and of a different design.

| Service Stripes | The uniform and chevron changes of 1872 also affected the design of service stripes. In the 1870s, an enlistment was for five years. Several years later, an enlistment was reduced to three years. The Army recognized completion of an enlistment, either three or five years, by diagonal service stripes worn on the lower sleeves of selected uniforms. Originally the Army authorized a service stripe for each enlistment, although the criterion later became each three years of service.[42] Throughout this period, soldiers used various colors and sizes of service stripes. Determining *which* ones were to be worn *when* is often difficult since the history of service chevrons is very complex. Staff members in the offices of the Quartermaster General and the Inspector General wrote several studies in the 1880s attempting to explain the system of service stripes.[43] These studies show that even the men in these offices were not sure what was to be worn in all cases.[44]

From the information now at hand, however, it appears that service stripes may be grouped into four categories: service, service-in-war, campaign, and war stripes. The first two were authorized throughout the 1872–1902 period and showed com-

75

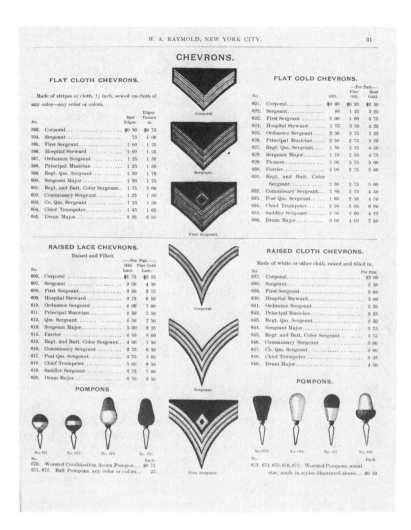

Figure 3-17. As shown in this page from an 1897 sales catalog, a wide variety of chevrons were available to militia units in the late nineteenth century.

pletion of one enlistment of either three or five years of "faithful and loyal" service. Campaign chevrons were authorized from 1879 through mid–1883 and were for soldiers who served in an announced campaign but had not yet completed their enlistment and for Civil War volunteer veterans who had served at least one field campaign.[45]

Soldiers initially wore service chevrons on overcoats and dress coats. These chevrons are ½-inch wide and of the appropriate color to show in which branch each enlistment was served. Table 3-4 at the end of this section summarizes these one-color service stripes. Since infantry overcoat chevrons were dark blue from 1876 through 1884, the service stripes worn on the overcoat were also dark blue. When the Army introduced gold lace chevrons (*see* Table 3-6 at the end of this chapter), a gold lace strip ½-inch wide was sewn on a ¾-inch-wide piece of dark blue cloth to show service. Simultaneously, regulations decreed the service chevrons would be worn only on the dress uniform

Figure 3-18. Samples of gold lace for Army and commercial chevrons. Gold lace used on Regular Army chevrons is shown on the top two rows. Below are two rows of gilt lace used by private firms to make chevrons for non-Regular Army organizations. On these nonstandard pieces, the lace was often sewn over padding to give the chevron a rounded three-dimensional effect.

coat.[46] The gilt or gold lace on dark blue continued in use until 1902, except for the Hospital Corps. When enlisted medical personnel discarded their dress uniforms in 1896, their gilt service chevrons were also eliminated, and these men had no way to show service. The Army then authorized a strip of emerald green facing cloth (the Hospital Corps color) with white stitching on the sides, for wear on the undress coat to designate peacetime service.[47]

Especially important to Regular Army men were service chevrons showing wartime enlistments. This was the only way of distinguishing who had seen service in the Mexican and Civil Wars. In 1879, men who served in active operations against the Indians were also authorized to wear service-in-war chevrons.[48] Initially, the pre–1872 practice continued of simply facing both sides of the enlistment chevron to show war service. Artillery stripes, which previously had light blue added to both sides of a service stripe to show a wartime enlistment, were changed so white was added on both sides, although the other branches still added red just as before 1872. The Quartermaster General continued this system of showing war service until 1884, when gilt lace came into use. Now service in war was to be shown by a ½-inch-wide strip of gold lace on top of a ¾-inch-wide piece of facing cloth the color of the branch in which the war service had been rendered.

All branches used this system until 1902, except for the Hospital Corps which dropped gilt chevrons in 1896.[49] Hospital Corps cloth service-in-war chevrons used from 1896 until 1902 were distinguished by an emerald green center stripe with piping beneath representing the branch of enlistment during war service. To show war service in the Hospital Corps, orange piped both sides of the green.[50]

Adjutant General orders authorized a "campaign chevron" from 1879 until 1883 by the scheme of simply making the service-in-war stripe narrower. When the Army authorized service-in-war chevrons for certain Indian campaigns, the question arose as to whether it was allowed for men to wear the service-in-war chevrons during the current enlistment or only after reenlistment. Military leaders decided a chevron of the same color combination as then worn for war service, but only ½-inch wide, would be authorized until reenlistment. Upon reenlistment, the standard ¾-inch service-in-war chevron would be worn instead of the ½-inch campaign chevron.[51] Table 3-5 summarizes these two- and three-color service stripes issued during this period.

Uniform Regulations of 1881 mention a "war stripe." The war stripe, intended to simplify the difference between campaign and service-in-war stripes, actually created confusion. The Office of the Quartermaster General could not decide how this "war stripe" related to the campaign stripe and this confusion finally led to their both being abolished in 1883.[52] As far as

TABLE 3-4
One-Color Service Stripes 1872–1902[c]

Color	Branch	Dates of Authorization
Light blue	Infantry	1872–1884
Red	Artillery	1872–1884
Light yellow	Cavalry	1872–1884
Crimson	Ordnance	1872–1884
Green	Hospital Corps	1872–1884
Orange	Signal Corps	1872–1884
Gray	Commissary Sergeant	1873–1884
Yellow	Service in USMC	1882–1884[a]
White	"War Stripe" (Civil War Volunteers)	1881–1883[b]

[a] Initially authorized by letter for an unnamed soldier in Captain Bascom's Company of the 13th Infantry.

[b] The "War Stripe" was rescinded in 1883 and Civil War Volunteers who served in at least one campaign in the field were authorized to wear a service-in-war stripe.

[c] NOTE: All one-color stripes were 1/2-inch wide.

can be determined, a "war stripe" was never issued by the Quartermaster Depot.

In 1884, service-in-war chevrons were worn next to the cuff, followed by service chevrons, with the campaign chevron on top. After the new dress uniform was introduced in 1885, the War Department specified that the stripes would be worn in the order earned and this practice continued through 1902.[53]

Some men stayed in the Army as long as they could, even as long as forty years, since there were no provisions for retirement. Thus in the 1880s, it was possible for some men to still be on active duty after serving in the Mexican War. Finally, in 1885, Congress passed a retirement law for the enlisted man.[54] Under its provisions, a soldier who had thirty years of service became eligible to retire. As a result, the use of stripes indicating more than thirty years of service became even more rare.

Precedence and Pay

Precedence
During the eighteenth century, there was little question of grade (rank) and precedence in the enlisted ranks. But as the NCO grades expanded and became more complex, the addition of special noncommissioned officers posed the question as to which sergeant ranked the other. Some grades were considered equal, and so in order to determine seniority among the men occupying these grades, date of rank was used.

78

TABLE 3-5
Two-Color and Three-Color Service Stripes 1872–1902

Center Color	Outer Color	Total Width (inch)	Branch	Dates of Authorization
Light blue	Red	¾	Infantry War Service	1872–1884
Dark blue[b]	Red	¾	Infantry (Overcoat) War Service	1876–1884
Red	White	¾	Artillery War Service/Engineers Service	1872–1884
Light yellow	Red	¾	Cavalry War Service	1872–1884
Crimson	Red	¾	Ordnance War Service	1872–1884
Orange	Red	¾	Signal Corps War Service	1872–1884
Gray	Red	¾	Commissary Sergeant War Service	1873–1884
White	Red[c]	¾	Engineers War Service	1872–1884
Yellow	Red	¾	USMC War Service	1883–1884
Green	Orange	¾	Hospital Corps War Service	1896–1902
Green	White[a]	½	Hospital Corps Service	1896–1902
Green	White	¾	Hospital Corps; War Service in Infantry	1896–1902
Green	Yellow	¾	Hospital Corps; War Service in Cavalry	1896–1902
Green	Crimson	¾	Hospital Corps; War Service in Ordnance	1896–1902
Green	Gray	¾	Hospital Corps; War Service as Commissary Sergeant	1896–1902
Green	Buff	¾	Hospital Corps; War Service as Post QM Sergeant	1896–1902
Green	Red	¾	Hospital Corps; War Service	1872–1884
Green	Red		Hospital Corps; War Service in Artillery	1896–1902
Green	Red[c]	¾	Hospital Corps; War Service in Engineers	1896–1902
Green	Black	¾	Hospital Corps; War Service in Signal Corps	1896–1902
Dark blue	White[a]	½	Infantry (Overcoat) Service	1876–1884
Dark blue[b]	Red	½	Infantry (Overcoat) Campaign Service	1879–1883
Light blue	Red	½	Infantry Campaign Service	1879–1883
Red	White	½	Artillery Campaign Service	1879–1883
Light yellow	Red	½	Cavalry Campaign Service	1879–1883
Crimson	Red	½	Ordnance Campaign Service	1879–1883
Green	Red	½	Hospital Corps Campaign Service	1879–1883
Orange	Red	½	Signal Corps Campaign Service	1879–1883
Gray	Red	½	Commissary Sergeant Campaign Service	1879–1883

[a] White is chain stitching.
[b] White chain stitching on sides of dark blue.
[c] White chain stitching on outer edges of red.

By the start of the Civil War, precedence among enlisted grades was very simple:

1. sergeant major
2. quartermaster sergeant (regimental)
3. ordnance sergeant and hospital steward
4. first sergeant
5. sergeant
6. corporal[55]

Figure 3-19. At left and center, *these sergeants of the Corps of Engineers each wear two service stripes on their lower sleeves, indicating two completed enlistments.*

In the 1880s, several titles were added to the growing list of enlisted grades. The trend was that sergeants major and regimental quartermaster sergeants were in the first two grades, followed by NCOs who were not members of line companies, and then, bringing up the last, were NCOs of the line. General Order No. 4, 1886, listed the precedence at that time:

1. sergeant major
2. quartermaster sergeant (regimental)
3. ordnance sergeant, hospital steward, commissary sergeant, post quartermaster sergeant, chief musician, principal musician, chief trumpeter, and saddler sergeant
4. first sergeant
5. sergeant
6. corporal

The Spanish-American War and the rapid proliferation of enlisted grades added many positions to the list of "who ranked who." In November 1901, the Adjutant General listed the grades of noncommissioned officers:

1. sergeant major (regimental) and sergeant major senior grade (Artillery Corps)
2. quartermaster sergeant (regimental)
3. commmissary sergeant (regimental)
4. ordnance sergeant, post commissary sergeant, post quartermaster sergeant, electrician sergeant, hospital steward, first class sergeant (Signal Corps), chief musician, chief trumpeter, and principal musician
5. squadron and battalion sergeant major and color sergeant, and sergeant major junior grade (Artillery Corps)
6. first sergeant, drum major, company quartermaster sergeant, and battery stable sergeant
7. sergeant and acting hospital steward
8. corporal

Seniority was certainly not sacred, and five months after the preceding order was published, the second and third ranking grades (regimental quartermaster and commissary sergeants) became "outranked" by men formerly their junior. This came about as a result of a regulations amendment in April 1902 which changed the order of grades to the following:

1. sergeant major (regimental), sergeant major senior grade (Artillery Corps)
2. ordnance sergeant, post commissary sergeant, post quartermaster sergeant, electrician sergeant, hospital stewards, first class signal sergeant
3. quartermaster sergeant and commissary sergeant (regimental), chief musician
4. squadron and battalion sergeant major, sergeant major junior grade (Artillery Corps), color sergeant, chief trumpeter, principal musician, battalion quartermaster sergeant (Engineers Corps)
5. first sergeant, drum major
6. sergeant, company quartermaster sergeant, battery stable sergeant, acting hospital steward
7. corporal

Pay
Pay for enlisted men reflected both the responsibilities of senior NCOs and the special skills of technically trained men. Longevity pay was given to men for service past the first few years, although the amount for extra pay varied.

TABLE 3-6

Gold Lace Service Stripes 1884–1902

Color of Backing[a]	Branch	Dates of Authorization
White	Infantry	1884–1902
Red	Artillery	1884–1902
Light yellow	Cavalry	1884–1887
Medium yellow	Cavalry	1887–1902
Red with white stitching	Engineers	1884–1902
Green	Hospital Corps	1884–1896
Crimson	Ordnance	1884–1902
Buff	{ Post QM Sergeant	1884–1902
	USMA Detachment	1900–1902
Black	Signal Corps	1889–1902
Orange	Signal Corps	1884–1889
Gray	Commissary Sergeant	1884–1902
White with red stitching	Indian Scouts	1890–1902

[a] Branch-colored backing indicated war service. Dark blue backing was used by all branches to show each service.

In 1872, enlistments were for five years, with an additional $1.00 per month earned during the third year, $2.00 per month the fourth year, and $3.00 per month the last year. (Table 3-7 summarizes monthly pay during the first year.) Two dollars was added to the monthly pay for men serving during their second and subsequent enlistments plus the standard longevity pay earned during the third, fourth, and fifth years. Depending on whether a man was on his first enlistment or was reenlisted, various amounts from one to three dollars were taken out of his monthly pay and held until he completed his enlistment "honestly and faithfully to the date of discharge." The monthly pay rates under the Pay Act of 1 July 1872 are given in Table 3-7. As can be seen, NCOs of Ordnance Corps and Engineers Corps and specialists such as hospital stewards and various band NCO's drew considerably more pay than did the line NCO.

In 1890, the same general pay rates as 1872 were still in effect, with the Signal Corps personnel drawing pay comparable to Engineers and Ordnance soldiers. Commissary sergeants and post quartermaster sergeants drew $34.00 a month, putting them on the same footing as ordnance sergeants. All hospital stewards drew $45.00 a month, while acting hospital stewards drew $25.00 each month.

TABLE 3-7
Summary of Monthly Pay by Grade (During First Year)[a]

Grade	Monthly Pay During First Enlistment
Sergeant Major and Quartermaster Sergeant Engineer Corps	$36
Ordnance Sergeant, Sergeants of Ordnance and of Engineer Corps	34
Hospital Stewards (First Class)	30
Sergeant Major and Quartermaster Sergeant of Cavalry, Artillery, and Infantry	23
Chief Trumpeter, Principal Musician, Saddler Sergeant, Hospital Steward (Second Class), First Sergeant (Cavalry, Infantry, Artillery)	22
Hospital Steward (Third Class), Corporals of Ordnance and Engineer Corps	20
Sergeants of Cavalry, Artillery, and Infantry; First Class Privates of Engineer and Ordnance Corps	17
Corporals of Cavalry, Artillery, and Infantry; Saddler; Farrier	15
Trumpeter, Musician, Second Class Privates of Engineer and Ordnance; Privates of Infantry, Cavalry, Artillery	13

[a] Pay is for first year of first enlistment. During the third, fourth, and fifth year, one, two, and three dollars per month were added to the pay. This sum, and some additional reenlistment pay, was retained until discharge.

CHAPTER 4

Catalog of 1872–1902 Chevrons: The Second Period

This chapter contains a detailed listing of chevron designs authorized from 1872 through 1902. Catalog numbers from 100 to 199 have been assigned to this 30-year period. The 1872-pattern chevrons are generally distinguished by their large size (approximately 9 inches wide) and the chain stitching used to mark the edge of each bar. Small shirt chevrons of a different manufacturing process are included in the designs identified in the catalog as type *i*. These authorized shirt chevrons, which were made in 1901 and 1902, are very similar to the type *k* chevrons authorized after 1902 and discussed in the next chapter. Type *i* chevrons usually include only Catalog Nos. 106–108, 111, 113–119, 122–123, 125–126, 129, and 138, unless the color of some other chevron indicates that it was made before mid–1902, as for example in the case of a sergeant of ordnance. This is because only the above-listed chevrons would have the specialty or distinguishing device correctly positioned with the rank insignia point down. In short, any chevron that could be either type *i* or *k* should be considered type *k*, so that only those chevrons that were clearly made for wear on shirts are cataloged as type *i*.

The pioneer's chevron is cataloged in this chapter as No. 151, although the over-all design did not differ from the pre–1872 pattern cataloged as No. 15 except in quality of material and workmanship. The Signal Service device (Catalog No. 16) is included in this chapter because it was worn unchanged from the Civil War until 1891. A brief discussion of candidate stripes and two armbands is also included here because these insignia were classified as chevrons by the Quartermaster General's Department in the last third of the nineteenth century.

The basic design is a continuation of the sergeant major's chevron established in 1847. In two regulations (1872 and 1881), the sergeant major's chevrons were described as having "an arc," but in all cases, this insignia with three arcs is the rank described. This chevron was worn initially by infantry, cavalry, and artillery regimental sergeants major.

The Corps of Engineers was authorized one battalion sergeant major, and evidently this chevron was worn by him as the annual price lists show the same price for Engineers Corps sergeant major's chevrons from 1884 to 1899 as for other branches. Before 1884 the price lists were written in such a way that comparisons of this type cannot be distinguished. In 1899 battalion sergeants major were authorized their own special chevrons.

Catalog No. 100 was retitled regimental sergeant major in 1899 when another chevron was established for battalion and squadron sergeants major. When retitled, the chevron was worn only by infantry, cavalry and artillery, as the Corps of Engineers was organized only as companies and battalions. In 1901, when the Corps of Artillery was reorganized into separate companies

Figure 4-1. Catalog No. 100: Sergeant Major, 1872–1899; Regimental Sergeant Major, 1899–1901; Regimental Sergeant Major (Infantry, Cavalry), 1901–1902; Sergeant Major, Senior Grade (Artillery), 1901–1902.

and batteries, artillery districts served as a higher headquarters for companies, generally corresponding to regimental head-quarters. In this reorganization an artillery regimental sergeant major became a sergeant major, senior grade.

Figure 4-2. Catalog No. 101: Quartermaster Sergeant, 1872–1899; Regimental Quartermaster Sergeant, 1899–1902.

The "three bars and a tie of three bars" used during this period is a continuation of the basic design established in 1847. Made in the 1872 pattern, it was used by infantry and cavalry from 1872 through 1902, and by the artillery from 1872 until 1901. The Corps of Engineers was also authorized a quartermaster sergeant for the engineer battalion who used this chevron until 1901 (despite the addition of the word "regimental" in the rank title). After 1901, a special chevron was established for the Corps of Engineers battalion quartermaster sergeant. When the artillery was reorganized in 1901 and this grade was abolished, the artil-lery gilt chevrons were modified by removing the three horizon-tal bars. The stripes that remained were issued to artillery sergeants.

Figure 4-3. Catalog No. 102: Regimental Commissary Sergeant, 1899–1902.

Regimental commissary sergeants were established by an Act of Congress on 2 March 1899, and the chevron was prescribed in General Order No. 80, April 1899. The chevron was worn in infantry and cavalry regiments through 1902. These chevrons were made in pairs so the cusps would face forward. Infantry and cavalry regiments continued to have regimental commissary sergeants through the uniform change of 1902. Although Con-gress did not authorize any artillery regimental commissary sergeants, the artillery chevron for this grade was made and issued by the Quartermaster's Department from 1899 through 1901.

Figure 4-4. Catalog No. 103: Squadron or Battalion Sergeant Major, 1899–1901; Squadron or Battalion Sergeant Major (Infantry, Engineers, Cavalry), 1901–1902; Sergeant Major, Junior Grade (Artillery), 1901–1902.

Prescribed by General Order No. 80, April 1899, this device was for battalion sergeants major of infantry and engineers, and for squadron sergeants major of cavalry. During reorganization of the Corps of Artillery in 1901, this rank—for the artillery—was retitled sergeant major, junior grade.

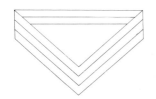

Figure 4-5. Catalog No. 104: Battalion Quartermaster Sergeant, 1901–1902.

The grade of battalion quartermaster sergeant was used only by the Corps of Engineers in the 1880s and 1890s. The one autho-rized battalion quartermaster sergeant of engineers wore chev-rons of the same design as regimental quartermaster sergeants of infantry, cavalry, and artillery from the mid–1880s until 1901. This rank insignia was established simultaneously with the expansion of the Engineers Corps to three battalions. After the 1902 uniform change, other branches were authorized battalion

Figure 4-6. Catalog No. 105: Battalion or Company Quartermaster Sergeant, 1872–1883; Company, Troop, or Battery Quartermaster Sergeant, 1898–1902.

quartermaster sergeants; however, in the 1872–pattern chevrons, this rank was worn only by the Engineers Corps.

This insignia was a continuation of Catalog No. 17, established in 1866 for company quartermaster sergeants. In 1873, the War Department published General Order No. 61, which stated that the men would no longer be promoted to this grade, but those holding the grade would be allowed to continue in the position so strength reduction would be gradual. After 1882, Uniform Regulations no longer mention this grade, and evidently all of the men who were battalion and company quartermaster sergeants in 1873 were by 1882 serving in other grades.

In July 1898, the design was reintroduced and used through 1902 for quartermaster sergeants of engineer, infantry, cavalry, and artillery of company-sized units.

Figure 4-7. Catalog No. 106:
Chief Musician, 1899–1902.

Although the pay grade and rank of chief musician was established in 1847, no special chevron was authorized until April 1899. When first authorized, this insignia was worn by chief musicians of infantry, cavalry, and artillery. Then in 1901, one chief musician for the Engineers Corps was added. A chief musician was assigned to each band, when bands were established, by a table of allowance. Prior to this time the chief musician position was simply allotted to the regiment, and band members were drawn from the various companies.

Figure 4-8. Catalog No. 107:
Chief Trumpeter, 1873–1902.

One of the first chevrons added after the 1872 Uniform Regulations was that for the chief trumpeter. Authorized at first only in mounted regiments, the one chief trumpeter was the senior regimental musician. In 1899, separate regimental bands were authorized and the chief trumpeter was assigned to this band, while before the band members had been drawn from companies of the line. With the authorization of men for regimental bands, the light artillery was also authorized a chief trumpeter. By 1902 chief trumpeters were assigned to all of the various regimental bands, along with other band musicians.

The bugle on the chevron was supposedly to be worn with the bell forward, but in practice the chevrons were sewn on arbitrarily. Early photos show some chief trumpeters wore the horn facing forward and some wore them reversed, although the chevrons were always made in pairs.

Figure 4-9. Catalog No. 108: Principal Musician, 1872–1902.

Authorized for over fifty years before being given a special chevron, the principal musician's title is self-explanatory. The chevron for principal musicians was initially created by the 1872 Uniform Regulations, the chevron being made in pairs so the bugle would face forward.

These men were authorized only in the dismounted regiments, and were the counterpart of the mounted chief trumpeters. As the senior musician in each infantry and artillery regiment, the NCOs of this rank acted as the drum majors of regimental bands before the rank of drum major was created in 1899. At the turn of the century, cavalry regiments and the engineers were also authorized principal musicians as a part of the concept of expanding the NCO ranks and recognizing specialists. As a result, in the twentieth century, each infantry, cavalry, artillery, and engineer band had a principal musician.

Figure 4-10. Catalog No. 109: Hospital Steward, 1872–1887.

The chevron worn by hospital stewards before 1887 is the only NCO chevron that does not conform to the general pattern of V-shaped bars. While the over-all design is the same as that used before the 1872 uniform changes, the yellow patented chain stitch used along the edges characterizes this chevron as typical of most hospital steward insignia made in green after 1872.

The chevron is 1¾-inches wide and 9–10 inches long with the caduceus 2 inches in length. Hospital stewards wore the chevrons in pairs so they ran at an angle approximately 30° below the horizontal, with the top of the caduceus facing up and to the rear.

In 1884, the Army established gilt dress chevrons; for the hospital steward's insignia, the edges were bound with gold tracing braid ⅛-inch wide and the caduceus was hand-embroidered with gold thread. Hospital stewards received a new chevron in August 1887, when the War Department established the grade of acting hospital steward. Throughout the 15-year period from 1872 to 1887, one hundred and fifty hospital stewards were authorized.

[See Figure 4-11.]

As a result of an Act of Congress and a decision of the Secretary of War, the Hospital Corps was reorganized in August 1887. General Order No. 56, 1887, specified that before a hospital steward could be appointed, the man must have served at least one year as an acting hospital steward. This created the need for a chevron to distinguish acting hospital stewards, and this in turn led to the making of a new chevron (Catalog No. 110) for hospital stewards. (Two years before, men appointed to act as hospital stewards wore a 2-inch by 2-inch red cross on a white armband, but this was not an official rank.)

Non-dress chevrons are of green with white chain stitching and a red Geneva cross in the center. The dress chevron created for hospital stewards used gold lace on green facing cloth, with

Figure 4-11. Catalog No. 110: Hospital Steward, 1887–1901.

Figure 4-12. Catalog No. 111: Hospital Steward, 1901–1902.

the cross made of red cloth; it is interesting to note that in the gilt chevrons, only those of hospital stewards and acting hospital stewards have the center device in cloth. At least one hospital steward was to be stationed at every post, and two if the garrison was of six companies or larger. Even so, it is questionable how often these gilt chevrons were worn because members of the Hospital Corps were not to attend reviews, parades, or similar functions. In August 1896, dress uniforms for the Hospital Corps were discontinued and instructions sent out that the gold chevrons rendered surplus by this action were to be turned in through quartermaster channels. The dress chevron of hospital stewards thus gathered were sold at public auction in Philadelphia a few months later.

[See Figure 4-12.]

In February 1901, the hospital steward's chevron was changed by replacing the red Geneva cross with a white-edged green Maltese cross. No gilt chevrons were used by Hospital Corps personnel during this time.

Figure 4-13. Catalog No. 112: Acting Hospital Steward, 1887–1901.

Acting hospital stewards were established in 1887 to test the capacity of men before appointing them as hospital stewards. Because of this, an acting hospital steward could administratively be reduced to a private in the Hospital Corps by a post commander. For field service, assistant hospital stewards and hospital stewards were mounted.

The chevrons, both cloth and gold lace, are identical to those worn by hospital stewards, except that the arc is omitted.

When the hospital steward's chevron was changed in February 1901, the insignia worn by the acting hospital stewards was altered in the same manner, replacing the red Geneva cross with a white-edged green Maltese cross. This change was established by General Order No. 19, 1901.

Figure 4-15. Catalog No. 114: Lance Acting Hospital Steward, 1901–1902.

The chevron of a lance corporal was in green cloth with trim of white chain stitching. The Maltese cross in the upper angle was the device then used to designate the Hospital Corps.

General Order No. 139, November 1901, the establishing order, stated, in part: *"To test the capacity of privates of the Hospital Corps for the duties of noncommissioned officers, the Surgeon General and chief surgeons may appoint lance acting hospital stewards, who will hold appointments not to exceed three months and will be obeyed and respected as acting hospital stewards. . . . "* In many respects, this rank was comparable to lance corporals of infantry, cavalry, artillery, and engineers.

[See Figure 4-16.]

The trend toward special chevrons for many soldiers resulted in the adoption of an insignia for privates of the Hospital Corps in February 1901. Prior to this, a white brassard with a red Geneva cross on it had been used to designate Hospital Corps privates.

Figure 4-14. Catalog No. 113: Acting Hospital Stewards, 1901–1902 (see man on the right).

Figure 4-16. Catalog No. 115: Privates of the Hospital Corps, 1901–1902.

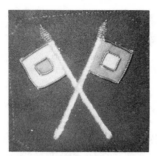

Figure 4-17. Catalog No. 16: Members of the Signal Service or Signal Corps, 1864–1891.

Figure 4-18. Catalog No. 116: Sergeant of First Class of Signal Corps, 1891–1902.

[See Figure 4-19.]

The names Signal Service and Signal Corps were used interchangeably during this time. Members wore a special device on the sleeves consisting of red and white flags ¾-inch square with a ¼-inch center; the centers and flags have bullion edges. The 3-inch staffs were made with bullion spears on the tips. Worn on all uniforms, the crossed flags device was on a 3-inch cloth square with rounded corners. When gilt chevrons were introduced in 1884, the same sleeve insignia continued to be used for both dress and work uniforms.

NCOs wore the insignia above their chevrons, privates of the first class wore the device on both sleeves, and privates of the second class wore it on the left sleeve only. The term *private first class,* or *first class private,* was introduced in 1872, although this insignia was used by Signal Corps privates before 1872. This insignia of two crossed flags was made in pairs, with one red flag and one white flag. No guidance was published as to which flag faced front, and the signal uniforms of the period show equal use of devices with white or red flags front. In all cases, however, opposed pairs appear to have been worn.

A flaming torch was added to other Signal Corps insignia in 1884, but because of stocks on hand, nothing was specified for enlisted chevrons until 1891, when the crossed flags were replaced by crossed flags and a flaming torch. Crossed flags continued to be used for several years by some state militia signal service. Those insignia made later, especially for militia use, have flags and staffs without bullion.

This long title was lengthened even more in 1900 to "sergeant of the first class of the Signal Corps." Before 1891, the highest enlisted rank in the Signal Corps was sergeant. Often the navy blue infantry overcoat chevrons are confused with the Signal Corps black, but the signal ranks are jet black and when compared with the infantry overcoat stripes, the difference is obvious. In addition, the signal device is in the upper angle of the black chevrons. This insignia was made so the white flag would be worn to the front. These beautifully made dress insignia were specified to have the crossed signal flags and a burning torch embroidered in silk and bullion in high relef. A pair of these gilt chevrons was the most expensive of all the dress ranks, costing over five dollars a pair under some contracts. The title of sergeant first class, which still endures, started with this grade.

The exact chevrons used by the Signal Corps NCOs before 1891 are difficult to trace; in 1891, however, the insignia of rank became clearly defined. There were only twenty signal sergeants second class authorized in 1891, and actual strengths were below that. Dress chevrons, as well as those for wear on campaign uniforms, were made in pairs (white flag worn to the front), the same as for sergeants of first class of Signal Corps, with the omission of the arc.

Figure 4-19. Catalog No.
117: Sergeant of Second
Class of Signal Corps,
1891–1896; Sergeant of
Signal Corps, 1896–1902.

Figure 4-20. Catalog No.
118: Corporal of the Signal
Corps, 1898–1902.

Figure 4-21. Catalog No.
119: Lance Corporal of
Signal Corps, 1898–1902.

During the summer of 1898, the first signal companies were organized, and the black chevron with the torch and flags was authorized to be made in pairs so that the white flag would face forward.

The Spanish-American War caused the establishment of the first companies of the Signal Corps. This concurrently established Signal Corps lance corporals who were on the same footing as lance corporals of other branches. This chevron consisted of a jet black V with white chain stitching on both sides of the signal device in the upper angle. These chevrons were made in pairs with the white flag worn forward.

Figure 4-22. Catalog No.
120: First Class Privates of
Signal Corps, 1898–1902.

The first class private rank (sometimes called private first class), initiated by the Signal Corps, was revised in 1898. This insignia was used during this revision with the white flag worn forward. Most photographs of these men show that the chevron actually used, especially on khaki uniforms, was simply the crossed flags and torch taken from a sergeant's chevron.

[See Figure 4-23.]

The ordnance sergeant, whose rank the Army established in 1851, continued to wear a star in the angle of his chevron after 1872. The star was shrunk and inverted, but the over-all chevron remained crimson in color.

The ordnance sergeant, along with the post commissary sergeant and the post quartermaster sergeant, constituted the post noncommissioned staff. Thus, the ordnance sergeant served as the ordnance NCO of a post. While ordnance sergeants wore this chevron, sergeants of ordnance simply wore a sergeant's three stripes in crimson. The two ranks should not be confused as the distinctions between them were great.

Gilt chevrons worn by ordnance sergeants in the late 1880s and early 1890s had the stars made from ten pieces of gold lace, each piece running along a side of the star, so no lace was wasted. Later, chevrons had the star made from five or six pieces of lace sewn together with a small cloth star covering the lace so the hollow star was formed, similar to first sergeant's chevrons.

The star was changed to represent color sergeants in 1901, as the star was deemed more appropriate for the NCOs who carried the national flag and the regimental colors. When the 1901 redesignation took place, this chevron was made in branch colors for infantry, cavalry, and artillery regimental color sergeants, and in red with white trim for the battalion color sergeants of the Engineers Corps.

This chevron superseded the ordnance sergeant's rank insignia with the star in February 1901. Although chevrons of this design were made in pairs, the direction in which the flames were to be worn was not specified. The flame, bomb, and stripes were in crimson. Ordnance sergeants continued in their status as members of the post noncommissioned staff and differed from sergeants of ordnance just as before 1901.

Figure 4-24. Catalog No.
122: Ordnance Sergeant,
1901–1902.

Figure 4-23. Catalog No. 121: Ordnance Sergeant, 1872–1901; Color Sergeant, 1901–1902.

Figure 4-25. Catalog No. 123: Regimental Color Sergeant, 1883–1885; Regimental and Battalion Color Sergeant, 1885–1901.

The Secretary of War established the color sergeant's chevron, containing a "sphere 1¼-inches in diameter," upon the recommendation of the Inspector General. Some correspondence[1] excerpts show how easily the Army made changes when the right person suggested them.

"12 March 1883: Respectfully returned to the Secretary of War. . . . The Regimental Color Sergeant I think should have an addition made to his chevron of a star. . . . Tactius says, the Color Sergeant is selected from the most distinguished for bravery and for precision under arms in marching. [signed] D. B. Sacket, Brig. & Inspector General."

"13 March 1883 [the next day]: The Secretary of War concurs in the recommendations of the Quartermaster General and the Inspector General. . . . "

The sphere was chosen simply because ordnance sergeants already used the star. On 29 March 1883, Captain Gill of the Philadelphia Quartermaster Depot sent two pairs of these chevrons in each branch color to the Quartermaster General. From inception to manufacture took seventeen days.

Regimental color sergeants of infantry, cavalry, and artillery, and engineers battalion color sergeants wore this chevron. In 1901, color sergeants changed to a chevron with an inverted star, the design originally considered best.

Figure 4-26. Catalog No. 124: Commissary Sergeant, 1873–1898; Post Commissary Sergeant, 1898–1902.

Congress first authorized commissary sergeants in 1873. The cadet gray chevrons were, according to regulation, made in pairs with the points to face forward. For the first twelve years or so, however, the crescent actually pointed up. The crescent worn on the forage cap and dress helmet pointed up and one can surmise that since the crescent was worn one way on the cap, the Quartermaster General sealed chevron samples with the crescent facing the same way. About 1885 the chevrons changed in that they were actually made in pairs with the crescent points forward.

In 1881, all but one of the authorized one-hundred and fifty commissary sergeant positions were filled. This number was substantially reduced, and in 1897 there were only ninety commissary sergeants. The rules governing examinations and appointments of commissary sergeants in 1897 stated, in part: "Commissary Sergeants are appointed from Sergeants in the line who have served at least 5 years in the Army, including 3 years as Noncommissioned Officers, and usually from those less than 45 years of age. . . . "[2] The requirements included demonstrating knowledge of subsistence regulations, the subsistence manual, general regulations, arithmetic, preparation of papers, penmanship, orthography, and general education.

In 1898, the title of commissary sergeant was changed to post commissary sergeant, emphasizing further the post noncommissioned staff type of duties required of the soldiers who wore the cadet gray chevrons.

[See Figure 4-27.]

For several years prior to 1884, the Quartermaster General recommended that sergeants be assigned to the Quartermaster General's Department for duty at various posts to assist in keeping records. Before 1884, all quartermaster sergeants were assigned to regiments. When a regimental headquarters left a post, or a station was manned by units not including the regiment's headquarters, a quartermaster sergeant was not present. This caused problems since several NCOs, at best, might keep records at a single post in a span of ten years because of the transfers of regiments. Often no NCO was available and the entire burden fell on one of the lieutenants.

In 1884, the rank of post quartermaster sergeant was created to alleviate this problem. Eighty men were authorized at this rank. These NCOs were the first enlisted men assigned to the Quartermaster's Department. Chevrons were buff with a yellow crossed key and quill pen in the upper angle. The key and pen were made in opposed pairs although it was not stated which way they would be worn. The grade of post quartermaster sergeant continued until 1912.

Before 1899, regiments were not entitled to bands per se. Men serving as band musicians did so as an additional duty, and the drum major normally was the chief trumpeter or principal musician. Personnel for regimental bands were authorized in

Figure 4-28. Catalog No. 126: Drum Major, 1899–1902.

Figure 4-27. Catalog No. 125: Post Quartermaster Sergeant, 1884–1902.

Figure 4-29. Catalog No. 127: Saddler Sergeant, 1873–1899.

1898, along with one drum major for each cavalry, infantry, and artillery regiment. The drum major's chevron was established in April 1899 and the distinguished device consisted of hand-embroidered crossed batons. In 1901, the Engineers Corps band was formed, and was led by the engineers drum major. The same year, the Corps of Artillery was reorganized and entitled to ten bands, each with a drum major.

This cavalry rank was added within a year after the adoption of the 1872 Uniform Regulations. The design in the angle represents a saddler's knife, handle up. The 1884-pattern dress chevrons had the gold lace placed so as to give the knife added realism. The lace representing the handle ran vertically, that representing the ferrule across, and the lace making the blade was crimped to run along the curved blade axis.

One saddler sergeant was authorized for each cavalry regiment, until 1899 when he was replaced by a saddler, who wore only the knife. Although only the cavalry was authorized saddler sergeants, the Philadelphia Depot ordered ninety-five pairs of this chevron for the artillery in 1900. These were never issued and after 1902 were sold at auction.

Figure 4-30. Catalog No. 128: Veterinary Sergeant of Battery of Field Artillery.

This chevron was authorized in July 1898 by General Order No. 106 which was written in response to a bill introduced in Congress that would have authorized one veterinary sergeant for each battery of field artillery. A number of chevrons, both cloth and gilt, were manufactured, but the bill failed and no one was ever issued the chevron.

Figure 4-31. Catalog No. 129: Stable Sergeant, Field Artillery, 1901–1902.

First authorized in February 1901, the grade of stable sergeant of field artillery existed for twenty years. For the first two years, the device was a sergeant's chevron with an outline of a red horse's head above. These chevrons were made in pairs, so the horsehead faced forward.

Figure 4-32. Catalog No. 130: First Sergeant, 1872–1902.
First sergeant's chevrons were changed in 1872 only to conform to standard materials and the newly introduced chain stitch. The patent of F. S. Johnston (*see* Appendix 3) discusses manufacture of this particular chevron in detail.

First sergeants were authorized for infantry, cavalry, artillery, and engineers in 1872. Although at this time the basic color for the Engineers Corps was red, with white as the trim, the lozenge for engineers first sergeants was white.

Until the Spanish-American War, first Sergeant's chevrons were made with the diamond almost square; after the war, the angles were made so that the diamond was taller.

Illustration a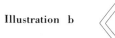

The usual design of cloth chevrons before the Spanish-American war is shown in *illustration a.*

Illustration b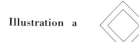

The cloth chevron design used after 1898 is shown in *illustration b.* This shape was occasionally used during the Indian Wars.

Illustration c

The dress 1884 lozenges were made of four pieces of gilt lace so that a minimum amount of lace was used. The effect made the lozenge appear as shown in *illustration c.*

Illustration d

Later, this gilt diamond was made from five or six pieces of gold lace sewn together, so that the center of wool completely covered the middle unused lace. These later chevrons can be distinguished by the pattern lozenge shown in *illustration d.*

When the Indian Scouts were authorized special uniforms in 1890, they began to wear white chevrons with red chain stitching. One first sergeant of Indian Scouts was authorized. The USMA

Figure 4-33. Catalog No. 131: Sergeant, 1872–1902.

Quartermaster Detachment's (QMD) first sergeant also wore a now-scarce chevron of buff color with black stitching. The Philadelphia Quartermaster Depot had only four pairs of cloth Indian Scout first sergeant's stripes, and two pairs of cloth USMA QMD chevrons in stock in 1901. The Philadelphia Depot also manufactured ordnance first sergeant's chevrons, and even included them in clothing specifications, although no ordnance first sergeants were authorized. Ordnance first sergeant's chevrons were even sealed as samples in the early 1880s. Ordnance first sergeant's chevrons were carried in stock until staff officers discovered that Congress had not provided for the rank of ordnance first sergeants. During revision of the chevron specifications in 1901, this illogicality brought strong words from the Quartermaster General, and the rank insignia for this unauthorized position was omitted from specifications and dropped from stock.

[See Figure 4-33.]

The backbone of the Army was and is the sergeant. More sergeants were authorized in the thirty years between 1872 and 1902 than any rank other than private. The strength of the Army in 1881 is typical of the NCO distribution during the last third of the nineteenth century. Each of the ten cavalry regiments were authorized sixty sergeants while NCOs of equal or greater rank in the regiment consisted of twelve first sergeants and one each chief trumpeter, saddler sergeant, chief musician, quartermaster sergeant, and sergeant major. During the same year, the artillery was authorized 260 Sergeants, the infantry 1,000, and the engineers 20.

Sergeants of ordnance (not to be confused with ordnance sergeants) wore crimson chevrons. Signal Corps sergeants before 1889 had orange chevrons, while "black silk braid" chevrons were called for from 1889 to 1891. Catalog No. 117 replaced the black silk braid chevrons in 1891. In 1890, Indian Scout sergeants began to wear this sergeant's chevron (Catalog No. 131) in white with red stitching. At the turn of the century, the six sergeants of the Army Service Detachment at West Point wore buff sergeant's chevrons. During the time between the uniform changes of 1872 and 1902, no other chevron was worn in more colors or by more men.

The Army had nearly as many corporals as sergeants. Men who wore the chevron of two bars were the junior NCOs, and many of the various NCOs served as corporals before promotion to higher ranks. Sergeants had either 1-inch-wide or 1¼-inch-wide stripes down the seam of their trousers while corporals were distinguished by ½-inch-wide trouser stripes.

All branches authorized sergeants also had corporals. For most of the time during the 1880s, the Army contained thirty-nine Signal Corps corporals who wore orange chevrons with separate signal flags above. Later authorizations reduced this

Figure 4-34. Catalog No. 132: Corporal, 1872–1902.

number to twenty men. The year 1889 saw a new chevron specified: one of "black silk braid." Other corporals who wore this design include those from the infantry, cavalry, artillery, engineers, ordnance, and Indian Scouts.

Lance corporals were first authorized in May 1891 by General Order No. 46, which read in part:

Figure 4-35. Catalog No. 133: Lance Corporal, 1891–1902.

> To test the capacity of Privates for the duties of noncommissioned officer, commanders of troops, batteries, and companies, including those at recruiting depots, may appoint Lance Corporals who shall hold such appointments not to exceed three months, and while holding the appointment shall be obeyed and respected as Corporals. . . . The appointment [may] . . . be renewed; but not more than one Lance Corporal at the same time for the same troop, battery, or company . . . [may be appointed].

A later order restricted reappointments to one 3-month term. Initially, lance corporals were found in artillery, infantry, cavalry, engineer, and Indian Scouts, and in 1893 or 1894, lance corporals of ordnance began to wear this special chevron. Other branches had lance corporals who had special chevrons, among them lance corporals of the Signal Corps and lance acting hospital stewards.

Figure 4-36. Catalog No. 134: Cook, 1898–1902.

One cook per company was authorized by Act of Congress in the summer of 1898. Cooks were to receive the pay and allowances of a corporal and were to "take the rank . . . of corporal." The insignia adopted represents a cook's cap outlined in the branch color. Infantry, cavalry, and artillery cooks wore the chevron in a single color; cooks of the engineers companies wore a red cap with white edges; and Signal Corps cooks had a black cap trimmed in white.

Figure 4-37. Catalog No. 135: Farrier, 1874–1903.

Figure 4-38. Catalog No. 136: Mechanic and Artificers (Artillery), 1899–1902; Artificer (Infantry), 1899–1902.

[See Figure 4-37.]

Farriers were in cavalry and artillery regiments before 1872 but had no special insignia. In September 1874, the Quartermaster General approved a sealed sample of the cloth horseshoe, and the chevron was officially established for farriers. The toe and heel pieces were made of gray cloth and the horseshoe itself was cut to show the underlying blue representing the nail holes. The chevron was not issued or worn in gold lace. The 4½-inch by 3¾-inch size continued through the 1902 uniform changes (*see* Catalog No. 317).

[See Figure 4-38.]

The War Department created this rank as a result of the Spanish-American War. Infantrymen who wore the crossed hammers were known as "artificers," while their artillery counterparts were known as "Mechanics and Artificers." The name "artificer" means one who works with arms and weapons, so the artillery title of "mechanic and artificer" was redundant. The reasoning behind the selection of this dual title is unknown. This design and the rank titles continued through 1902.

Figure 4-39. Catalog No. 137: Saddler, 1899–1902.
Saddlers replaced saddler sergeants in the spring of 1899. Only cavalry regiments were authorized saddlers. This rank was authorized through the 1902 chevron changes.

Figure 4-40. Catalog No. 138: Electrician Sergeant, 1899–1902.

Technical advances, combined with sudden interest in coastal defenses caused by the Spanish-American War, created an immediate need for an NCO capable of performing specialized duties at coastal artillery works. Thus, one hundred electrician sergeants were authorized. Although considered part of the post noncommissioned staff and not officially belonging to the Artillery Corps, the electrician sergeants did submit personal reports to the Chief of Artillery and worked exclusively with defense fortifications.

To train electrician sergeants, a special division was established at the School of Submarine Defense, Fort Totten, New York. At this school, candidates studied electrician sergeant's duties for six months, with classes limited to forty students a year. Before a soldier could apply for the Electrician Sergeant School, he had to prove he had studied a practical course in electricity for at least one year and be recommended by his commanding officer. A civilian could enlist as a private of artillery with the intent of attending the school, provided he was accepted by the school commandant. A man so enlisting could be discharged at his option at the end of the course if he failed the final examination. Electrician sergeants appointed prior to the school's founding were required to attend the course. If these NCOs failed, they could not reenlist as electrician sergeants, although some were permitted to remain as sergeants of the line.

The chevrons prescribed for these specially trained men were standard artillery sergeant's chevrons with five white bolts of lightning above. Clothing specifications called for the lightning chevrons to be made in pairs, but this was not always done.

Figure 4-41. Catalog No. 151: Pioneer, 1851–1899.

Pioneers were the only privates who wore a specialty chevron before 1872. This sleeve device set the precedent for others; however, just when the cook's, mechanic's, and saddler's insignia became authorized, the Army eliminated the precedent-setting pioneers. Men designated as pioneers wore the cloth crossed hatchets on both sleeves in the same location as other chevrons. A few pioneers were corporals and they wore the hatchets "above and just resting on the chevrons."

The crossed hatchets were made in the primary colors for infantry, cavalry, artillery, engineers, and ordnance. The dark blue background for the pioneer's device was 9 inches long and 5½ inches high but often wearers cut off much of the background material to make it smaller. The insignia was made only in cloth, as were other specialty marks, so the crossed hatchets did not exist in gold lace for the post 1884 dress uniform.

Company Bearer, 1887–1890; Company Litter Bearer, 1890–1899.
Each company commander, with the concurrence of the post surgeon, designated four privates to receive at least four hours' instruction each month in litter bearing and first aid. These men were distinguished by a red brassard worn on the left arm above the elbow and were known as company bearers or company litter bearers.

The bearers had to be men who could qualify as privates in the Hospital Corps, so they could transfer to that corps if they desired. After the Army's experience in the Spanish-American War, it was determined that special company litter bearers were unnecessary.

[See Figure 4-42.]

The red cross brassard had several titles and was worn by a variety of men from 1884 through 1902. The brassard was first prescribed in August 1884. It was to be worn by all neutrals (in terms of the Geneva Convention) on the left arm above the elbow, in addition to any chevron of rank. The next June the brassard was prescribed for acting hospital stewards, and the following month, it was moved from the left arm to the left cuff. Three years later, in February 1888, hospital stewards stopped wearing the brassard, and the Army directed that it be worn by company litter bearers on the left cuff. Just six months before, the Army had authorized company bearers a red arm band to be worn *above* the elbow. Evidently, quartermaster personnel discovered this duplication and in March 1890, the red cross brassard was prescribed for "privates of Hospital Corps and for all personnel neutralized by terms of the Geneva Convention." At

Figure 4-42. Red Cross Brassard, 1884–present.

this same time, it was specified to be worn above the left elbow again. The next year, regulations further clarified that only personnel transferred to the Hospital Corps could wear the brassard. In 1892, the brassard was prescribed only for privates of the Hospital Corps.

During 1892, the Adjutant General published the provisions of the Geneva Convention in a General Order to the Army. The convention included the stipulation that a red cross on a white arm band would be worn by individuals neutralized by the convention. During the Spanish-American War, all persons connected with the Medical Department habitually wore the brassard. Three years later, the insignia was prescribed to be worn "in time of war with a signatory of the Geneva Convention by all persons in the military service by terms of the Geneva Convention."

Photographs show the brassard often sewn onto the blouse sleeve, rather than pinned in place.

Candidates, 1878–1904.

Congress authorized the appointment of new officers from enlisted men in 1878, and the Army in turn authorized a candidate insignia. Established by General Order No. 62, 1878, was "a single stripe of gilt lace similar to that worn by commissioned officers" to be worn on each sleeve. Candidates who became ineligible for commissions by reason of age continued to wear the stripe on the left sleeve only.

In 1889, the candidate stripe was described as a "double stripe running the length of the cuff, pointed at the end, with a small button below the point of the stripe."[3] The stripes, ¼-inch wide with an ⅛-inch space between, were worn on dress coats in gilt lace, and on the blouse and overcoat in branch colors made of cloth. Evidently, very few men qualified for or wore these candidate stripes, as the Philadelphia Depot only had thirty pairs of cloth stripes and four pairs of gilt ones in June 1900.

Starting in 1892, hopeful enlisted men appeared before a board of officers at Fort Leavenworth once a year. Men selected as candidates were placed on a list and, as vacancies occurred, promotions to second lieutenant were made. These same stripes, both gold and cloth, continued to be worn on the new uniforms adopted in 1902.

CHAPTER 5

History of Chevron, Uniform, and Service Stripe Development 1902–1920: The Third Period

In 1902 a board to rewrite the Army Uniform Regulations convened in Washington. The Quartermaster Depot at Philadelphia made various uniform samples proposed by the board, which then sent letters and occasionally samples to regimental commanders for their opinions.[1] On 17 July 1902, the Adjutant General published the resulting regulations as General Order No. 81. This general order was far reaching in its effects, drastically changing enlisted uniforms and the accompanying chevrons.

No sooner was the new uniform order published than President Theodore Roosevelt and the Commanding General, Nelson Miles, objected to portions of the new regulations.[2] General Miles wanted the new regulations suspended and another set made. Accordingly, the War Department published new regulations on 31 December 1902, as General Order No. 132. All of the controversy involved officers' uniforms. Since no senior official questioned the suitability of the new enlisted uniforms, the Philadelphia Quartermaster Depot started to make them in the summer of 1902, along with the great variety of new chevrons. Lieutenant Colonel William Patten, Deputy Quartermaster General, directed officers at Philadelphia to make and seal new chevron sample books. Problem areas not covered in the new regulations were worked out through correspondence.[3]

The authorization of new chevrons increased dramatically during World War I, when Congress gave the President special powers to expand the Army for conduct of the war. The President created temporary branches of service and the War Department established new chevrons for each pay grade in the temporary branches, continuing the inefficient practice of stocking chevrons for each separate branch. Included were chevrons for men assigned to the Tank Corps, the Aviation Service, two different transportation services, plus a myriad of smaller sections. The Quartermaster Department's supply problem became overwhelming in the attempt to outfit over a hundred different ranks with distinctive chevrons.

The cost and confusion was just too much, and finally in 1920 Congress radically revised the enlisted grade structure by declaring that all enlisted ranks would be consolidated into seven pay grades. The resulting new chevrons marked an end to the concept that position or job was to be shown by a chevron: from then on only pay was involved.

Uniforms and Chevrons

Old Uniforms and Chevrons

America after the Spanish-American War was a new power in the world, flexing its muscle from the Pacific to the Caribbean, having won battles halfway around the world. United States troops became involved in battles in the Philippines, initially taking over from the Spanish and then fighting the native insur-

Cavalry,Private   Hospital Corps,Private,First Class   Signal Corps, Sergeant   Infantry,Private   Coast Artillery Corps, Sergeant   Quartermaster Corps, Sergeant
Full Dress   Full Dress   Full Dress   Service Uniform   Full Dress   Full Dress

Figure 5-1. Uniforms and chevrons in use between 1902 and World War I.

gents, while the 9th Infantry, elements of the 6th Cavalry, and others campaigned in China. The cost of this new involvement was huge, and the military spent money as it had not done since the Civil War. This abnormal condition of money increases and an Army stretched around the globe clashed with the ingrained workings of the War Department. How could new uniforms be introduced when there were stocks of the older-pattern clothing still available and in good condition? Even the Secretary of War became personally involved on several occasions, writing letters to point out how many hats, coats, buttons, and other quartermaster supplies were available. New world power or not, the War Department had always watched the pennies and it would continue to do so.

The Secretary of War's office prevailed. The engineers and the artillery were selected to wear the old uniforms, while other troops were to receive the new 1902-pattern clothing.

In 1903, the Quartermaster General reported that "under existing orders, the Artillery Corps and Engineer troops serving in the United States wear the old dress uniform. This will

*Figure 5-2. The last soldier
to see George Custer alive
who lived to tell about it is
former Trumpeter Martin,
shown here upon his
retirement. He wears a coast
artillery dress coat with
gold lace chevrons point up.
The Coast Artillery Corps
was selected in 1903 to wear
out the remaining stock of
1885-pattern coats, gilt
chevrons, and gilt service
stripes. These were worn
from 1902 through 1911 until
the stocks were depleted.*

continue until the stock on hand is exhausted, except in the case
of battalions or companies returning from the Philippines."[4] In
mid–1904, the War Department announced a policy change,
stating the artillery alone would wear out the old uniforms, and
all other units would be issued new coats which they would
wear with the old trousers. Men wore small 1902-type chevrons
on the artillery 1885-pattern coats. Some confusion existed in
the various coast artillery companies despite explicit War Department instructions; as always, someone did not get the word.
A few coast artillery units began to wear the 1902 chevrons on
the old coats in December 1905, but most companies continued
using the old gold lace for dress and the 1872-pattern cloth
chevrons for service wear. Simply by virtue of being stationed
with non-artillery units, some companies obtained the new
rank insignia. As the Quartermaster's Department supplied infantry and field artillery regiments with the 1902-pattern uniforms, any coast artillery unit stationed at the same post was also
supplied with the new uniform and chevrons. By 1907, owing to
many misunderstood directives and a fair amount of finagling

by company commanders, some coast artillery units wore new chevrons on old coats, some wore 1884 gold chevrons, and at least two companies wore 1872 cloth chevrons on their dress coats. The War Department's policy then became one of "keep what you have—no more changes."[5]

The Chief of Artillery continually tried to obtain new-pattern clothing but to no avail. By April 1908, there remained 19,000 dress coats in the Quartermaster's Department stocks. The Quartermaster General, replying to a request by the Chief of Artillery for release of the 1902-pattern coats by June 1908, stated: "In the opinion of this office, these dress coats [in stock] should be utilized, and it is not believed that 19,000 recruits will join the Coast Artillery during the next fiscal year."[6] The all-powerful logic of saving money won again, for a time at least, and issue of old coats continued—much to the chagrin of the artillerists. Finally, the systematic issue of some 1902 dress coats to coast artillery troops began in the fall of 1909; and by 1912 all companies were furnished with the newer coats for dress occasions, although the old-style blouses continued to be worn for a few more years as a non-dress uniform.[7]

1902 Chevrons

On 15 March 1901, Brigadier General Charles Bird, the Acting Quartermaster General, wrote the Adjutant General suggesting that the recently adopted small shirt chevrons be adopted for wear on all uniforms except where gilt chevrons were used. Bird had written at the urging of subordinates in the Philadelphia Depot, who had come up with the idea as a way of reducing the huge stockage of rank insignia then required. Samples were made and sent to field commanders, so when the 1902 Uniform Board met, the concept of small chevrons had been in circulation for a year. Besides cost savings, the small size was attractive because NCOs could not become sniper targets during civil distrubances or on battlefields like the Philippine Islands. Why the chevrons were changed to "point up" (inverted V) is not clear, other than they were "more attractive."[8]

The shirt chevron could continue to be used in most cases without modification. Nevertheless, by pointing the chevron up, a few changes were made. Buglers, trumpeters, drum majors, electricians, and a few others had their distinctive insert at the juncture of the bars inverted; but other NCOs, including the color sergeants, simply inverted the entire shirt chevron to acquire the "new" 1902 chevron.

The 1902 Uniform Board originally planned on continued use of the sleeve-engulfing gold lace chevrons for the dress uniforms and placed the smaller shirt-sized insignia on other uniforms. Owing to the high cost of the gold lace, coupled with the fact that the gold quickly tarnished and lost its attractive appearance, the board finally recommended that all chevrons be cloth.[9] Even so, economy dictated the remaining 1884 gold

Figure 5-3. In 1902, four hundred pairs of the 1902-size chevrons were made in the 1901-pattern for the Hospital Corps (green and white bars and Maltese cross). The PFC in the front row wears a 1898-pattern chevron, while two PFCs in the back row wear the 1902-pattern insignia. Note the absence of corporals, there being only twenty authorized.

chevrons on hand be used by the hapless Coast Artillery Corps.

Regulations of 1902 specified four types of uniforms requiring chevrons: dress blues, field olive drab for winter, field khaki for summer, and white duck. Additionally, chevrons could be worn on the flannel or chambray shirt as was done in the Philippines. In all cases, soldiers continued to wear colored stripes to show their branch of service, the chevrons differing only as to background color, which matched the garment.

The longest lived of the four types was the chevron on blue cloth for the dress uniform coat. These branch-colored stripes for the blue uniform (manufacturing code k) continued in use until the War Department suspended their use at the outset of World War I. Table 5-1 provides a summary of the manufacturing codes relevant to this third period of chevron history as a whole.

Besides dress blue chevrons, 1902 regulations authorized three other types. NCO stripes colored according to branch of service were worn on olive drab wool backgrounds (manufacturing code e) to go with the winter field uniform and on cotton khaki backgrounds (manufacturing code m) for wear on the summer field uniform. The fourth distinctive chevron had the branch-colored stripes sewn onto white cotton duck (manufacturing code n) to match that summer uniform.[10]

Introduction of these 1902 chevrons was slow and sporadic, as stock of the old chevrons first had to be used up while the new designs were slowly manufactured. As a result, by June 1904 only the following units had been issued the new uniforms and small colored chevrons: 5th Infantry; 26th Infantry; 1st Caval-

Figure 5-4. Between 1902
and 1904, small chevrons
were worn on the lower
sleeve of the overcoat. The
corporals in this late 1904
photograph wear such
chevrons on their coats.

ry, 5th Cavalry; 6th Cavalry; 15th Battery, Field Artillery; 6th
Band, Artillery Corps (dress uniform only); 2nd Battalion,
Engineers; 2nd Squadron, 15th Cavalry (Fort Myer); West Point
Detachment; Company B, 9th Infantry (Peking, China); 3rd and
4th Batteries, Field Artillery (Fort Myer). Priority was given to
units returning from overseas and to the Fort Myer Garrison.[11]

On the olive drab overcoat chevrons continued to be worn
below the elbow as had been done on the blue overcoat. Rather
than 2 inches above the cuff, however, these chevrons were now
to be midway between the elbow and the end of the sleeve. The
branch-colored overcoat chevrons themselves were the same as
those worn on the wool service coat.

The supply problems caused by the use of four different
chevrons for each branch was formidable, especially during
the initial outfitting of the entire Army. Additionally, the colors
ran badly when washed, affecting the entire sleeve of a coat. In
an attempt to solve these problems, as well as reduce costs, the
15th Cavalry at Fort Myer began to test chevrons with olive drab

bars and designs. The Quartermaster General wrote on 4 January 1904:

> *The Squadron of 15th Cavalry at Fort Myer, Virginia, will be completely equipped with olive drab overcoats and service uniforms as prescribed by General Order 132, 1902, with the following additions and modifications: Brown chevrons for NCOs [are] to be worn with the olive field coat and overcoat. . . .* [12]

By mid–1904, even though a quantity of branch-colored chevrons on the white duck, olive drab wool, and khaki cotton backgrounds had been made, the Quartermaster General reported that because of the dye problems, and as a result of the Fort Myer test, "the color of olive drab [for making the chevrons design] was decided as best. Bars made of olive drab shirting flannel upon a background of olive drab serge . . . will be sufficiently distinctive. Bars of the same cloth sewn upon a groundwork of either cotton khaki or white duck will harmonize with the khaki service and white summer coats."[13] Thus, within two years, three of the four styles of chevrons introduced were generally discarded so only the dress blue chevron remained. A few units actually drew the 1902–1904 colored field chevrons as late as 1910, although most of the supply of chevrons remaining in the Philadelphia warehouse was sold in 1907, and among collectors, these three types are still common.[14]

Also authorized by General Order No. 81, 1902, was a brown cotton duck fatigue coat. On it, soldiers working at gun emplacements were to wear "the usual" chevrons. The coats carried brown rank insignia on a matching "rust" or brown background, rather than branch-colored bars.[15] Manufacturing code *o* has been assigned these chevrons for cataloging.

1904 Chevrons
In December 1904, the War Department published a General Order which instituted several changes found to be necessary during the introduction of the 1902 uniforms. All branches received the same olive drab chevron bars on a background matching the service coats, overcoats, and white coats.[16] The following three types of chevrons, manufacturing codes *p*, *q*, and *r*, replaced types *l*, *m*, and *n* by virtue of the 1904 change. All enlisted rank were now specified to be worn centered on the sleeve between the elbow and the shoulder, thus eradicating the overcoat with a chevron below the elbow. Chevrons for the dark blue dress coat and those for the canvas fatigue coat remained unchanged.

1907 Chevrons
The blue, khaki, and olive drab chevrons formalized in 1904 continued for many years, but the Secretary of War rescinded

Figure 5-5. Starting in 1910, chevrons on a denim background were available for certain branches for wear on denim work uniforms. The designs were chain stitched in branch colors. Cooks and bakers wore similar rank chevrons on white backgrounds, as shown in the center.

the dark brown fatigue rank devices in the spring of 1907 by directing that the standard khaki rank insignia be worn, as the color difference was "immaterial."[17] Philadelphia Depot, unaware of the edict, continued to manufacture brown fatigue chevrons until April 1908, when work was halted in anticipation of a change of fatigue uniforms.[18] Money again shaped the Secretary of War's decision, and in 1907 the olive drab stripes on white uniforms—just authorized in 1904—were withdrawn from use except for members of the Hospital Corps.[19] The recruiting service's efforts to attract new men relied in part on the natty looks of the recruiters, who usually wore dress uniforms. For more comfortable summer wear, in the spring of 1908 recruiting parties were authorized white uniforms.[20] Corporal's and sergeant's bars in brown were applied to white cotton duck backgrounds for wear on this uniform, just as in the case of Hospital Corps chevrons. The authority for wearing these white recruiting uniforms was annulled in March 1914, thereby removing from use the olive drab-on-white sergeant's and corporal's chevrons. Recruiters then switched to blue uniforms.[21]

In early 1908, the coast artillery began to phase out the dark brown canvas work uniforms and the associated chevrons, blue denim clothing being substituted.[22] Initially, men wore the standard khaki chevrons on these denim coats, but in November 1909, the Philadelphia Depot started experiments to make blue denim chevrons. All trials were unsatisfactory until the unique approach of simply outlining the bars was discovered. By the spring of 1910, standardized samples had been made, and troops were being supplied with the new denim insignia.[23]

The final concept for the artillery denim chevrons that proved successful was to chain stitch the design outline with mercerized cotton on blue denim. This type of manufacture set a precedent to be used later by other branches prior to World War I. All chain-stitched chevrons on blue denim are cataloged as manufacturing code *t*.

In 1911 the Army began to replace khaki uniforms with

116

those made from olive drab cotton. Chevrons originally made for the khaki uniforms were to be issued "until the supply is exhausted." This change from khaki uniform to olive drab cotton caused the creation of olive drab cotton chevrons, although the supply of some khaki chevrons lasted until the start of World War I.[24]

1911 and 1912 Regulations
The War Department published "Regulations of the Uniform of the United States Army" on 26 December 1911. This marked the first time since the Civil War that the Army had published uniform regulations in other than General Orders. The booklet contained guidance on *how* to wear the articles of uniform, while the next publication, issued on 25 January 1913, "The Uniform Specifications," specified *what* constituted the uniform articles. Authorized by virtue of these 1911 regulations were chevrons for wear on sweaters in the field, and on the olive drab shirt when it was worn without the coat.

In 1913 cook and bakers in the Quartermaster Corps began to wear special white work uniforms with the various quartermaster rank insignia outlined in buff chain stitching, on white cotton duck, similar to the style developed for the coast artillery denim uniforms. These white cotton chevrons have been designated manufacturing code *u* to distinguish them from chevrons on a blue denim background. At the same time members of the Quartermaster Corps whose "classification calls for manual labor" were authorized the blue denim fatigue uniforms with chevrons of buff chain stitching on blue denim backing.[25]

In the summer of 1914 the Commanding Officer, 1st Aero Squadron, requested denim chevrons also be approved for men of the Air Service since Signal Corps men had recently received blue denim work uniforms. As the Signal Corps used two colors, their denim chevrons were chain stitched twice, once using orange and once with white thread. The infant Air Service at that time was part of the Signal Corps and had no special color or insignia other than the distinctive badge worn by pilots. There was an attempt to put a flying eagle in place of the flags and burning torch, but a strong rebuke from the War Department staff halted the attempt.[26]

The War Department published new Uniform Regulations in December 1914, along with new Uniform Specifications in January 1915, although no chevron changes were introduced. By this time though, actual wear of the blue dress uniform had decreased so at many posts that the men actually wore their dress blues only once or twice a year.[27] A Uniform Board met in March 1916, and decided to study the possibility of eliminating the enlisted blue uniform. Letters were sent to the Army's generals and senior field grade officers so a consensus could be obtained on the desirability of keeping a special uniform. During the summer, replies came in indicating most commanders favored discarding the blue dress uniforms. To actually get the last traditionally colored blue uniforms out of the Army, however, took a catastrophic event—the World War.[28]

World War I Uniforms and Chevrons

With the entry of the United States into World War I in April 1917, the pretense of a parade Army was flung aside; and that same month, an edict went out that new soldiers would not draw dress uniforms. The next month the Army prescribed the service uniform for all occasions except White House wear. The wartime look was in and the peacetime look was out. The edict halting the issuance of the blue uniforms was quite sudden, and a large stock of the dress uniforms remained on hand. One proposal was to issue these suddenly obsolete uniforms to black stevedore regiments and labor battalions for wear on the docks. These units had been formed because there was a manpower shortage in Europe after three years of fighting. The blue uniforms could be issued to these troops because there was a shortage of precious olive drab uniforms which could not be "wasted" far behind the front.[29] Whether a certain number of blue uniforms went this way is not known, but some books devoted to the World War I black experience make no mention of the cast-off uniforms, and the few known photos of black soldiers working on the docks show the olive drab uniform in use.

Officers in the Army Chief of Staff's Office began a series of actions in early 1918 with the goal of simplifying Army supply problems. In April 1918 the issue and manufacture of special chevrons for the various denim work uniforms was eliminated to ease the supply situation. Staff officers decided the service uniform chevrons then worn on the olive drab cotton coats could just as well show on denim jackets the rank of the wearer. In this way, the Army removed denim chevrons from stocks. At the same time and for the same reason, Chief of Staff planners withdrew the white chevrons worn by medical NCOs. These steps left soldiers only the dress blue and the service chevrons; since the dress uniform was suspended from use, only the olive drab cotton and wool chevrons remained in general use.[30]

In addition to simplifying the issue of enlisted rank insignia through the elimination of chevrons made on white duck and blue denim backgrounds, the Army moved to save material. The magnitude of the problem of simply supplying chevrons to an expanding Army was expressed in a memo written for the Chief of Staff in late April 1918: "The Quartermaster General . . . has informed this office that the manufacture of chevrons for the next fourteen months [until the end of the fiscal year 1919] will take approximately 750,000 yards of cloth, enough to make nearly 250,000 uniforms, and in order to conserve cloth he suggests that chevrons be worn on one arm only, as is now the case in the Navy and in the British Army."[31] Accordingly, on 30

April 1918, the War Department notified the American Expeditionary Force that rank chevrons would henceforth be worn on the right sleeve only.

1919–1920 Chevron Changes

Using the knowledge gained during World War I, the General Staff and the Quartermaster Corps set about establishing various new insignia, including chevrons, with the goal of minimizing future supply problems. In fact, by 1919 so many chevrons had been introduced few men could identify all the authorized grade insignia. In August 1919, staff officers in the General Staff and the Quartermaster General's Office agreed upon the following points as a basis for a new set of chevrons:

1. Only one kind of chevron would be used for both woolen and cotton service coats.

2. Single chevrons would be worn, not pairs.

3. The background for all chevrons would be olive drab felt.

4. Bars would be of a lighter shade of olive drab felt than the backing felt, making a distinct contrast.

5. Insignia of staff departments would conform to the established colors of the respective arms of service.

6. There would be elimination of several chevrons by the consolidation of similar grades from the different arms of service.[32]

Most of these concepts were quite revolutionary. Up to this time, attempts had usually been made to match the chevron to the coat. Chevrons of a single color and a single material (and those not the same as any coat) were a giant step away from the earlier practice. Elimination of some designs by combining several grades was also a unique and notable effort to ease the supply problem. By consolidating some chevrons, it was hoped, a logical scheme could be adopted. As a first step, the Chief of Staff approved the new PFC insignia, common for all branches, in September 1919, although work on the other new designs was just beginning.[33] Under this plan, several of the different grades would have a single chevron. For example, master engineers senior grade were authorized for both the Tank Corps and the Coast Artillery Corps, but these men traditionally wore different chevrons, the design of which included an indication of branch. Because these men held a common grade, War Department officials now considered a single chevron appropriate regardless of branch.[34]

The drab service uniform was for wear on all occasions; in these 1919 proposed chevron changes, some color was added to the chevrons of certain senior NCOs. This addition of color to the chevron was probably influenced by the pre–World War I practice of having dress chevrons made in the various branch

Figure 5-6. Some of the colored 1920 chevrons that were approved but not issued are shown here.

colors. In this proposed 1919 change, chevrons adopted different color schemes.[35]

The most notable change incorporated in these new designs was the addition of the United States eagle. The original suggestion was to use a flying eagle of the type used on the Quartermaster Corps insignia. However, the final decision was to use an eagle identical to the one on a Navy petty officer's rate.[36]

Samples of these new chevrons were made in November and December 1919 and formally approved by the Secretary of War on 6 January 1920. The Quartermaster Corps prepared official drawings and additional samples were made, with official sample books being sealed 18 May 1920.[37] Before orders could be issued to make the general announcement of these changes, Congress passed an Army Reorganization Act which the President approved 4 June 1920. Under the provisions of this act, all enlisted men were grouped into seven grades.

Almost immediately, Colonel Robert Wyllie of the Clothing and Equipage Branch proposed a set of chevrons that were eventually adopted in August 1920.[38] With the rapid adoption of chevrons intended to implement the concept of seven enlisted grades, the Army forgot the recent 1919 and early 1920 chevron changes, even though some of the colored 1919–1920 senior NCO rank insignia had been made in quantity. So quick was the change that most people did not learn of the colored 1920 chevrons, and a 1921 note on an official drawing stated the 1920 designs were never used.[39]

Chevron Identification

Determining when a particular chevron was made may be a vital key in evaluating a uniform or other item that may accompany a chevron, or even the chevron itself. The color and material of a chevron's background, the manufacturing process, as well as the shape and color of the central design, can be used to help identify the date a chevron was made. One element such as shape may indicate a particular chevron was manufactured from 1902 through 1907, for instance, while another factor such as the central design may show the chevron was authorized from 1905 through 1920. A consideration of both of these time factors, then, reveals the particular chevron was made during the three years between 1905 and 1907. By using two or more various means in this way, an initially wide time span may be reduced to a

TABLE 5-1
Manufacturing Code Letters for 1902–1920 Chevrons

Background Material	Design Material and Color	Dates of Authorization	Remarks	Code Letter
Dark blue wool	Branch colors[a]	1902–1918	Uniforms out by April 1917	*k*
Olive drab wool	Branch colors[a]	1902–1904	[c]	*l*
Khaki cotton	Branch colors[a]	1902–1904	[c]	*m*
White duck	Branch colors[a]	1902–1904	[c]	*n*
Rust duck	Tan or brown	1902–1908	Wearout thru 1910; Coast Artillery only	*o*
White duck	Olive drab wool or felt	1904–1907	Also refer to next two entries	*p*
White duck	Olive drab wool or felt	1904–1918	Used only by Medical Corps. Machine embroidered cotton caduceus distinguish this exception to the 1907 withdrawal (see above entry)	*p**
White duck	Olive drab wool or felt	1908–1914	Corporal and Sergeant; Recruiting Service only	*p*
Khaki cotton	Medium khaki flannel bars or hand-embroidered khaki wreaths and specialty devices	1904–1911	Some ranks issued thru 1916 until stocks depleted	*q*
Olive drab wool or felt	Olive drab flannel or felt	1904–1920		*r*
Khaki or Olive drab cotton[d]	Olive drab flannel or felt[d]	1911–1920		*s*
Blue denim	Red chain stitch	1910–1918	Coast Artillery only	*t*
White duck	Buff chain stitch	1913–1918	QM Cooks and Bakers only	*u*
Blue denim	Branch colored chain stitching	1913–1918	QM, Signal and ASSD only	*t*
Olive drab felt	Branch colors[b]	1920	Not actually worn	*v*

[a] All wreaths yellow (except Artillery Chief Mechanic which was red).
[b] All wreaths green, all lyres yellow, special Coast Artillery insignia red.
[c] Very limited actual wear when compared to official authorizations.
[d] Colors vary considerably, from light khaki to dark olive drab, including greens and browns, especially in privately made World War I insignia.
[e] If a projectile is included in the design, the projectile may be red.

*NOTE: The same code letter is applied to chevrons produced by the same manufacturing process and in use at the same time. Such chevrons are said to constitute a set.

much briefer period. It must be remembered, however, that many militia units wore chevrons considered obsolete by the Regular Army,[40] and that before a new design was released to the field, any current stock of "old" chevrons on hand had to be either issued to the militia or the regular troops or sold at auction for scrap. Usually this last option was not acceptable to the War Department staff which forced many obsolete chevrons to continue in use for several years.[41]

Design

Most 1902-type chevrons for other than the line troops had distinctive devices as a part of their basic design. Ordnance bombs, medical caducei, signal devices, and the like served to identify branches other than infantry, cavalry, artillery, and engineers. Cooks, farriers, mechanics, and other men in the lower grades who served in the combat arms had chevron designs related to their work rather than to any particular branch of service. The senior men wore chevrons that distinguished the wearer's specialty by the addition of a device in the angle of the sergeant's three bars. Sergeants major added arcs, supply men added horizontal bars, color sergeants added a star, first sergeants added a diamond, and so forth.

Basically, until 1907, most chevrons consisted either of V's (with or without devices added as noted) or of a simple design used alone. In 1904 a wreath on the sleeve was introduced for master gunners.[42] The wreath came to signify a high degree of excellence for a special skill. In 1908 the Artillery Corps introduced stars and more wreaths on various chevrons,[43] and soon this practice spread to other branches. These wreaths and stars indicated rank, and as such were equivalent to the arcs and bars in use by noncommissioned officers. A simple design in the center of the chevron (e.g., a projectile, a mechanical governor) continued to show the specialty of the wearer. Initially, the star was placed in the top of the chevron, and a wreath was placed below to help balance the design of the chevron as a whole. In 1909, master signal electricians were authorized crossed flags in a wreath, with five lightning bolts above (Catalog No. 243).[44] This chevron was the first grade insignia for special skills that had something other than a star as the top portion of the design.

In 1916, a set of similar chevrons came into wide use for men of intermediate level special skills. These chevrons were similar, often even identical, to those for highly skilled men, except for the omission of a star.[45] During World War I the War Department introduced some new chevrons consisting only of a simple device (e.g., bugle, wheel, lyre). These chevrons were intended to distinguish three or four grades of men who without these insignia would have simply been PFCs.[46] All in all, by 1920 some chevrons were a far cry from those based on the more traditional V's.

Figure 5-7. This 1904 master gunner's insignia was the first chevron to use the wreath to note excellence or a high grade. By 1920 the chevrons for several dozen different ranks included wreaths.

TABLE 5-2
Shape and Date of Manufacture for Special Chevron Backgrounds 1902–1920

Shape	Dimensions	Dates of Manufacture
▭	4 × 2 inches to 5 × 3½ inches	1902 to August 1908
○	2½ to 2¾ inches in diameter	August 1908 to August 1920
⬡	About 3½ inches wide	September 1907 to August 1920
⌂	About 3½ inches wide	1918 to 1919 (made in Europe for the AEF)

Shape

Initially, the private first class and other low-ranking specialty insignia were modeled after the pre–1902 practice of placing a simple design on a rectangular background. Soldiers often trimmed off the excess cloth so that with a minimum of material around the design, they would consequently have less sewing to do. But with or without the trimming, most of the cloth *was* unnecessary. Officials at the Quartermaster Depot in Philadelphia finally recognized the waste and when the Philadelphia Depot ordered a new machine for cutting and folding chevron backgrounds, the machine was designed so the backing material would be made in the shape of a disk rather than a rectangle. This change was made in 1908; therefore, all of the PFC chevrons and coast artillery ratings made between 1902 and August 1908 were round.[47] These two basic shapes are of great assistance in determining when a chevron was made. (Table 5-2 lists manufacture dates by shape.) One must still consider, however, that those devices in stock on the rectangular background had to be issued before the Army issued round chevrons. An examination of the illustrated uniform plates published in October 1908 by the Quartermaster General reveals that some of the chevrons are on the newer circular background, while others are on the older rectangular backing.

Color

As a result of the 1902 regulations, colors changed for several branches. Most noticeable was the infantry which in 1899 had converted completely to white chevrons, but in 1902 returned to light blue. Light blue was the primary infantry color and so chevrons intended for the doughboy were made in that shade. Because of the severe fading of chevrons made in the 1880s and 1890s, white had been adopted for the infantry; now a return to the infantry blue was made by those with short memories. Officers and men immediately complained, and in October 1903, General Order No. 37 stated a reversal of position by announcing white as the infantry color again. Issuance of the white chevrons was gradual, starting with the regiments returning from the Philippines.

Figure 5-8. First class gunner ratings. Rectangular backgrounds were manufactured before August 1908, circular backgrounds after that date.

In 1902, the Signal Corps went back to its original orange, but white was added as a second color. Signal chevrons were made with orange bars, white chain stitching being added around each of the bars. This technique of making the bars of the major color with piping of the second color was used on dress chevrons throughout the 1902–1920 period for those departments or branches represented by two colors.

Other branches beside the Signal Corps changed colors. Ordnance Corps personnel switched from crimson to black piped with red. A change by the Hospital Corps from green to maroon was made on the basis that green was traditionally a color used by riflemen.[48] The United States Military Academy Band wore infantry chevrons, either light blue or white depending upon the time in question, but even so the West Point Band was listed separately in most specifications and regulations.

It is interesting as a sidelight to note that infantry chevrons were initially prescribed for the West Point Band.[49] The fact the United States Military Academy Band chevrons were white was simply because the infantry wore white chevrons.

The Quartermaster General listed the West Point Band separately in chevron specifications and regulations because the authorized designs differed between the band and the infantry. When the rest of the Army changed to olive drab uniforms, the West Point Band continued to wear dress chevrons and blue uniforms and this was why the use of the infantry white chevrons continued. Today the band still wears white chevrons that can be traced back to the introduction of the 1903 white infantry chevrons.

For the period 1902–1904, all of the branches were to have four types of chevrons for each grade, one to match each uniform: dark blue (manufacturing code k), white (manufacturing code i), khaki (manufacturing code m), and olive drab (manufacturing code n).[50] During the manufacture of standard samples in September 1902, the question arose as to which chevrons Indian Scouts should wear. Since the 1902 Uniform Board had not specified any color for Scouts, the Quartermaster General decided white chevrons with red chain-stitched piping would be made for the Scouts, but only on backgrounds to match the two service uniforms—khaki cotton and olive drab wool.[51] With this decision on the Indian Scouts, all 1902 chevrons executed in branch colors other than for infantry, ordnance, Hospital Corps, and Signal Corps were done in the same colors as before 1902.

Congress authorized an Army Service School Detachment in 1909 so that the Army would have school troops at the various service schools. For all Army Service School ranks, green dress chevrons were authorized, and all normal colors associated with a branch were thus replaced. This called for green crossed Signal Corps flags with a green torch, a green caduceus, and even an all-green Quartermaster insignia.[52]

TABLE 5-3
Colors for Branch Use on 1902–1917 Chevrons

Color	Branch	Dates of Authorization
Light blue	Infantry	1902–1903
White	Infantry	1903–1917
White	USMA Band	1903–1917
Yellow	Cavalry	1902–1917
Scarlet	Artillery	1902–1917
Scarlet piped with white[c]	Engineers	1902–1917
Black piped with scarlet[c]	Ordnance	1902–1917
Buff[c]	Post QM Sergeants	1902–1912
Buff	USMA Detachment[b]	1902–1909
Buff[c]	Quartermaster Corps	1912–1917
Gray[c]	Post Commissary Sergeant	1902–1912
Maroon piped with white[c]	Hospital Corps	1902–1917
Orange piped with white[c]	Signal Corps	1902–1917
Green	Army Service School Detachment	1909–1917
Green piped with white	Army Service Detachment, USMA	1909–1917
White piped with red	Indian Scouts	1902–1904[a]

[a] Never authorized by Regulations but made for khaki and olive drab uniforms 1902–1904. Doubtful if worn.

[b] Only First Sergeant, Sergeant, Corporal, Lance Corporal, and Cook chevrons were made, all without the QM device.

[c] Includes Department/Corps insignia in design.

Before 1909, the Military Academy Detachment soldiers wore buff chevrons, the color of the Quartermaster General's Department, but without the Quartermaster eagle, wheel, key, and sword.[53] When Congress created the Service School Detachment, the West Point soldiers became a part of that branch. To continue a means of distinguishing Military Academy members of the Army Service School Detachment, white piping was added to the new green chevrons, replacing the older buff stripes.[54]

One goal of the 1919 chevron consolidation scheme was to return some color to the drab enlisted rank insignia. The senior grade special skill chevrons were to be dressed up by making wreaths green and by returning colors to the specialty devices. In addition, the three standard chevrons contained yellow embroidered lyres, while coast artillery insignia bore red designs on an olive drab background.[55] Table 5-3 summarizes dates of authorization for branch colors used on chevrons during this period as a whole.

Titles of Ranks

Congressional acts, Army regulations, and other official sources often used two or three titles for one grade. For example, originally a man in a certain grade was known as a sergeant of the first class. Through the effort to eliminate extraneous words, this title became informally shortened to sergeant, first class. Eventually, the shortened title appeared in some and then all official documents and correspondence. It became the official title by virtue of its wide use over a period of time. Simultaneously, the familiar name "sergeant first class" began to creep into usage (note the omission of the comma). No document announced a change from one title to another as this was an evolutionary process. Because of these phenomena, it is usually impossible to state firmly when one title went out and a similar one replaced it. It has only been since 1920 that the Army has placed much significance on exact titles and really distinguished between such names as first class privates and privates first class.

Publications

There are few publications showing chevrons in use between the Spanish-American War and 1917, since the Army received little publicity at that time. Consequently, finding illustrations of chevrons in use during this time is very difficult, although the chevrons themselves are not scarce, even today.

H. A. Odgen undertook to update his illustrated history of Army uniforms in 1907.[56] Despite elimination of branch colors in the 1904 uniform regulations, Odgen labeled the field uniform with the 1904–1907 chevrons as 1902–1907. This was probably prompted by the fact that few units actually wore the colored field chevrons. Although Mr. Ogden did not intend primarily to show various chevrons, his twentieth-century illustrations clearly show many of the various enlisted rank insignia designs.

Quartermaster General James B. Alshire published a set of color plates in 1908 to show the actual chevrons in use at that time. The excellent publication includes color illustrations showing all chevrons for the dress uniforms as well as for both the khaki and olive drab service uniforms, and the stripes worn by recruiting party members.

In February 1914 the War Department printed a booklet entitled *Illustration of Chevrons*. This publication has a photograph of each chevron design used by each branch. It is the last set of illustrations published by the War Department specifically to show all chevrons.

Many books privately published during World War I include various unofficial illustrations. Unfortunately, most of these books are neither comprehensive nor accurate, and contemporary catalogs and photographs provide a much better source of identification when determining what was actually worn. These sources must be balanced with information from War Department and Quartermaster memos, letters, inventories, and the like, as well as the ordinary Uniform Regulations. During World War I, a great many new designs appeared, both official and unofficial, and determining what soldiers actually wore is now very difficult.

*Chevron
Procurement*

The Quartermaster Corps continued to be the official supplier of chevrons, but the techniques of sealing samples and, more important, their *significance*, changed. Mass civilian manufacturing of chevrons produced an immediate disruption of the flow of well-made chevrons at the start of World War I. Because by 1918 unofficial chevrons were worn widely, privately made chevrons must be fully considered for the first time. Also many companies under government contract produced chevrons of poor quality that did not meet Army specifications.

Samples

The surviving nineteenth-century samples are from various War Department collections or from the Stokes-Kirk Store of Philadelphia. Mr. Kirk had the foresight to preserve those obsolete sealed samples that did fall into his hands at government auctions and today they are the property of the Smithsonian Institution. Still, there are no known surviving samples sealed from 1902 through 1917. Because of this gap, other evidence must be considered when trying to determine what was actually manufactured by the government before World War I.

In 1902, Quartermaster officials began placing examples of all authorized chevrons in a book and then sealing the entire sample book rather than sealing individual chevrons. This technique naturally made for a more comprehensive history since when a chevron fell into disuse, it was not included in subsequent books. Although books were a better means of showing officially authorized chevrons, sample books were not always 100 percent inclusive, owing to human oversight. A set of sleeve devices for exclusive use by the Army Mine Planter Service was sealed in May 1920, but when the Quartermaster General supposedly sealed a complete sample book of Army chevrons, the chevrons used solely by the Army Mine Planter Service were not included.[57] In a similar manner, the Quartermaster General did not consider chevrons for the Army Harbor Boat Service and the Army Transport Service when rank chevron samples were sealed, even though various Coast Artillery Corps ratings, which indicated a specialty but not a rank, were included.

After sample books were assembled by the Army, some were sent to uniform manufacturers who bid on government contracts so the firms could see what was authorized and exactly how a

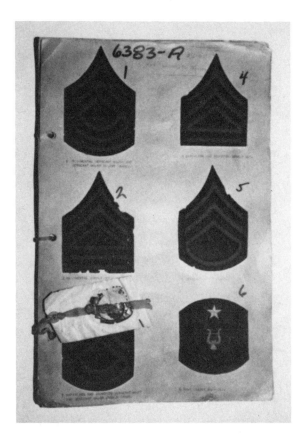

Figure 5-9. A sample book, sealed in May 1920.

design was to look. Many of these sample books intended for manufacturers did not carry official Quartermaster seals, but the books still served their intended function. As noted, however, the chevrons actually fielded in 1918 and later often were very different from official Quartermaster samples.

Specifications

Just as in the nineteenth century, post–1902 Clothing and Equipage Specifications were intended to go hand-in-hand with the sample books to assist dealers in making the desired chevrons. In truth, the specifications usually reflected what was being made when the specifications were written rather than what should have been made. As a result, whenever a change in the manufacture of chevrons occurred, staff officers at the Philadelphia Quartermaster Depot considered whether or not the specifications had to be amended to reflect the change.[58] Consequently, chevron specifications, although rather detailed, occasionally had a few omissions.

The twentieth-century specifications were more detailed than those from the preceding century. This included stating whether embroidery of a specific design was to be by hand or machine for each chevron, because the practice varied from dress, service cotton, and service wool insignia. Also, some of the specifications contained photographs of chevrons so that more complete details would be seen. Although not as common as Uniform Regulations, today the Clothing and Equipage Specifications are the best and readiest source for detailed chevron information.

Manufacture

Excellent workmanship characterized most issue chevrons made prior to World War I. Women hand embroidered all designs on dress blue chevrons except for some PFC's disks. This resulted in beautifully made chevrons for those specialists whose insignia of grade included a wreath, or a department device, as seamstresses neatly hand stitched these designs in vivid colors. Initially, most embroidery for service chevrons was also hand done, and the pride in workmanship is still very evident in even these dull-colored insignia. Simultaneously with the Army expansion and increased need for chevrons, engineers were able to design machines that could embroider more easily. This led to machine embroidery of some service chevrons. As machinery improved, more and more designs were machine embroidered, until even the most complicated devices were automatically stitched during World War I.

The comparatively minor supply problem of providing chevrons was virtually neglected by the Quartermaster staff in World War I; quite properly, clothing, ammunition, and food took priority. As a result, several new problems appeared during the war insofar as the supply of chevrons was concerned. Since the increased demand for chevrons could not be fully met, in 1917 the private manufacture of rank insignia began rapidly to fill the gap. The well-made pre–World War I chevrons, easily distinguished by their fine workmanship and high quality materials, generally disappeared. Chevrons made commercially during World War I, usually of poor quality and often manufactured from substandard material, came into wide circulation.

In 1918 the Army let several contracts with private companies. What resulted was that poorly made substandard chevrons were issued through official supply channels—or sold as surplus after the war. Additionally, many of those chevrons contracted for in 1918 and delivered in 1919 were never used owing to the 1920 chevron change. These privately made chevrons are the most common of all the 1917–1920 chevrons and can most easily be identified by examining several points.

1. Several commercially made chevrons were of unauthorized design, while War Department rank insignia were listed in specifications and regulations. Most unauthorized chevrons of this period are cataloged in Chapter 6, along with official designs.

2. The size of many privately made and contract-made chevrons was too small. The official PFC's disks were 2⅝ inches in diameter and the sergeant's chevrons were 2⅝ inches wide.

3. During the years that chevrons were worn in pairs (before May 1918), Quartermaster insignia were sewn together at the edge by hand with two or three stitches. Many chevrons sold commercially were fastened together by metal clips or staples, and today traces of rust from these fastenings may show.

4. Government colors were closely controlled (even if they did fade, however, after washing or exposure to sunlight). Cotton cloth was a dark khaki, while wool chevrons were olive drab. Even though all colors were tinted olive drab, the color of commercial chevrons varied widely, especially in the cloth and thread used to make a special design. Various hues of green, chocolate, and tan were widely used in these insignia.

5. War Department chevrons made at the Philadelphia Depot present a generally neat appearance and strike one as being of good workmanship. Privately manufactured PFC's disks are often not round and look poorly made over-all. Simplified manufacturing processes and designs are other marks of these poorly made commercial chevrons.

6. Properly made wool and felt chevrons were of high quality, the weave of the wool not being easily discernible to the naked eye. The government cotton chevrons had neatly trimmed and stitched edges, while poor edges on chevrons are usually a mark of private manufacture.

Figure 5-10. These two examples reveal the manufacturing-quality differences experienced in World War I. The chevron on the left was made between 1905 and 1911 when few chevrons were required and high quality control was possible. The chevron on the right is typical of those made during World War I, when manufacturers rushed out poor quality insignia to meet the large demand of the expanded Army.

Fielding

The slow introduction of the 1902 chevrons because of the prolonged wear-out period of the 1872 chevrons has already been discussed. In December 1904, when the Army replaced the branch-colored field chevrons by the totally drab khaki and olive drab chevrons, a stock of the then obsolete 1902–1904 chevrons was left surplus. Supply personnel continued to issue some of the 1902–1904 chevrons with the khaki and olive drab backgrounds to the appropriate branches for the next few years in order to deplete Army stock. Photographs taken as late as 1911 show some Signal Corps members wearing the 1902–1904 colored khaki chevrons, while other photographs taken in 1908 show the later (post–1904) khaki and olive drab Signal Corps chevrons in use.[59] Information of this type tends to support an assumption that until about 1905 or 1906, the Army allowed the issue of the 1902–1904 chevrons already in the possession of units, while the 1902–1904 chevrons in stock at Philadelphia were sold at auction as surplus. New units and new posts may have received the newer chevrons while older units kept the 1902–1904 insignia.

Gradual phase-in of several years' length was typical of all new chevrons up to 1917. When a new design was introduced for a particular rank, the existing stocks usually had to be issued before that new design was released. Another factor that influenced the speed with which a new chevron was fielded was the number of insignia issued to a soldier during an enlistment. A man could draw only one pair of dress chevrons every three years, so if a soldier reenlisted and six months later the Army replaced his chevron it would be at least 2½ more years before a pair of the *new* chevrons would be issued to him gratuitously—and then only if the older stock had been depleted. If the older chevrons were still in stock, these would be issued, and it would be a total of 5½ years before the new insignia was issued. Nevertheless, except for the slow start from 1902 through 1905, the Quartermaster General's Department adequately supplied the Army's chevrons until World War I.

Non-Army Chevrons

Catalogs show that before World War I a person could order virtually any chevron design or color he might want. Military schools and various quasi-military organizations, state militias, veterans' groups, and police could select from a myriad of chevron designs and colors, many identical to Regulation Army insignia. Gray was evidently the most popular color and several chevrons found today in any of these nonstandard color schemes probably were made for such organizations.

Some cadet organizations wore miniature metal chevrons about 1 inch wide. These devices were pinned onto the collar and came both in bronze metal and in enameled metal of

Figure 5-11. Typical miniature metal chevrons worn by military school cadets in the early twentieth century.

various colors. Even such special chevrons as those for Signal Corps sergeants and ordnance sergeants were made in the form of these miniature insignia.

Army Organization: Effects on Enlisted Ranks

In 1901 a major reorganization of the Army had taken place. New infantry and cavalry regiments had been organized to increase the over-all size of the Army. The Artillery Corps was divided into the Coast and the Field Artillery, with all units organized as companies or batteries.[60] To support this larger military establishment there was created a series of new grades and even a new branch (the Army Service School Detachment). The largest single effect on enlisted grades, and consequently on chevrons, however, came several years later (the National Defense Act of June 1916). What was driving the Army organization throughout this time was the conversion from an Army oriented towards fighting on the frontier to a modern Army ready to fight anywhere in the world. This phenomenon called for the creation of new grades for specially skilled men. Examples include chief mechanics, highly paid Hospital, Ordnance, and Signal Corps men, and sea coast defense specialists.

1907 Artillery Reorganization

Congress passed a Reorganization Act in January 1907 providing for the separation into two corps of the coast and field artillery, that since 1901 had been subdivisions of the Army Artillery Corps. The six field artillery regiments were organized into two battalions of three batteries each, with the necessary battalion and regimental NCOs (e.g., battalion quartermaster sergeants, color sergeants). Field artillery NCOs wore chevrons of the same design as men of other branches, but the new coast artillery grades required new chevrons.

Congress charged the Coast Artillery Corps, as it then became known, with the care and use of the coast fortifications, including submarine mines and torpedo defenses. To allow proper accomplishment of this mission several new ranks were created. Twenty-six master electricians, sixty engineers, seventy-

132

four electrician sergeants first class, seventy four electrician sergeants second class, forty two master gunners, and sixty firemen constituted the newly authorized grades.[61]

The new law stated that the Coast Artillery Corps would have twenty one sergeants major with the rank, pay, and allowances of an infantry regimental sergeant major, and forty two sergeants major equal in rank and pay to an infantry battalion sergeant major. Organization-wise the entire Coast Artillery Corps consisted of over one hundred numbered companies and did not lend itself to the familiar regimental and battalion structure of most organizations of this period. As a result the Army assigned men of the two sergeants major ranks (sergeants major senior grade and sergeants major junior grade) to artillery districts, with these districts functioning similarly to regimental headquarters.

Another important factor of the 1907 artillery reorganization was authorization for several special ratings. Forty-four casemate electricians were allowed along with one-hundred-seventy observers first class and one-hundred-seventy plotters, all of whom received $9.00 a month in addition to their regular pay. The law also authorized the ratings of chief planter, chief loaders, observers second class, gun commanders, gun pointers, first class gunners, and second class gunners.

Recruiting and training of men for the high skill required in conjunction with the new senior grades proceeded slowly, and the seven-month delay between authorization of the grades and design of the chevrons caused no problem. An August 1907 General Order described the new rating insignia in detail, but manufacture of sample insignia had not even been attempted at this time. Some designs proved so intricate that the Quartermaster General considered cutting by dies an impossibility and hand manufacture too costly.[62] Accordingly, the ratings were redesigned in January 1908, when a new order was issued prescribing the sleeve insignia.[63]

School Detachments and Quartermaster Corps, 1909 and 1913
While passing the appropriations for the 1910 fiscal year, Congress finally recognized the pleas of the War Department and authorized the organization of detachments at each service school. This allowed the Army to form a new branch, known as the Army Service School Detachment. Prior to this time, the enlisted men serving at the schools had often been assigned to and carried on the rolls of a troop unit not assigned near the service school. With the creation of the Army Service School Detachment, men could be assigned to a school staff and not reduce the strength of a particular regiment.

Although the Army did not increase its over-all strength, the President was authorized to appoint noncommissioned officers, mechanics, artificers, farriers, horse shoers, and cooks as necessary for administration of the schools. The grades autho-

Figure 5-12. Senior noncommissioned officers at a California Coast Artillery Corps post in 1912. The men in the front row all wear chevrons created as a result of the 1907 artillery reorganization.

rized were those required for the continued smooth operation of the various schools. For instance, Hospital Corps lance corporals and sergeants first class were authorized for the medical school, but corporals and sergeants were not. Green was selected as the branch color for the Service School Detachment, and it was used on chevrons worn with dress and denim uniforms. In June 1909, the War Department set the initial allotment for the Army Service School Detachment at 550 men.[64]

In 1912 the Army organized the Quartermaster Corps as such, with the enlisted men coming from post quartermaster sergeants and post commissary sergeants. Several new ranks came into being as a result of this reorganization, and each grade was then authorized a new chevron incorporating the Quartermaster Corps insignia.[65]

1916 Defense Act and World War I
A major expansion of the Army resulted from the 1916 National Defense Act. Several new regiments were authorized for the infantry, cavalry, field artillery, and Corps of Engineers, while

134

the Coast Artillery, Quartermaster, Medical, and Signal Corps were increased. This 1916 expansion caused several new grades and chevrons to come into being.

The Corps of Engineers was increased to seven regiments, two mounted battalions, and a band. Consequently, several new grades were authorized, with most newly required chevrons adopted from designs then in use by other branches. Only master engineers of the senior and junior grades and the drum major required totally new chevrons (Catalog Nos. 260, 261, and 215).

The National Defense Act authorized privates first class for most branches, with the most noticeable additions being the authorizations for infantry, cavalry, and artillery. These new PFC grades replaced lance corporals, with the Army adopting crossed rifles, sabers, and cannons for rank insignia. Only the West Point Band was left with lance corporals, since the Act of 3 June 1916 stated that no change could occur in the West Point Band and other special organizations unless specifically listed. Even though Army regulations and not a statute had established lance corporals, the Judge Advocate General ruled lance corporals should continue to be authorized for the West Point Band.[66]

Other minor changes occurred in most branches, with the Coast Artillery Corps authorized assistant engineers and radio sergeants for the first time, in addition to the redesignations of the various coast artillery rated positions.

During World War I the National Army included temporary branches, although only the grades of the permanent branches were used. Consequently, when the Army formed various new temporary corps, all of the grades were related to existing ranks and branches. The Chief of Staff authorized sergeants first class, sergeants, corporals, PFCs, and one or two senior enlisted grades for most branches. Senior NCOs included the ranks of master engineers (senior and junior grades) and quartermaster sergeants (senior and junior grades), although the Tank Corps, unlike all of the other temporary branches, was allotted master engineers only of the senior grade. This policy of adopting enlisted grades parallel to permanent branches caused extremely long titles. As an example, the highest enlisted grade in the Motor Transport Corps was a quartermaster sergeant senior grade, but because several branches had men of this grade, the full title became "quartermaster sergeant senior grade, Motor Transport Corps." This full name described a rank and, of course, is necessary to describe completely the appropriate chevron.

Service Stripes

Soldiers continued to wear large 10-inch-long service chevrons after 1902, the major changes being the elimination of gilt lace and the adoption of new color schemes. Under the 1902 regulation, a soldier wore a ½-inch-wide stripe colored according to the branch in which he had served. Service in wartime was shown by a ¾-inch-wide branch-colored stripe bearing a ½-inch white center. Cloth service chevrons were used except for those of coast artillery men who continued to wear gold lace stripes in an effort to use up existing stocks.

In a repeat of late-nineteenth-century history, in 1902 a service chevron was worn on each sleeve for each enlistment of either three or five years, but in 1907 the Army changed this so again a stripe would indicate each three-year period of service completed, the color to be of the branch in which the majority of the time was spent.[67]

The issue of campaign medals, which began in 1905, influenced the wear of service-in-war stripes. Service medals showing a soldier's war experience rendered the need for service-in-war chevrons obsolete. In November 1907, the War Department decided service-in-war chevrons would not be worn to indicate service for which a campaign medal had been authorized. Since only those soldiers in and en route to Cuba and the Philippines earned campaign medals, the Army allowed the men who stayed in the United States to wear war service chevrons but not the medal. The net result was that enlisted men who served in the Army from 21 April 1898 until 11 April 1899 and who were not entitled to a campaign medal could continue to wear a service-in-war chevron.[68] Finally, in May 1910, the service-in-war chevrons were completely discontinued, with only service chevrons continuing.[69]

Because the wide service stripes so filled the space on sleeves, the Army created a narrower stripe in June 1910.[70] The new service chevron, still 10 inches long and running from seam to seam, was only ⅜-inch wide. Also, no extra cloth backing was used so the coat sleeve would not become too heavy and thick when a man wore several enlistment stripes. Table 5-4 lists the 1902–1910 ¾-inch-wide service stripes along with authorization dates. Table 5-5 lists the narrower 1910–1917 service chevrons.

When the Army discarded the dress uniform at the start of World War I, there was no means for an old soldier to show his many enlistments. To revive the custom of showing enlistments, service uniform coats were authorized enlistment stripes in 1920.[71] The attractive new color combination of olive drab bars on a navy blue background for service stripes eventually led to the adoption of the same color scheme for rank chevrons.[72]

Precedence and Pay   Soldiers' pay did not substantially change from 1872 through 1908, although Congress did vote new grades and some new pay rates prior to 1908. A summary of the 1907 pay shown in the Secretary of War's *Annual Report* constitutes Table 5-6.

Figure 5-13. These noncommissioned officers of the 16th Infantry wear 10-inch-long stripes on their sleeves to show their many enlistments. Until 1920, service stripes ran across the entire outside width of the sleeve, as do these insignia.

TABLE 5-4

Colors of Service and Service-in-War Chevrons 1902–1910[a]

Color[b]	Branch	Dates of Authorization
Yellow	Cavalry	1902–1910
Scarlet	Artillery	1902–1910
Light blue	Infantry	1902–1910
Scarlet piped with white	Engineers	1902–1910
Black piped with scarlet	Ordnance	1902–1910
Buff	{ Post QM Sergeant	1902–1910
	{ Army Service Detachment, USMA	1902–1909
Gray	Post Commissary Sergeant	1902–1910
Maroon piped with white	Hospital Corps	1902–1910
Orange piped with white	Signal Corps	1902–1910
Green	Army Service School Detachment	1909–1910
Green piped with white	Army Service Detachment, USMA	1909–1910

[a] Chevrons measure ¾-inch wide, 10 inches long.

[b] Colors of ½-inch wide applied to dark blue background ¾-inch wide were for service. The colored strip ¾-inch wide with a ½-inch white center stripe indicated a wartime enlistment.

TABLE 5-5
Colors of Service Chevrons 1910–1917[a]

Color	Branch	Dates of Authorization
Yellow	Cavalry	1910–1917
Scarlet	Artillery	1910–1917
White	Infantry and USMA Band	1910–1917
Scarlet stitched with white	Engineers	1910–1917
Black stitched with scarlet	Ordnance	1910–1917
Buff	Post QM Sergeant	1910–1912
	Quartermaster Corps	1912–1917
Gray	Post Commissary Sergeant	1910–1912
Maroon stitched with white	Hospital Corps	1910–1917
Orange stitched with white	Signal Corps	1910–1917
Green	Army Service School Detachment	1910–1917
Green stitched with white	Army Service Detachment, USMA	1910–1917
Red stitched with yellow	Navy Service	1913–1917
Yellow stitched with red	USMC Service	1913–1917

[a] Chevrons measure ⅜-inch wide, 10 inches long.

With the creation of the special 1907 ranks for the Coast Artillery Corps, Congress authorized special-skill pay for selected soldiers. This information is summarized in Table 5-7. In a further effort to improve the Army, and at the urging of the Secretary of War, Congress finally—on 11 May 1908—passed the first new pay rates for enlisted men to be approved since 1872. Compared to the ranks in existence thirty-five years before, the Army's growth is startling. An extract from the 1908 Act of Congress giving the authorization and limitations for pay provided that:

> Hereafter the monthly pay of enlisted men of the Army during their first enlistment shall be as follows, namely: Master electricians, master signal electricians, seventy-five dollars; engineers, sixty-five dollars, sergeants first class Hospital Corps, fifty dollars; regimental sergeants-major, regimental quartermaster-sergeants, regimental commissary-sergeants, sergeants-major senior grade coast artillery, battalion sergeants-major of engineers, post quartermaster-sergeants, post commissary-sergeants, post ordinance-sergeants, battalion gunmaster-sergeants of engineers, electrician-sergeants first class, sergeants first class Signal Corps, and first sergeants, forty-five dollars; battalion sergeants-major of infantry and field artillery, squadron sergeants-major, sergeants-major junior grade coast artillery, battalion quartermaster sergeants, field artillery, and master gunners, forty dollars; electrical-sergeants second class, sergeants of engineers, ordnance, and

138

TABLE 5-6
Summary of 1907 Monthly Pay by Grade and Years of Service

Grade	First & Second	Third	Fourth	Fifth	Sixth to Tenth	Eleventh to Fifteenth	Sixteenth to Twentieth	Twenty-First to Twenty-Fifth	Twenty-Sixth to Thirtieth
					YEARS				
Master Signal Electrician	$75	$76	$77	$78	$80	$81	$82	$83	$84
Master Electrician, Coast Electrician	75	76	77	78	80	81	82	83	84
Engineer, Coast Artillery	65	66	67	68	70	71	72	73	74
Chief musician, Band, Engineers, Cavalry, Artillery, Infantry	60	61	62	63	65	66	67	68	69
Sergeant, First-Class, Hospital Corps	45	46	47	48	50	51	52	53	54
Electrician-Sergeant, First-Class, Coast Artillery	45	46	47	48	50	51	52	53	54
Sergeant, First-Class, Signal Corps	45	46	47	48	50	51	52	53	54
Battalion Sergeant Major, Engineers	36	37	38	39	41	42	43	44	45
Battalion Quartermaster-Sergeant, Engineers	36	37	38	39	41	42	43	44	45
Electrician-Sergeant, Second-Class, Coast Artillery	35	36	37	38	40	41	42	43	44
Ordnance-Sergeant, Post Noncommissioned Staff	34	35	36	37	39	40	41	42	43
Commissary-Sergeant, Post Noncommissioned Staff	34	35	36	37	39	40	41	42	43
Quartermaster-Sergeant, Post Noncommissioned Staff	34	35	36	37	39	40	41	42	43
Regimental Sergeant-Major, Cavalry, Field Artillery, Infantry	34	35	36	37	39	40	41	42	43
Regimental Quartermaster-Sergeant, Cavalry, Field Artillery, Infantry	34	35	36	37	39	40	41	42	43
Regimental Commissary-Sergeant, Cavalry, Field Artillery, Infantry	34	35	36	37	39	40	41	42	43
Senior Sergeant-Major, Coast Artillery	34	35	36	37	39	40	41	42	43
Master Gunner, Coast Artillery	34	35	36	37	39	40	41	42	43
First Sergeant, Engineers	34	35	36	37	39	40	41	42	43
Sergeant, Engineers, Ordnance, Signal Corps	34	35	36	37	39	40	41	42	43
Quartermaster-Sergeant, Engineers	34	35	36	37	39	40	41	42	43
Fireman, Coast Artillery	30	31	32	33	35	36	37	38	39
Drum Major, Band, Engineers, Cavalry, Artillery, Infantry	25	26	27	28	30	31	32	33	34
Sergeant, Hospital Corps	25	26	27	28	30	31	32	33	34
Squadron, Sergeant-Major, Cavalry	25	26	27	28	30	31	32	33	34
Battalion Sergeant-Major, Field Artillery, Infantry	25	26	27	28	30	31	32	33	34
Battalion Quartermaster, Sergeant, Field Artillery	25	26	27	28	30	31	32	33	34
Color Sergeant, Cavalry, Field Artillery, Infantry	25	26	27	28	30	31	32	33	34
Junior Sergeant-Major, Coast Artillery	25	26	27	28	30	31	32	33	34
First Sergeant, Cavalry, Artillery, Infantry	25	26	27	28	30	31	32	33	34
Chief Trumpeter, Cavalry, Artillery	22	23	24	25	27	28	29	30	31
Principal Musician, Engineers, Cavalry, Artillery, Infantry	22	23	24	25	27	28	29	30	31
Corporal, Hospital Corps	20	21	22	23	25	26	27	28	29
Corporal, Engineers, Ordnance, Signal Corps	20	21	22	23	25	26	27	28	29
Cook, Engineers, Signal Corps	20	21	22	23	25	26	27	28	29

TABLE 5-6 (Continued)

	YEARS								
	First & Second	Third	Fourth	Fifth	Sixth to Tenth	Eleventh to fifteenth	Sixteenth to Twentieth	Twenty-First to Twenty-Fifth	Twenty-Sixth to Thirtieth
Sergeant, Band	18	19	20	21	23	24	25	26	27
Cook, Band	18	19	20	21	23	24	25	26	27
Private, First-Class, Hospital Corps	18	19	20	21	23	24	25	26	27
Sergeant, Cavalry, Artillery, Infantry	18	19	20	21	23	24	25	26	27
Quartermaster-Sergeant, Cavalry, Artillery, Infantry	18	19	20	21	23	24	25	26	27
Cook, Cavalry, Artillery, Infantry	18	19	20	21	23	24	25	26	27
Mechanical, Coast Artillery	18	19	20	21	23	24	25	26	27
Chief Mechanic, Field Artillery	18	19	20	21	23	24	25	26	27
Stable Sergeant, Field Artillery	18	19	20	21	23	24	25	26	27
Private, First-Class, Engineers, Ordnance, Signal Corps	17	18	19	20	22	23	24	25	26
Private, Hospital Corps	16	17	18	19	21	22	23	24	25
Corporal, Band	15	16	17	18	20	21	22	23	24
Corporal, Cavalry, Artillery, Infantry	15	16	17	18	20	21	22	23	24
Farrier and Blacksmith, Saddler, Cavalry	15	16	17	18	20	21	22	23	24
Artificer, Infantry	15	16	17	18	20	21	22	23	24
Mechanic, Field Artillery	15	16	17	18	20	21	22	23	24
Wagoner, Cavalry	14	15	16	17	19	20	21	22	23
Trumpeter, Cavalry	13	14	15	16	17	19	20	21	22
Musician, Engineers, Artillery, Infantry	13	14	15	16	17	19	20	21	22
Private, Band	13	14	15	16	18	19	20	21	22
Private, Signal Corps, Cavalry, Artillery, Infantry	13	14	15	16	18	19	20	21	22
Private, Second-Class, Engineers, Ordnance ..	13	14	15	16	18	19	20	21	22

TABLE 5-7
Coast Artillery Additional Pay Authorized, January 1907[a]

Grade	Additional Monthly Pay	Number of Men Authorized
Casemate Electrician	$9	44
Observer First Class	9	170
Plotter	9	170
Chief Planter	7	44
Chief Loader	7	44
Observer Second Class	7	170
Gun Commander[b]	7	378
Gun Pointer	7	378
First Class Gunner	2	No limit
Second Class Gunner	1	No limit

[a] Annual Report of the Secretary of War, 1907.[73]
[b] Appointed from sergeants by company commander.

Signal Corps, quartermaster sergeants of engineers, and color-sergeants, thirty-six dollars; sergeants and quartermaster-sergeants of cavalry, artillery, and infantry, stable-sergeants, sergeants, and acting cooks of the Hospital Corps, firemen, and cooks, thirty dollars: Provided, *That mess sergeants shall receive six dollars per month in addition to their pay; corporals of engineers, ordnance, Signal Corps, and Hospital Corps, chief mechanics, and mechanics, coast artillery, twenty-four dollars; corporals of cavalry, artillery, and infantry, mechanics of field artillery, blacksmith and farriers, saddlers, wagoners, and artificers, twenty-one dollars:* Provided, *That not to exceed one blacksmith and farrier in each troop of cavalry and one mechanic in each battery of field artillery shall receive nine dollars per month additional for performing the duty of horseshoer; private first class of engineers, ordnance, Signal Corps, and Hospital Corps, eighteen dollars; privates, Hospital Corps, sixteen dollars; trumpeters, musicians of infantry, artillery, and engineers, privates of cavalry, artillery, infantry, Signal Corps, and private second class, engineers and ordnance, fifteen dollars.*

That hereafter any soldier honorably discharged at the termination of an enlistment period who reenlists within three months thereafter shall be entitled to continuous-service pay as herein provided, which shall be in addition to the initial pay provided for in this Act and shall be as follows, namely: For those whose initial pay as provided herein is thirty-six dollars or more an increase of four dollars monthly pay for and during the second enlistment, and a further increase of four dollars for and during each subsequent enlistment up to and including the seventh, after which the pay shall remain as in the seventh enlistment. For those whose initial pay as provided herein is eighteen, twenty-one, twenty-four, or thirty dollars an increase of three dollars monthly pay for and during the second enlistment, and a further increase of three dollars for and during each subsequent enlistment up to and including the seventh, after which the pay shall remain as in the seventh enlistment. For those whose initial pay as provided for herein is fifteen and sixteen dollars, an increase of three dollars monthly pay for and during the second and third enlistments, and a further increase of one dollar for and during each subsequent enlistment up to and including the seventh, after which the pay shall remain as in the seventh enlistment: Provided, *That hereafter any soldier honorably discharged at the termination of his first or any succeeding enlistment period who reenlists after the expiration of three months shall be regarded as in his second enlistment; that an enlistment shall not be regarded as complete until the soldier shall have made good any time lost during the enlistment period by unauthorized absences exceeding one day, but any soldier who receives an honorable discharge for the convenience of the Government after having served more than half of his enlistment shall be considered as having served an enlistment period within the meaning of this Act; that the present enlistment period of men now in service shall be determined by the number of years continuous service they have had at the date of approval of this Act, under existing laws, counting three years to an enlistment, and the former service entitling an enlisted man to reenlisted pay under existing laws shall be counted as one enlistment period:* And provided further, *That hereafter any private soldier, musician or trumpeter honorably discharged at the termination of his first enlistment period who reenlists within three months of the date of said discharge shall, upon such reenlistment, receive an amount equal to three month's pay at the rate he was receiving at the time of his discharge.*

That hereafter enlisted men now qualified or hereafter qualifying as marksmen shall receive two dollars per month; as sharpshooters, three dollars per month; as expert riflemen, five dollars per month; as second-class gunners, two dollars per month; as first-class gunners, three dollars per month; as gun pointers, gun commanders, observers second class, chief planters and chief loaders, seven dollars per month; as plotters, observers first class, and casemate electricians, nine dollars per month, all in addition to their pay, under such regulations as the Secretary of War may prescribe, but no enlisted man shall receive at the same time additional pay for more than one of the classifications named in this section: Provided, *That nothing in this Act shall be construed to increase the total number of gun pointers, gun commanders, observers, chief planters, chief loaders, plotters, and casemate electricians now authorized by law.*

That increase of pay for serivce beyond the limits of the States comprising the Union, and the territories of the United States continguous thereto, shall be as now provided by law.

That hereafter the monthly pay during the first enlistment of enlisted men of bands, exclusive of the band of the United States Military Academy, shall be as follows:

Chief musicians, seventy-five dollars; principal musicians and chief trumpeters, forty dollars; sergeants and drum majors, thirty-six dollars; corporals, thirty dollars; and privates twenty-four dollars; and the continuous-service pay of all grades shall be as provided in this Act:

Provided, *That army bands or members thereof shall not receive remuneration for furnishing music outside the limits of military posts when the furnishing of such music places them in competition with local civilian musicians.*

CHAPTER 6

Catalog of 1902–1920 Chevrons: The Third Period

While this chapter is a catalog listing of chevrons authorized from 1902 through 1920, a few common unauthorized chevrons are included for the sake of over-all clarity. Generally, the NCO chevrons approximately 3 inches wide fall into this period, except those with arcs or bars embroidered, or those with olive drab bars on a dark blue background (World War II or later, 1920 to 1951). Also included in this chapter are PFC's insignia on rectangles about 4½ by 2¼ inches and PFC's disks which are usually 2⅝ inches in diameter. (Artillery and marksmanship insignia from this era that have similar shapes are listed in Chapter 8.)

Chevrons cataloged in this chapter are broken into subgroups as follows:

Catalog Number	User
200–219	Bands and Musicians
220–229	Quartermaster Corps and associated personnel
230–239	Ordnance Corps
240–249	Signal Corps
250–259	Hospital Corps
260–269	Corps of Engineers
270–289	Coast Artillery Corps
290–299	Chemical Warfare Service
300–339	General use, not previously designated, including Cavalry, Infantry, and Field Artillery
340–354	Tank Corps
355–359	Air Service
360–369	Motor Transport Corps
370–379	Transportation Corps
380–391	Intelligence Police and Corps of Interpreters
396–399	Special 1920 Chevrons

Chevrons for Bands and Musicians

Figure 6-1. Catalog No. 200: Sergeant of Band and Assistant Leader, USMA, 1904–1918; Assistant Band Leader, 1917–1918.

Established by letter authorization in January 1904 for the United States Military Academy Band, this dress chevron was made only in white: "The lyre . . . as designated would be distinctive of West Point. . . . " Picked up in Clothing Specifications in 1911, the design was dropped in May 1918. From December 1917 until May 1918, this chevron was also authorized for assistant band leaders. In 1918 it was replaced by Catalog No. 210. After 1920, some National Guard band personnel wore this unofficially with the lyre and bars in olive drab and the background of navy blue.

Figure 6-2. Catalog No. 201: Sergeant of Field Music, USMA, 1910–1918. In this 1913 photograph, the Sergeant of Field Music for the USMA Band was acting as the drum major. This is the only known photograph of this chevron actually worn.

Authorized in January 1904 for the Military Academy Band only, this chevron was made in pairs so the bell of the trumpet would face forward. The chevron, which was made in white, was first published in specifications in 1911, and was replaced in May 1918 by Catalog No. 204. This insignia is similar to Catalog No. 203, except a trumpet was used here while an old-style bugle was on the chief trumpeter's chevron.

Figure 6-3. Catalog No. 202: Chief Musician, 1902–1916; Band Leader, 1916–1917. Shown here is the dress chevron for Chief Musician. This particular chevron was for the left sleeve.

The basic design is an inverted continuation of the 1901 shirt chevron based on the 1899 design for chief musicians. The chevron was made in pairs so the bugle would face forward. In colors, the chevron was made in both blue (1902–1904) and white (1904–1917) for infantry, yellow for cavalry, red for artillery, and red with white piping for engineers. The 1916 National Defense Act of Army reorganization did away with the grade of chief musician and created band leaders in coast and field artillery, cavalry, infantry, and engineers. This chevron was accordingly retitled in 1916 and used until December 1917, when it was replaced by Catalog No. 208. Chief musicians were the highest paid men in bands, receiving $75.00 per month in 1908, with the next highest paid band members, principal musicians and chief trumpeters, far behind at $40.00 a month.

Figure 6-4. Catalog No. 203: Chief Trumpeter, 1902–1916; Sergeant Bugler, 1916–1917.

The basic design is an inverted continuation of the 1901 shirt chevron based on the 1873 design for chief musicians. Originally, chief trumpeters were only in mounted units (artillery and cavalry) but they were added to the coast artillery in 1908. As a result of the 1916 National Defense Act of Army reorganization, the chevron was retitled sergeant bugler, that grade then being authorized for engineers as well as for cavalry and artillery. The chevron, which was made in pairs, was dropped in December 1917, although the title of sergeant bugler was restored in May 1918 and associated with Catalog No. 204.

Figure 6-5. Catalog No. 204: Principal Musician, 1902–1916; Assistant Band Leader, 1916–1917; Sergeant Bugler (general application), 1918–1920; Sergeant of Field Music (USMA Band), 1918–1920. These chevrons were made in pairs; the example shown here was for the right sleeve of an Engineer.

The basic design, although inverted in 1902, was established in 1872 for principal musicians. Made in pairs, the chevron was worn by NCOs in the artillery, cavalry, infantry, and engineers. Congress did away with the grade of principal musician in 1916 and created assistant band leaders. In December 1917, this chevron was discarded, only to be reinstituted the following May for use by sergeant buglers of all branches, and for use by sergeants of field music of the USMA Band.

Figure 6-6. Catalog No. 205: Corporal Bugler, 1918–1920.

This design was established for general application in May 1918.

Figure 6-7. Catalog No. 206: Bugler First Class, 1918–1920.

This design was established for general application in May 1918.

Figure 6-8. Catalog No. 207: Bugler, 1917–1920.

Established in December 1917, this design was unofficially used earlier in World War I and was manufactured by private companies.

Figure 6-9. Catalog No. 208: Band Leader, 1917–1918.

This short-lived chevron was instituted in December 1917 and replaced May 1918 by Catalog No. 209. This grade of band leader took the place of drum major, which had been rescinded in 1916.

Figure 6-10. Catalog No. 209: Band Leader, 1918–1920.

In May 1918, this rank insignia replaced Catalog No. 208 and was authorized for all branches until August 1920. In January 1920, the star was changed to white, the lyre to yellow, and the wreath to green. Prior to 1920, the normal World War I practice of using subdued embroidery on a matching background was followed.

Figure 6-11. Catalog No. 210: Assistant Band Leader, 1918–1920.

Instituted in May 1918 for general application, this chevron replaced Catalog No. 200. Until 1920 the chevron was entirely in olive drab, but at that time the design was changed to a green wreath and a yellow lyre on a wool olive drab background.

Figure 6-12. Catalog No. 211: Sergeant Bugler, 1917–1918.

Used by the field artillery from December 1917 until May 1918, the title of sergeant bugler was previously used with Catalog No. 203. In May 1918, all branches which were authorized sergeant buglers switched to Catalog No. 204. This particular chevron was commonly worn in the 1920s and 1930s by staff sergeants assigned to National Guard bands, just as was done with Catalog No. 200. Staff sergeants assigned to the Army Music School were authorized this chevron in the 1920s (*see* Catalog No. 595).

Figure 6-13. Band Corporal (left) *and Band Sergeant* (right) *chevrons. Catalog No. 212: Band Sergeant, 1917–1920; Catalog No. 213: Band Corporal, 1917–1920.*

Catalog No. 212. Created in December 1917, this band sergeant's chevron in olive drab continued until 1920, when the lyre was changed to yellow, although the stripes remained olive drab. Catalog No. 213. This band corporal's chevron was created in December 1917 for the field artillery and was expanded to all branches in May 1918. The chevron was initially all olive drab, but the lyre was changed to yellow in January 1920.

Figure 6-14. Catalog No. 214: Drum Major, 1902–1916; Drum Major (USMA Band), 1918–1920.

Used by artillery, cavalry, infantry, engineers, and the USMA drum majors from 1902 through 1916, this grade was consolidated with headquarters company first sergeants, by the National Defense Act of 1916 (*see* Catalog No. 215). A 1918 interpretation of the 1916 act resulted in the decision that the USMA Band was still authorized a separate drum major and accordingly in May 1918, Special Regulation No. 42 was changed to reflect this new situation. During World War I, several firms made this chevron for wear by all drum majors and band leaders, although it was unauthorized for all but the West Point drum major. After World War I, some National Guard organizations wore this design on a navy blue background, although unauthorized.

Figure 6-15. Catalog No. 215: First Sergeant (Drum Major), 1916–1917.

The 1916 National Defense Act of Army reorganization stated that the first sergeant of headquarters companies would be the drum major. Consequently, this combination design bearing the First Sergeant's diamond and the drum major's crossed batons was created. Since the coast artillery did not have regimental organization and their bands were organized separately, the title in the coast artillery was "first sergeant of band (drum major)." In 1917, this chevron was prescribed for the USMA Band drum major. Whether the West Point drum major actually wore this chevron or Catalog No. 214 during those two years is unknown; however, the question is academic since the USMA Band wore white infantry chevrons throughout this period.

Figure 6-16. Catalog No. 216: Musician. (First, Second, and Third Class), 1920.

Approved 7 January 1920 by the Secretary of War, this yellow lyre on an olive drab disk was never worn. Later a similar design, in different colors, was used to designate men at the Army School of Music (Catalog No. 595).

Chevrons for the Quartermaster Corps and Associated Personnel

For branch-colored insignia, the Quartermaster Corps chevron was hand embroidered in yellow, with the felloe (the outer wooden portion of the wagon wheel) in blue and X's (representing stars) in white on the felloe. When these chevrons were made in pairs prior to about 1912, the hilt of the sword was to the wearer's front, and the eagle was looking forward. By 1914, most Quartermaster Corps chevrons were made with sword hilt on the chevron's right and only the eagle made in pairs. The Quartermaster Corps was formed in 1912, as the Pay Department, the Quartermaster General's Department, and the Commissary General's Department were combined.

Quartermaster cooks and bakers wore special white chev-

rons on their working uniforms with the ranks outlined in buff chain stitching. In addition to Catalog Nos. 221, 222, 227, and 228 in this section, Catalog No. 316 (cook) was made using this buff chain stitching on white. Quartermaster men "whose classification calls for manual labor" wore buff stitched chevrons on blue denim with their work clothing. This included Catalog Nos. 221 through 223 and 225 through 228.

Figure 6-17. Shown here are typical chain-stitched chevrons for wear on white uniforms by Quartermaster Corps cooks and bakers.

This chevron is a continuation of the basic design instituted in 1883 for post commissary sergeants. On chevrons made in branch colors, the stripes and crescent were gray. From 1910 through 1913, the chevron was also made in green for the Army Service School Detachment. Originally, the chevrons were made in pairs and were worn points forward, but in 1911 the chevrons were reversed so the cusps of the crescent would be toward the rear.

Post commissary sergeants were members of the post noncommissioned staff during the entire time the grade existed. In 1912, all post commissary sergeants were transferred to the Quartermaster Corps with the grade of quartermaster sergeant. However, former post commissary sergeants could continue to wear their chevrons until they were worn out, at which time Catalog No. 223 was to be worn. Additionally, despite their 1912 transfer, these two hundred former post commissary sergeants were "continuing members of the Post Noncommissioned Staff."

Various companies continued to make and sell—and men wore—chevrons of this design until 1920. During World War I and afterward, this then-unofficial chevron was usually worn by company mess sergeants.

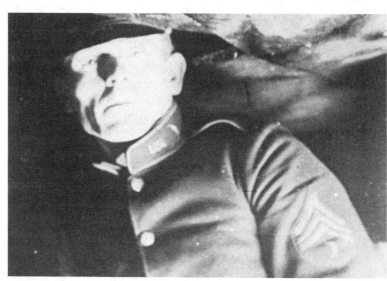

Figure 6-18. Catalog No. 220. Post Commissary Sergeant, 1902–1912.

Figure 6-19. Catalog No. 221: Post Quartermaster Sergeant, 1902–1912; Quartermaster Sergeant, Quartermaster Corps, 1912–1913; Sergeant, Quartermaster Corps, 1913–1918.

The grade of post quartermaster sergeant was established prior to 1902 when a key and pen were worn in the angle of the chevron. In July 1902, as an experiment and at the request of the Uniform Board, the Quartermaster Corps insignia was embroidered on small chevrons. When it proved feasible to use the entire Quartermaster Corps insignia, the 1902 regulations were written to reflect this fact and this chevron was estabished, to be made in pairs with the eagle facing forward. Usually the key and sword were also made in pairs with the hilt of the saber to the front.

In color, the stripes were buff, with the basic design in yellow. The felloe of the wheel was blue with white X's to represent stars. From 1910 through 1917, the stripes and entire device were made in green for the Army Service School Detachment at Fort Leavenworth.

During the 1912 reorganization of the Quartermaster General's Department into the Quartermaster Corps, this chevron was briefly worn by quartermaster sergeants; however, in 1913, this grade was given another chevron (Catalog No. 223). From 1913 through 1917, both the grades and chevrons existed for quartermaster sergeants of the QMC, and for sergeants of the QMC. In 1916, sergeants of the QMC made up 25 percent of the Quartermaster Corps strength, while quartermaster sergeants made up 6 percent of the Quartermaster Corps enlisted strength.

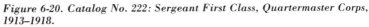

Figure 6-20. Catalog No. 222: Sergeant First Class, Quartermaster Corps, 1913–1918.

First specified in 1913, the chevron was originally made in pairs. As of 1916, this grade was not to exceed 2½ percent of the Quartermaster Corps strength. The chevron, although unauthorized after 1918, was worn well into 1919 by some men.

When the rank was established as of 1 January 1913, men of this rank were the following: electricians, clerks, packmasters, superintendents of transportation, *or* foremen of engineers, plumbers, mechanics, blacksmiths, carpenters, wheelwrights, painters, and horseshoers; they were also train masters and interpreters.

Figure 6-21. Catalog No. 223: Quartermaster Sergeant, 1913–1918.

After the consolidation of the post commissary sergeant with the Quartermaster Corps in 1912, the grade of post quartermaster sergeant was retitled quartermaster sergeant. In 1913, this chevron replaced Catalog No. 221 for quartermaster sergeants. These men were not to exceed 6 percent of Quartermaster Corps strength and were still considered members of the post noncommissioned staff.

In color, the three bars were buff, the wreath yellow, and the Quartermaster Corps insignia "natural" colors. The quartermaster sergeant of the Army Service School Detachment at Fort Leavenworth wore this chevron with the bars, wreath, and insignia in green, starting in 1915. Catalog No. 224 replaced this insignia in May 1918.

Figure 6-22. Catalog No. 224: Quartermaster Sergeant, 1918–1920.

In May 1918, this chevron replaced Catalog No. 224 for quartermaster sergeants; however, this design was also mentioned in Uniform Specifications of 1913 and 1915, but the insignia intended was Catalog No. 225. Catalog No. 395 was to replace this chevron in 1920; however, before orders could be published to implement this change, chevrons for the seven pay grades came into use.

Figure 6-23. Catalog No. 225: Master Electrician, Quartermaster Corps, 1912–1916.

Fifteen master electricians were authorized—under the Army Appropriation Act of 24 August 1912—and given this insignia. This was the highest paid grade in the Quartermaster Corps and the men were appointed by the Secretary of War on the recommendation of the Chief of the Quartermaster Corps.

The entire chevron was hand embroidered for dress uniforms, the wreath was made in yellow, the five lightning bolts in buff, and the central insignia in yellow and white. In June 1916, master electricians of the Quartermaster Corps were all transferred to the new grade of quartermaster sergeant senior grade, and given the chevron cataloged as No. 226.

Figure 6-24. Catalog No. 226: Quartermaster Sergeant Senior Grade, 1916–1920.

Created in June 1916, this grade actually was a change of title for master electricians of the Quartermaster Corps. NCOs who wore this insignia in 1916 were paid the top enlisted salary: $75.00 a month. Men occupying this grade could not exceed ½ percent of the Quartermaster Corps strength.

Figure 6-25. Catalog No. 227: Corporal, Quartermaster Corps, 1913–1918.

A pair of corporal's chevrons of the Quartermaster Corps—made about 1919—is pictured here, showing the old style of having the keys and sword crossed in opposite directions. When the Army formed the Quartermaster Corps, authorization included 650 Corporals, and these men wore this chevron. In 1918, the War Department instructed men of this grade to switch to a plain corporal's insignia, but many NCOs continued to wear these distinctive insignia until 1920.

Figure 6-26. Catalog No. 228: Private First Class, Quartermaster Corps, 1913–1919.

The Philadelphia Quartermaster Depot made this chevron for dress and service (both wool and khaki) uniforms, as well as the buff chain-stitched devices on white and on blue denim for work uniforms. During 1918, the Army also prescribed this insignia for PFCs in supply trains—until the universal PFC arc was prescribed in July 1919.

Figure 6-27. Catalog No. 229: Lance Corporal, Quartermaster Corps (unauthorized). This chevron is from the National Collection at the Smithsonian Institution and is included as an example of unauthorized chevrons made during World War I.

**Chevrons for the
Ordnance Corps**

Figure 6-28. Catalog No. 230: Ordnance Sergeant, 1902–1917.

This rank was a continuation of the same grade (Catalog No. 122) authorized before 1902. The ordnance sergeant was a member of the post noncommissioned staff; therefore there was only one man of this grade for each post. This rank should not be confused with that of sergeant of ordnance, who wore the chevron cataloged as No. 231. In October 1917, the Adjutant General approved a change to No. 235 for ordnance sergeants, the change taking effect two months later.

Men already in the Army who wished to apply for this grade took a standard test the first of December of each year. Those who passed the test had their names put on a list in the order of their test scores. A soldier's name could remain on the appointment list for three years, and as vacancies occurred, men were promoted to the rank of ordnance sergeant with this list as the basis of selection.

Figure 6-29. Catalog No. 231: Sergeant of Ordnance.

The ordnance sergeant's chevron shown here was for wear on the white uniform, while the sergeant of ordnance's chevron was for wear on the khaki uniform. Both are of the 1902–1904 type with black bars piped in red and a black bomb with red flames. It was in 1902 that sergeants of ordnance were first authorized to wear chevrons of a special design. Prior to this, standard design sergeant's chevrons, in ordnance crimson, had been worn. The new Ordnance Corps colors were used on the 1902 chevrons: black with red piping for the stripes, a black bomb, and red flames. In May 1918, this chevron was superseded by the plain three stripes of a sergeant (Catalog No. 312).

Figure 6-30. Catalog Nos. 232 and 233: Corporal (left) and Lance Corporal (right) of Ordnance—for wear on the khaki uniforms, 1905–1916.

The plain corporal's chevrons for general application to all branches replaced this insignia (No. 232) in May 1918, although many men wore this chevron as late as 1920. Lance corporals were authorized their chevron (No. 233) initially only where there was a company organization. However, in the Ordnance Department and the Quartermaster Department, there was some question as to the validity of this restriction. Uniform and clothing specifications from 1905 through 1908 made allowances for this grade, and the appropriate chevrons were manufactured and issued by the Quartermaster depots.

Figure 6-31. Catalog No. 234: First Class Private of Ordnance, 1902–1915; Private First Class (Ordnance), 1915–1919.

In 1902 the Ordnance Corps flaming bomb was selected to represent this new grade. At that time, all of the other Ordnance Corps chevrons were made with a hand-embroidered insignia, but owing to the large number of first class private insignia required and the cost of hand embroidery, the new device was made by cutting the design out in colored cloth and sewing it to the background. Within a few years, this practice was replaced by having the bomb embroidered by machine.

Figure 6-32. Catalog No. 235 (1917–1918): Ordnance Sergeant (left). Catalog No. 237 (1917–1918): Sergeant First Class, Ordnance Department (right). Both chevrons were introduced in the fall of 1917 and rescinded in mid–1918.

In September 1917, the Chief of Ordnance recommended that this chevron for ordnance sergeant replace Catalog No. 230, and although the request was not approved until the next month, private companies began to make this insignia immediately. Various companies continued to sell this insignia until 1920 despite the fact it was officially replaced by Catalog No. 236 in the summer of 1918. For the sergeant first class, a new rank, this chevron was first made in September or October 1917 and was replaced in May 1918 by Catalog No. 323, which was to be used by all sergeants first class.

Figure 6-33. Catalog No. 236: Ordnance Sergeant, 1918–1920.

This chevron replaced Catalog No. 235 when Change 4 to Special Regulation No. 42 was published in May 1918. This action was in line with the trend of having the senior NCOs and former post noncommissioned staff grades designated by a wreath and the branch insignia. In January 1920, the Secretary of War approved a new set of chevrons, including this one, having colored embroidery on an olive drab background. The wreath was in green, the bomb in black, and the flame in two shades of red.

Chevrons for the Signal Corps

All of the branch-colored Signal Corps chevrons had orange stripes with white piping and the signal devices in "natural colors." Made in pairs, the chevrons were to be worn so that the white flag with red center was at the wearer's front. Owing to the stocks of the pre–1902 black and white shirt chevrons already made, the orange and white insignia were not introduced for enlisted men at the Signal School until 1905.

Chevrons cataloged as Nos. 240 through 243 were also made in green for members of the Army Service School Detachment at the Signal School, with the entire signal insignia as well as the stripes embroidered in green. In the summer of 1914, the War Department approved Signal Corps denim chevrons for wear on blue denim work uniforms. The bars and devices on these denim chevrons were outlined in white chain stitching and piped in orange. In addition to chevrons cataloged as Nos. 240 through 247, master signal electricians wore No. 308 prior to 1909.

Figure 6-34. Catalog No. 240: Sergeant First Class of Signal Corps, 1902–1908; Sergeant First Class, Signal Corps, 1908–1918.

This chevron was a continuation of the basic design used by men of the same grade prior to 1902 (Catalog No. 116), with the chevron points up (inverted V) in the standard 1902 change.

*Figure 6-35. Catalog No. 241: Sergeant of Signal Corps, 1902–1913;
Sergeant, Signal Corps, 1913–1918.*

Instituted in 1902, this chevron was continuously authorized
only until 1918 although it was actually worn well past the end
of World War I.

*Figure 6-36. Catalog No. 242. Corporal of the Signal Corps, 1902–1913:
Corporal, Signal Corps, 1913–1917.*

This design of insignia was authorized from 1902 to the end of
1917, although it was actually used by many men until 1920. The
chevrons of this design were made to be worn on the khaki
uniform. Colored chevrons (like those shown in Figure 6-36)
were made in pairs, with the white flag intended to face the
wearer's front.

Figure 6-37. Catalog No. 243: Master Signal Electrician, 1909–1918.

General Order No. 11, published in January 1909, created a new
chevron to replace Catalog No. 308, giving men of this grade
their own distinctive chevron. Initially the entire design was
hand embroidered for both dress and service uniforms, but by
1915 the wreath and lightning for chevrons for service uniforms
were embroidered by machine, leaving only the flags and staffs
to be sewn by hand. In May 1918 the torch was added to the flags
by Change 4 to Special Regulation No. 42, creating Catalog No.
245 as a replacement for this chevron. Despite this change, many
stores continued to sell this chevron in 1918 and 1919 as the
insignia for master signal electricians.

*Figure 6-38. Catalog No. 244: Lance Corporal of Signal Corps, 1902–1913;
Lance Corporal, Signal Corps, 1913–1916.*

Figure 6-39. Catalog No. 245: Master Signal Electricians, 1918–1920.

This chevron replaced Catalog No. 243 in May 1918 and was
authorized through 1920.

Figure 6-40. Catalog No. 246.

Made by various manufacturers during World War I, this chevron was never authorized by regulations. According to the
scheme generally in use, this chevron would have been worn by
a master signal sergeant senior grade, or someone of similar
title, but the Signal Corps was not authorized personnel of
master sergeant grades other than the electricians who wore
chevrons cataloged as Nos. 243 and 254.

Figure 6-41. Catalog No. 247: Privates of the Signal Corps, 1902–1911; Private First Class, Signal Corps, 1911–1919.

From 1902 through mid–1918, this chevron was used by privates or privates first class of the Signal Corps, including the infant aviation section. In July 1918, the aviation section was split from the Signal Corps, and PFCs of that branch were given their special chevron. The standard PFC insignia adopted for all branches in July 1919 replaced this chevron.

Chevrons for the Hospital Corps

Maroon bars and the caduceus with white piping were used on branch-colored Hospital Corps chevrons. The Surgeon General instituted special chevrons with olive drab bars and a caduceus on white cotton cloth for wear on the hospital white uniforms through World War I. Army Service School Detachment members who were sergeants first class and PFCs of the Hospital Corps at the medical school also wore green bars and caduceus on dress uniforms.

Figure 6-42. Catalog No. 250: Hospital Sergeant, 1916–1918.

In June 1916, the grade of hospital sergeant was authorized, and the following month this chevron was authorized. In mid–1918, hospital sergeants changed from this chevron to that cataloged as No. 257.

Figure 6-43. Catalog No. 251: Hospital Steward, 1902–1903; Sergeant First Class of the Hospital Corps, 1903–1905; Sergeant First Class, Hospital Corps, 1905–1918.

The title of hospital steward, used for many years during the nineteenth century, was changed in March 1903 to conform with other NCO titles then in use. The chevron cataloged as No. 257 replaced this insignia in May 1918.

Figure 6-44. Catalog No. 252: Acting Hospital Steward, 1902–1903; Sergeant of the Hospital Corps, 1903–1918.

Initially sergeants of the Hospital Corps, like SFCs, could only be appointed by the Secretary of War on the recommendation of the Surgeon General. In 1918 this distinctive chevron was officially replaced by the three bars used by all sergeants.

Figure 6-45. Catalog No. 253: Corporal of the Hospital Corps, 1903–1918.

In March 1903, Congress authorized hospital corporals and paid the men $20.00 a month, the same as other corporals of special skill. In 1918, standard corporal's chevrons officially replaced this special insignia.

Figure 6-46. Catalog No. 254. Lance Acting Hospital Steward, 1902–1903; Lance Corporal of the Hospital Corps, 1903–1916.

The awkward title of lance acting hospital steward was a carry-over from the 1890s. A new title, in line with others in general Army use, was introduced in 1903 and used until Congress abolished the grade of lance corporal in 1916.

Figure 6-47. Catalog No. 255. Private of the Hospital Corps, 1902–1903; Private First Class of the Hospital Corps, 1903–1917; Private First Class, Medical Department, 1917–1919.

The 1¼-inch-high caduceus was used by privates or PFCs until replaced by the universal PFC chevron in July 1919. Starting in May 1910, this chevron was made in green for the dress uniform for use by PFCs in the Army Service School Detachment at the medical school.

Figure 6-48. Catalog No. 256: Master Hospital Sergeant, 1916–1920.

As authorized by Congress in the summer of 1916, NCOs of this grade received the highest pay then given to enlisted personnel, $75.00 a month. When colored chevrons were proposed for service wear in early 1920, this insignia was included with a white star, a maroon caduceus, and a green wreath.

Figure 6-49. Catalog No. 257: Hospital Sergeant, 1918–1920.

This chevron replaced Catalog No. 250 in May 1918. A colored version was approved in January 1920 for wear on service uniforms, until Congress consolidated the enlisted grades in August 1920.

Chevrons for the Corps of Engineers

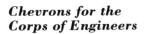

Figure 6-50. Catalog No. 260: Master Engineer Senior Grade, 1916–1920.

Two NCOs of the rank of master engineer senior grade were authorized for each of seven Engineer Corps regiments when the grade was created in 1916. The men received $75.00 a month, the highest pay authorized NCOs at that time. During the expansion of the Army during World War I, this pay grade was authorized for several other branches and master engineers senior grade, not in the Corps of Engineers, were given chevrons of other designs. This chevron, along with several others, was scheduled to be replaced by the chevron cataloged as No. 396 in 1920.

Figure 6-51. Catalog No. 261: Master Engineer Junior Grade, 1916–1920.

Master engineers junior grade were paid $65.00 a month, the second highest pay authorized for enlisted men in 1916. Each engineer battalion was initially authorized three men who wore this chevron. When temporary branches were created during World War I, several branches besides the Corps of Engineers were authorized men of this grade, although other chevrons were worn. In 1920, this chevron was to be replaced by No. 397, but this did not actually take place.

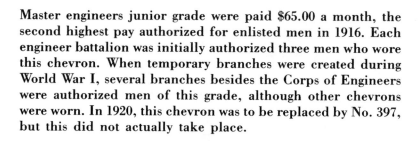

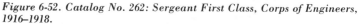

Figure 6-52. Catalog No. 262: Sergeant First Class, Corps of Engineers, 1916–1918.

This chevron was replaced by No. 312 in May 1918. Despite this fact, some men continued to wear the sleeve insignia with the castle device until 1920.

Figure 6-53. Catalog No. 263: Sergeant, Corps of Engineers.

Figure 6-54. Catalog No. 264: Corporal, Corps of Engineers.

Never authorized by regulations, these chevrons were commonly worn during World War I.

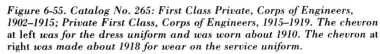

Figure 6-55. Catalog No. 265: First Class Private, Corps of Engineers, 1902–1915; Private First Class, Corps of Engineers, 1915–1919. The chevron at left *was for the dress uniform and was worn about 1910. The chevron at right was made about 1918 for wear on the service uniform.*

The castle in red cloth, 1½ inches long, piped with white, was initially worn only on the right sleeve, although by 1912 it was worn on both sleeves. Also worn by engineer PFCs of supply trains in 1918 and 1919, this insignia was replaced in July 1919 by the chevron cataloged as No. 336.

Chevrons for the Coast Artillery Corps

After the Spanish-American War, the coast artillery became a separate branch in the Army and expanded rapidly, becoming almost an army within an Army. Some coast artillery units wore the old 1885-pattern coats and the large nineteenth-century chevrons as late as 1912, but, especially after 1907, many special rank insignia unique to the Coast Artillery Corps were also created. Chevrons of this branch have thus continued to stand out.

The following pages on Catalog Nos. 270–283 contain only the chevrons of rank worn exclusively by members of the Coast Artillery Corps. Those chevrons cataloged as Nos. 500 through 521, also used solely by the sea coast defense units, showed position and ratings, however, and not ranks. Many of the standard chevrons (those cataloged here as Nos. 300 through 330) were also used by the Coast Artillery Corps.

Figure 6-56. Catalog No. 270: Electrician Sergeant, 1902–1907; Electrician Sergeant Second Class, CAC, 1907–1908; Radio Sergeant, 1916, 1918–1920.

This chevron is a continuation of Catalog No. 138 in the 1902 pattern. Prior to 1903, electrician sergeants were the only NCOs who were specialists in power and electrical work, but in that year, master electricians were first appointed and these men outranked electrician sergeants.

Circular No. 5, January 1904, spelled out the responsibilities of the men who wore the electrician sergeant's chevrons:

> His duties comprise the supervision of the care and use of steam and oil engines, motors, dynamos, storage batteries, searchlights, submarine mine equipment, and the other electrical apparatus found at seacoast fortifications, for the proper and serviceable condition of which he is held responsible.

Initially, electrician sergeants were simply appointed from the Army. However, in August 1905 tougher standards were established. Before a new enlisted man could be appointed an electrician sergeant, he had to pass a 6-month course for electrician sergeants taught at the School of Submarine Defense, Fort Totten, New York. Those NCOs who were already electrician sergeants had to complete the course, and anyone who failed could

159

not be reenlisted as an electrician sergeant. In 1907, electrician sergeants were retitled electrician sergeants second class, C.A.C., and in January 1908, a new, more distinctive chevron, cataloged here as No. 272, was given these men.

Catalog No. 270 was reintroduced in 1916 when Congress established the grade of radio sergeant. The next year, another chevron, cataloged here as No. 308, replaced this insignia of grade, but 1918 saw this chevron reintroduced for radio sergeants. These men were to care for and operate radio stations, conduct instruction in signaling, and perform other duties. Some radio sergeants were assigned to mine planters and Army cable ships. In 1920, it was proposed that the design be modified so that the lightning bolts were to be white, while the rest of the chevron was to remain olive drab.

Figure 6-57. Catalog No. 271: Electrician Sergeant First Class, 1908–1918.

Electrician sergeants first class supervised portions of electrical installations, including searchlights, and were in charge of "more important power plants." In addition they performed other duties in connection with electrical installations. All electrician sergeants first class were appointed from electrician sergeants second class.

NCOs of this grade were authorized chevrons cataloged as No. 271 in January 1908. The stripes and ¾-inch bar were in Artillery Corps red, while the sparks were white and the wreath yellow. In 1908, the Artillery School portion of the Army Service School Detachment was authorized NCOs of this grade who wore the design executed entirely in green, except for the five white lightning bolts. Catalog No. 273 replaced this chevron in May 1918.

Figure 6-58. Catalog No. 272: Electrician Sergeant Second Class, 1908–1918.

This chevron is identical to No. 271 with the omission of the small horizontal bar beneath the sparks. Specifically charged with the care, repair, and maintenance of electrical installations, including minor power plants, electrician sergeants second class also supervised linemen. To qualify for appointment, a man had to be a graduate in electrical work of the School of Enlisted Specialists. Electrician sergeants first and second class, although noncommissioned staff officers of the Coast Artillery Corps, were verbally addressed as "sergeant," the form of address "electrician" being reserved for master electricians by regulation.

This chevron was also used by certain men of the Army Service School Detachment who were part of the Artillery School's staff from 1909 until 1918. After ten years' service, this chevron was replaced by that cataloged as No. 308.

Figure 6-59. Catalog No. 273: Electrician Sergeant First Class, 1918–1920.

Established in May 1918 by Change 4 to Special Regulation No. 42, this chevron superseded No. 271. Originally the design was executed entirely in olive drab, as was the World War I practice; this made the chevron virtually indistinguishable from that cataloged as No. 308 except upon close inspection. In 1920, authorization was granted to embroider the sparks in white (manufacturing code "*o*") although chevrons of this kind were not actually worn.

Figure 6-60. Catalog No. 274: Master Electrician, 1907–1908.

Although prescribed in 1907, this chevron was not manufactured at that time. The wreath was to be gold, the lightning silver. In January 1908, the Quartermaster General's Department specified Catalog No. 276 as a replacement since officials judged the original too difficult to make.

During World War I, various private companies sewed the design cataloged as No. 274 on automatic machines, evidently in the belief most chevrons with stars above were also authorized without stars for lower grade personnel. In such cases, the chevron was not authorized.

Figure 6-61. Catalog No. 275: Master Gunner, 1908–1920.

A yellow wreath enclosing a red projectile with a white star above was selected as the design for coast artillery master gunners in 1908. A green shell replaced the one of red for members of the Army Service School Detachment at Fort Monroe in 1909. During the 1919 revision of chevrons, this design was specified to be made with a red projectile, a green wreath, and a white star, all embroidered on a background of olive drab felt.

Only forty-two master gunners were authorized prior to World War I. Their duties included photographic work, seacoast engineering, preparation of tables, charts, and maps, and other similar technical artillery work. To become a master gunner a coast artillery soldier had to complete a comprehensive enlisted course at the Coast Artillery School and be recommended for the grade. In 1908, for instance, nineteen out of twenty-one who started finished the course, but only eight were recommended for the grade of master gunner, even while the other men were considered highly qualified enlisted men.

Figure 6-62. Catalog No. 276: Master Electrician, 1908–1920.

Before World War I, the Army had only twenty-six men in this grade, four of whom were members of the Army Service School Detachment at the Artillery School. The dress chevrons had yellow wreaths and white stars, with green lightning bolts for ASSD members and lightning bolts of red for other master electricians. When the Army proposed a return to colored chevrons after World War I, the star and lightning bolts were made in white with the wreath green.

Of the several NCOs whose specialty centered around electricity, the most senior was the master electrician. Master electricians served as supervisors and inspectors of electrical and power installations of an artillery district. Appointment to this grade was by competitive examinations which open only to engineers, electrician sergeants first class, and electrician sergeants second class who had served in that grade at least one year.

Figure 6-63. Catalog No. 277: Fireman, 1907–1908.

Authorized in 1907, this was originally intended to be a rating in the Coast Artillery Corps. The chevron cataloged as No. 280 replaced No. 277, which was never manufactured.

Figure 6-64. Catalog No. 278: Engineer, CAC, 1908–1920.

The red mechanical governor enclosed in the center of the chevron was symbolic of the engineer's duties. He supervised and operated power plants, machines, and mechanical apparatus used for power purposes. Although this was a rank used exclusively by the coast artillery, the select few engineers who were members of the Army Service School Detachment at the Artillery School wore a green governor. In 1920, the wreath was changed to green, although the star remained white.

Engineer's appointments were based on the results of competitive examinations that were open to electrical sergeants first class, electrical sergeants second class, and firemen who had served as such for at least one year.

Figure 6-65. Catalog No. 279: Assistant Engineer, CAC, 1916–1920; Oiler, Mine Planter Service, 1920.

Assistant engineers were first authorized by Congress in 1916. In 1920, colored embroidery was proposed for use on service chevrons, the governor to be red and the wreath green. Assistant engineers were assigned to power plants to perform duties as necessary to care for and operate these plants.

Figure 6-66. Catalog No. 280: Fireman, CAC, 1908–1914.

Authorized in 1908, firemen were appointed from graduates of the School for Enlisted Specialists and were to operate boilers and associated accessories. Equating NCOs who served in this grade with other soldiers is extremely difficult. Pay, precedence of rank, and other insignia worn by firemen all run counter to each other. Initially, firemen were somewhat equated to corporals, but later it was decided firemen were above this junior NCO standing. By World War I, the decision was reversed and firemen were considered a special and separate grade, but somewhat akin to corporals.

The dress chevron was made in red for the coast artillery—and in green for members of the Army Service School Detachment—until replaced in 1914 by Catalog No. 281.

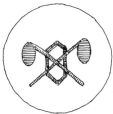

Figure 6-67. Catalog No. 281. Fireman, CAC, 1914–1917.

This design replaced that cataloged as No. 280 as a result of the effort to upgrade the standing of this unusual NCO. Because stocks of the previous chevrons were still on hand, this design saw only limited use until it was replaced by that cataloged as No. 282.

Figure 6-68. Catalog No. 282: Fireman, CAC, 1917–1920.

Chevrons of this design were worn during World War I. The design itself was the last of three in use during the twelve years firemen were authorized. Initially this chevron was made with an olive drab design on an olive drab background as were all World War I chevrons. In 1920 the chevron was authorized to have a red bar and governor on an olive drab felt background.

Figure 6-69. Catalog No. 290: Sergeant First Class, Chemical Warfare Service, 1918. Catalog No. 291: Sergeant, Chemical Warfare Service, 1918. Catalog No. 292: Corporal, Chemical Warfare Service, 1918.

Authorized in February 1918 by Change 3 to Special Regulation No. 42, chevrons cataloged as Nos. 290, 291, and 292 were officially replaced in May of the same year, although men continued to wear these chevrons well into the following year.

Figure 6-70. Catalog No. 293: Private First Class, Chemical Warfare Service, 1918–1919.

Authorized from February 1918 through July 1919, this design was instituted shortly after the Chemical Warfare Service was founded and was officially replaced by Catalog No. 336. Many AEF members who should have worn this insignia wore in its place the chevron cataloged here as No. 294.

Figure 6-71. Catalog No. 294: Private First Class, Gas Service, 1917–1919.

The design of a dragon's head and two shells became the insignia of the Gas Service, a branch initially separate from the Chemical Warfare Service in the American Expeditionary Force but not separate in the Army in the United States. The AEF Gas Service was responsible for the actual firing of chemical ammunitions, while members of the Chemical Warfare Service served as staff members of headquarters and worked on development of chemical weapons. The AEF proposed that the Army split the Gas Service from the Chemical Warfare Service but this failed, and in Europe some men in the Gas Service acted as if they were not in the Chemical Warfare Service by wearing the dragon head and shells. Although the War Department did not authorize the chevron, it was commonly worn by Gas Service PFCs in France and was issued by the AEF Quartermaster.

Figure 6-72. Catalog No. 295: Master Chemical Sergeant, 1918.
Men of this rank, which was authorized from February through May 1918, were sometimes known as master chemists.

Figure 6-73. Catalog No. 296.
Although not officially recognized, this insignia was made by some companies during World War I.

Chevrons for General Use (Cavalry, Infantry, Field Artillery)

Figure 6-74. Catalog 300: Regimental Sergeant Major (all branches except Coast Artillery); Sergeant Major, Senior Grade (Coast Artillery only), 1902–1920.

Starting in 1902, this chevron was worn by the most senior NCOs of infantry, artillery, and cavalry. In 1910, regimental sergeants major and sergeants major, senior grade were authorized for the Army Service School Detachment. Engineer regimental sergeants major were added in 1916. After 1920, the Quartermaster Corps issued the remaining chevrons to master sergeants.

Each cavalry and infantry regiment was authorized one of these NCOs until the field artillery reorganization in 1907. After that, all three of these branches had one regimental quartermaster sergeant in each regiment. Green dress chevrons for members of the Army Service School Detachment were added in May 1910. The National Defense Act of 1916 changed the title and added a regimental supply sergeant to each engineer regiment. Most members of the regimental noncommissioned staff were assigned to headquarters company in 1916, but because of the duties of this NCO, he was a member of the regimental supply company.

Figure 6-76. Catalog No. 302: Regimental Commissary Sergeant, 1902–1916.

Regimental commissary sergeants followed the same branch development as regimental quartermaster sergeants from 1902 through 1916. In 1916, however, Congress withdrew authorization for these men and the rank ceased to exist. Some men who functioned like a regimental commissary sergeant continued to wear the chevron through World War I even though this was unauthorized. Initially, the older pattern of wearing the cusps to the front was followed, but by 1911 the crescent on the sleeves had been turned around.

Figure 6-77. Catalog No. 303: Squadron or Battalion Sergeant Major (branches other than Coast Artillery), 1902–1920; Sergeant Major, Junior Grade (Coast Artillery), 1902–1920.

Figure 6-78. Catalog No. 304: Battalion of Engineers, Quartermaster Sergeant, 1902–1907; Battalion Quartermaster Sergeant, 1907–1916; Battalion Supply Sergeant, 1916–1918; Battalion or Squadron Supply Sergeant, 1918–1920.

From 1902 through 1920, each infantry, cavalry, and engineer battalion had a sergeant major who was distinguished by two arcs beneath the sergeant's bars. In 1901, artillery regiments were abolished and the senior NCOs who had been battalion sergeants major became sergeants major, junior grade. After the 1907 artillery reorganization, a field artillery man who wore this chevron became known as a battalion sergeant major, even though he wore the same red dress chevrons as a sergeant major, junior grade. Starting in 1919, the Army Service School Detachment was authorized men as squadron sergeants major, battalion sergeants major, and sergeants major, junior grade.

Until 1907, only the Corps of Engineers considered the battalion other than just a tactical organization. For this reason other arms had regimental and not battalion supply NCOs. When the field artillery was formed as a separate arm in 1907, that branch was authorized a supply NCO at battalion level. The Field Artillery Service School Detachment added battalion quartermaster sergeants in May 1910. When Congress reorganized the Army in 1916, in the process the title of this grade was changed and again the grade was restricted to one mounted engineer battalion and the Engineer Service School Detachment. During the World War I expansion, some men acted as battalion supply sergeants and wore this chevron unofficially. In May 1918, most battalions and squadrons were authorized supply sergeants, and these men were officially authorized to wear this chevron.

Figure 6-79. Catalog No. 305.

Made by some private companies during and after World War I, this chevron was never authorized by the United States Army. Chevrons of this design were worn by men acting as battalion commissary sergeants.

Figure 6-80. Catalog No. 306: Troop, Battery, or Company Quartermaster Sergeant, 1902–1916; Supply Sergeant, 1916, 1918–1920.

This chevron is the 1902 insignia that replaced Catalog No. 105. At first this chevron was worn by infantry, cavalry, artillery, and engineers. In 1910, selected members of the Army Service School Detachment began to wear this chevron with green stripes.

This grade was redesignated supply sergeant in 1916; NCOs of this grade were to change officially to chevrons cataloged as No. 312 a few months later. Many manufacturing companies made chevrons of this design (No. 306) during the unauthorized period from 1916 through 1918, and naturally many NCOs wore the device. The chevron was reauthorized in May 1918.

Figure 6-81. Catalog No. 307.

Made by the Walter Reib Company in 1918 and 1919, and perhaps by other manufacturers during and after World War I, this unofficial chevron was intended for company commissary sergeants. Even though this grade was not authorized, some company mess sergeants and supply sergeants used this insignia.

Figure 6-82. Catalog No. 308: Master Electrician, 1903–1908; Master Signal Electrician, 1904–1909; Electrician Sergeant First Class, CAC, 1907–1908; Radio Sergeant, 1917–1918; Electrician Sergeant Second Class, 1918–1920.

Congress, in March 1903, provided "that there shall be added to the Artillery Corps twenty-five Master Electricians, to be enlisted by the Secretary of War, after such examination as he may prescribe, who shall receive seventy-five dollars per month. . . . " Red artillery bars and white lightning were the colors of this chevron for coast artillery master electricians. The next year this same design was used to designate master signal electricians, but the bars were orange, piped with white. In January 1909, Catalog No. 243 replaced this insignia for master signal electricians although replacement of the chevrons was not immediate.

Electrician sergeants first class, authorized in April 1907, were initially to wear this chevron although the new year (1908) saw a new design, Catalog No. 271, intended for NCOs of this grade. Simultaneously, master electricians were authorized chevron No. 276; this caused No. 308 to fall into disuse.

Revived in 1917, this chevron was authorized for radio sergeants of the coast artillery until May 1918, when Catalog No. 270 was authorized for radio sergeants. The May change also retitled this insignia so that it became the rank device for electrician sergeants second class, replacing Catalog No. 272. The

World War I all-olive-drab chevron was modified in 1920 by making the five lightning bolts white.

Figure 6-83. Catalog No. 309: Color Sergeant, 1902–1920.

Color sergeants were selected to carry the national and regimental colors because they were some of the most distinguished soldiers in a regiment. These men were in regimental organizations, and accordingly only cavalry and infantry units had these men until the 1907 artillery reorganization, when field artillery regiments were again formed. In 1916, when engineer regiments were organized, engineer color sergeants became authorized.

[See Figure 6-84.]

A horsehead silhouette below the juncture of the sergeant's bars distinguished this field artillery rank, with chevrons made in pairs, left and right. In October 1915, the Fort Leavenworth Army Service School Detachment was authorized a green chevron of this design.

Congressional reorganization of the Army in June 1916 resulted in stable sergeants' also being authorized for mounted engineer units; however, the Uniform Regulations resulting from this legislation abolished the special chevron for stable sergeants and prescribed the chevron be the "same as other Sergeants." Men unofficially wore this chevron during the 1916–1918 period, and in mid–1918 the chevron was again prescribed by regulations for stable sergeants.

Figure 6-85. Catalog No. 311: First Sergeant, 1902–1920.

In 1907, the Secretary of War reported:

> The First Sergeant is a selected Sergeant, but more valuable to a company than all other Sergeants combined. In Germany, he is the "mother" of a company, as the Captain is the "father." He is no less important with us. In executive and administrative ability and in knowledge of his trade, he must rise superior to every enlisted member of his organization. . . .

Infantry, cavalry, artillery, and engineer companies had first sergeants throughout this period. The Army Service Detachment at West Point was authorized one first sergeant during these eighteen years; but after 1909, the dress chevron for this one soldier differed from all other first sergeant stripes. All but the USMA first sergeant dress stripe had the diamond in the major branch color only. For instance, an engineer first sergeant would have stripes of red with white piping, but the lozenge would be only of red. When the Secretary of War reviewed a sample chevron for the West Point first sergeant in 1908, he noted the chevron was satisfactory, but commented that the diamond should be chain stitched like the bars. The Quartermaster Depot dutifully made the chevron that way, but other branches were not modified. Up to that time, the West Point

Figure 6-84. Catalog 310: Stable Sergeant, 1902–1916, 1918–1920.

Detachment had worn buff chevrons, but these were replaced by the green and white since the Quartermaster General's Department also wore buff.

One Indian Scout first sergeant was authorized, and from 1902 through 1904, white stripes with red piping were made for this man. The Scout chevrons were made only on olive drab wool and on khaki, rather than on the usual four different background materials authorized during these three years. Until 1916, the West Point Band first sergeant wore infantry chevrons, although the band was listed separately in regulations. Catalog No. 215 replaced this insignia for the USMA and other bands in 1916. The various Army Service School Detachment first sergeants began to wear their green chevrons in 1910, completing the list of distinctively colored chevrons worn by various "top sergeants."

Figure 6-86. Catalog No. 312: Sergeant, 1902–1920. The three bars of a sergeant are on this soldier's right sleeve only, indicating this photograph was taken after April 1918. The three V's on the left cuff indicate eighteen months' overseas service, which further shows this picture was taken after the end of World War I. The star on the cuff was an unauthorized device worn by some soldiers to indicate they volunteered (i.e., were not draftees).

All branches authorized a first sergeant were also authorized two or more sergeants. Additionally, the recruiting service had sergeants after 1904 who wore the white duck uniform with stripes of olive drab.

In 1916, stable sergeants, supply sergeants, mess sergeants, band sergeants, and sergeants of the line wore this chevron. This chevron was established for general application to all branches in 1918, replacing chevrons cataloged as Nos. 221, 231, 241, 252, 291, 383, and 389.

Figure 6-87. Catalog No. 313: Corporal 1902–1920.

The history of this rank device is parallel to that of the sergeant's chevrons. Any organization authorized chevrons cataloged as No. 312 also had corporals who wore this chevron, including the recruiting service's olive drab bars on a white duck background. In 1916, several grades of sergeants began to wear chevrons cataloged as No. 312, but at this time only band corporals and recruiting corporals wore the two stripes previously reserved for junior line NCOs. Catalog No. 213 was later introduced for band corporals.

Corporals of various branches were to wear chevrons of this kind (No. 313) after May 1918, replacing Nos. 227, 232, 242, 253, 292, 384, and 390.

Figure 6-88. Catalog No. 314: Lance Corporal, 1902–1920.

Used by the infantry, cavalry, artillery, recruiting service, engineers, school detachments, USMA Band, and Indian Scouts. In the summer of 1902 the question arose whether or not Indian Scouts were authorized lance corporals. An affirmative decision was reached, and accordingly in August of that year this chevron was made for Indian Scouts, but only on khaki and olive drab backgrounds.

In 1916, Congress abolished the rank of lance corporal and created in its place first class privates. However, the law stated that the USMA Detachment at West Point would not be affected, and the War Department staff concluded that lance corporals were still authorized in the USMA Band. Regulations were written accordingly authorizing the lance corporal only at West Point until the entire rank structure was overhauled in 1920.

Figure 6-89. Catalog No. 315: Farrier, 1908–1918.

Approved by the Secretary of War in September 1908, this chevron was for coast and field artillery farriers. The Army Service School Detachment was authorized chevrons of the same design in 1910. Often, this field artillery grade was known as mechanic-farrier because the law provided only for mechanics in that branch.

Artillery and ASSD farriers were withdrawn in 1916, but the Medical Department simultaneously authorized this chevron. Officially, this chevron was eliminated in early 1918, but many soldiers continued to wear the horsehead.

Figure 6-90. Catalog No. 316: Cook, 1902–1920.

A cook's cap was the device used to designate cooks. Their status was generally parallel to that of a corporal since in the Signal Corps and the Engineers Corps, a cook's pay was $20.00 a month (in 1905); but in the infantry, cavalry, and artillery, cooks drew $18.00 a month, $3.00 more than corporals.

By letter authorization, the Indian Scouts had cooks and Scout chevrons were made for them until at least 1904. Two

171

cooks were authorized the West Point Detachment; for them a buff cook's cap design was used until 1909, when a change was made to a green cap piped with white. Hospital Corps cooks were established in March 1909, and the Army Service School Detachment's cooks began to wear their green insignia in May 1910. Under the reorganization of the Quartermaster Corps in 1912, cooks were authorized for that branch also. In short, this insignia was worn by more branches than any other chevron. In addition to the standard types of chevrons, this insignia was outlined by buff chain stitching on white duck cloth for wear on QMC cooks' clothing.

Figure 6-91. Catalog No. 317: Farrier, 1902–1908; Horseshoer, 1908–1920.

A continuation of Catalog No. 135, this chevron was unusual in that the 1902 regulations did not reduce the size of the horseshoe from 4½ inches by 3¾ inches until a special amendment was made on 10 April 1903 (General Order No. 54), by which it was reduced to 1⅜ inches by 1⅛ inches.

Only the cavalry had men who wore this insignia until 1907, when mechanics of the field artillery who performed duties as farriers and blacksmiths were directed to wear this chevron rather than that cataloged as No. 318. From 1904 until 1908, this rank was often called a "Farrier and Blacksmith," especially in the cavalry. Farriers were authorized Catalog No. 315 in September 1908, and No. 317 was to be worn by the newly authorized horseshoers, who were in both cavalry and field artillery units. In 1910, the Army Service School Detachment was authorized men in this grade along with several others. The Medical Department, engineers, Signal Corps, and infantry all gained horseshoers in 1916.

172

Figure 6-92. Catalog No. 318: Mechanic and/or Artificer, 1902–1916; Mechanic, 1916–1920.

Various offices in the War Department went to great lengths to ensure that appropriate titles were used by the men who wore this chevron. Unfortunately, all of the written memos and orders only confuse the titles used by the various branches. The field artillery vacillated between "mechanic" and "mechanic and artificer," seemingly changing between the two names every year or two. "Mechanic" was consistently used by the coast artillery, with the infantry switching back and forth between "mechanic" and "artificer." In March 1909, Fort Leavenworth was authorized the only men in the Army Service School Detachment who wore this chevron, and their title varied among all three designations. Finally, Congress—in its National Defense Act of June 1916—redesignated all men of this grade as mechanics and added the Medical Department to those branches authorized the crossed hammers.

Figure 6-93. Catalog No. 319: Chief Mechanic, 1907–1918.

Established in 1907 as a field artillery rank, this NCO grade was not considered equivalent to a sergeant, although the same pay was drawn. Presumably, a soldier of this rank was between a corporal and a sergeant.

The background for this chevron initially was rectangular, with the long sides forming the top and bottom. In July 1908, however, the more familiar outline shown above was adopted. Colors were unusual on this dress chevron, since the wreath—as well as the hammers—was red rather than the yellow used on other chevron wreaths. In 1910 men of this grade were authorized for the Field Artillery Corps School. Their crossed hammers were the usual green of the Army Service School Detachment, but the wreath was embroidered in yellow (a change from other school chevrons). This chevron—Catalog No. 319—was replaced by No. 320 in May 1918.

Figure 6-94. Catalog No. 320: Chief Mechanic, 1918–1920.

Established by Change 4 to Special Regulation No. 42, May 1918, this insignia superseded Catalog No. 319.

Figure 6-95. Catalog No. 321: Saddler, 1902–1920; Mechanic-Saddler, 1907–1916 (Field Artillery only).

Originally, only the cavalry had saddlers, but the 1907 Uniform Regulations stated that "Mechanics of Field Artillery performing duties of Saddler will wear [the] device of this duty and not [the] Mechanic." This continued until 1916 when other branches besides cavalry were authorized saddlers. These included: infantry, engineers, Medical Department, and field artillery. The Army Service School Detachment of the Cavalry School had a few men of this rank after 1910; they were known by the cavalry title of saddlers. The device represents a saddler's knife, blade up.

Figure 6-96. Catalog No. 322: Wagoner, 1910–1920.

In 1910, the War Department authorized wagoners in cavalry regiments and the ASSD of the Cavalry School to wear this sleeve insignia of an eight-spoked wheel. The wheel is 1⅜ inches across and differs considerably from the chauffeur's insignia instituted during World War I. In June 1916, Congress put wagoners in engineer, infantry, and field artillery supply companies. Although Congress withdrew authorization for cavalry wagoners at the same time, the War Department did not take note of this, and consequently, issue of cavalry wagoner chevrons continued for the next few years. The Army Service School Detachment was authorized two wagoners in 1910, but correspondence indicates this dress chevron was not made through 1916.

Figure 6-97. Catalog No. 323: This is an unauthorized chevron made during World War I.

Figure 6-98. Catalog No. 324: Motor Sergeant, 1918–1920.

The impact of the automobile is suggested by the fact that chevrons of this design and of the next three (Catalog Nos. 325, 326, and 327) were authorized in May 1918 for general application to all branches of the service.

Figure 6-99. Catalog No. 325: Chauffeur First Class, 1918–1920.

This design was established in May 1918 for general application.

Figure 6-100. Catalog No. 326: Chauffeur, 1918–1920.

Established in May 1918 for general application, the 1918 and 1919 design is on a semirectangular background. The round background was adopted in 1920.

Figure 6-101. Catalog No. 327: Assistant Chauffeur, 1918–1920.

This chevron can be distinguished from the wagoner's rank insignia, Catalog No. 322, by the wide tire and the twelve spokes. The insignia shown here is from an official 1920 sample book.

Figure 6-102. Catalog No. 328: Mess Sergeant, 1918–1920.

Prior to mid–1918, mess sergeants were authorized the three inverted V's of a line sergeant. In practice, however, some mess sergeants wore this chevron or those of Catalog No. 220, and the authorization for this chevron was more to acknowledge what was being worn rather than to institute a new chevron.

Private First Class, 1916–1919.

Selected to replace the grade of lance corporal, the grade of private first class of infantry, cavalry, and artillery was first authorized in 1916. Special chevrons were designed to indicate the individual branch. All special PFC insignia were officially replaced by Catalog No. 336 in July 1919 although the initial PFC chevrons authorized during World War I were actually worn through 1920.

Figure 6-103. Catalog No. 329: Private First Class, Infantry.

Chevrons of this design were used by PFCs of infantry, pioneer infantry, Philippine scouts, machine gun battalions, discipline battalion guards, United States guards, headquarters of territorial departments, infantry divisions, infantry brigades, and infantry division trains.

Figure 6-104. Catalog No. 330: Private First Class, Cavalry.

Chevrons of this design were used by PFCs of cavalry units, including headquarters troops of cavalry divisions, machine gun squadrons, headquarters of cavalry brigades, and cavalry division trains.

Figure 6-105. Catalog No. 331: Private First Class, Artillery.

Chevrons of this design were used by PFCs of artillery units, including ammunition trains, artillery parks, headquarters of army artillery, artillery brigades, and coast artillery districts.

Figure 6-106. Catalog No. 332: Private First Class, Service Schools and USMA Detachment, 1917–1919.

Instituted in December 1917, this design incorporated the symbol from the cap and collar insignia worn by enlisted men of the various posts of the Army Service School Detachment. Catalog No. 336 officially replaced this and other PFC insignia in July 1919, although men probably continued to use this chevron until at least 1920.

Figure 6-107. Catalog No. 333: Private First Class, General Recruiting Service, 1918–1919.

Authorized in May 1918 for PFCs of the recruiting service, this chevron was officially replaced in July 1919.

Figure 6-108. Catalog No. 334: Private First Class, General Headquarters, 1918–1919.

Instituted in May 1918, this chevron was worn only at army and corps headquarters, chevrons cataloged as Nos. 329, 330, and 331 being used at lower levels.

Figure 6-109. Catalog No. 335: Private First Class, Provost Marshal General's Department, 1919.

Authorized only during the first seven months of 1919, this was one of the last branch-designed PFC chevrons authorized.

Figure 6-110. Catalog No. 336: Private First Class, all arms, and Deckhand Mine Planter Service, 1919–1920.

On 22 July 1919, Colonel Robert Wyllie, Chief of the Chief of Staff's Equipment Branch, recommended that "an arc of one bar" become the insignia for all privates first class. "In addition, the only other grades which have the insignia of the arm of service in the chevrons are those of the very highest rank, such as Master Engineers, Master Hospital Sergeants, etc., so that it is anomalous to have the lowest grades with a chevron of the same character as that of the highest," Colonel Wyllie continued. The War Department approved an official sample on 3 September 1919. Because of the large stocks of branch-oriented chevrons still on hand, the Quartermaster Corps made few of these insignia other than for samples. This design was replaced in 1920, but the idea of a common chevron for all men of the same grade, regardless of branch, had been furthered by this chevron.

Figure 6-111. Catalog No. 337: Sergeant First Class, 1918–1920.

The Army formed many new branches during World War I and, under the concept of the time, each required an entire set of rank chevrons. The supply problem became overwhelming and in May 1918, a change in the Uniform Regulations established this chevron for all sergeants first class, regardless of branch. After the 1920 consolidation of grades, this design continued in use.

Chevrons for the Tank Corps

Figure 6-112. Catalog No. 340: Master Engineer Senior Grade, Tank Corps, 1918.

Congress authorized the President to create temporary arms of service during World War I, with the men in the new branches to hold existing grades authorized for other arms. One of the resulting chevrons was this insignia, based on the combination of Catalog No. 260 and the first type of Tank Corps insignia. The central figure represents an oncoming French tank. Other chevrons bearing the side views of Mark VIII tanks soon replaced chevrons of this design.

It is interesting to note the Tank Corps was the only branch authorized master engineers senior grade that was not also authorized master engineers junior grade.

Figure 6-113. Catalog No. 341: Private First Class, Tank Corps, 1918.

Authorized from February through May 1918, this chevron was replaced by Catalog Nos. 343 and 345.

Figure 6-114. Catalog No. 342: Master Engineer Senior Grade, Tank Corps, 1918–1919.

An abbreviated version of the Tank Corps insignia distinguished this chevron from the official version, Catalog No. 344. As far as can be determined, War Department staff officers never intended chevrons of this style to be worn, but such chevrons were nevertheless made under local contract to the AEF in Europe.

Figure 6-115. Catalog No. 343: Private First Class, Tank Corps, 1918–1919.

An unauthorized variation of Catalog No. 345, this chevron is much more common than the correct official insignia. Evidence indicates chevrons of this style were made in Europe during 1918. The insignia was officially replaced by Catalog No. 336 in 1919, although in practice this chevron continued to be worn.

Figure 6-117. Catalog No. 345: Private First Class, Tank Corps, 1918–1919.

Established in May 1918 by Change 4 to Special Regulation No. 42, this chevron replaced Catalog No. 340. The Tank Corps officially adopted this chevron, but in practice, soldiers usually wore chevrons cataloged as No. 342 with just the tank rather than with the entire Tank Corps device.

Figure 6-116. Catalog No. 344: Master Engineer Senior Grade, Tank Corps, 1918–1920.

Although authorized from May 1918 until July 1919, this chevron was not widely used.

Left to right: *Figure 6-118. Catalog No. 346: Sergeant First Class, Tank Corps. Figure 6-119. Catalog No. 347: Sergeant, Tank Corps. Figure 6-120. Catalog No. 348: Corporal, Tank Corps.*

Never officially authorized, these three early Tank Corps chevrons (Catalog Nos. 346, 347, 348) followed the earlier practice of adding the branch insignia below the angle of a standard insignia.

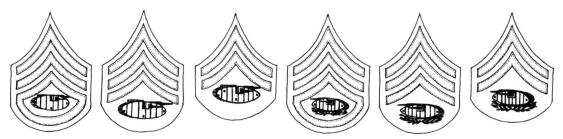

Figure 6-121. Catalog No. 349: Sergeant First Class,
Tank Corps.   Figure 6-122. Catalog No. 350: Sergeant, Tank
Corps.   Figure 6-123. Catalog No. 351: Corporal, Tank Corps.
Figure 6-124. Catalog No. 352: Sergeant First Class, Tank
Corps.   Figure 6-125. Catalog No. 353: Sergeant, Tank Corps.   Figure
6-126. Catalog No. 354: Corporal, Tank Corps.

Chevrons displaying a side view of a tank were made and worn
after mid-1918. Two versions exist: a tank alone, as shown in
Catalog Nos. 349, 350, and 351, and a tank supported by two
dragons, on a wreath, as shown in Catalog Nos. 352, 353, and 354.

Chevrons for the Air Service

Figure 6-127. Catalog No. 355: Master Signal Electrician, Air Service,
1918–1920.

Late in the war, the War Department separated the Air Service
from the Signal Corps and made a distinctive arm of service.
Because the highest pay grade in the Signal Corps had been a
master signal electrician, these men continued with the grade in
the new aviation branch, and in July 1918, this chevron was
created.

Left to right: Figure 6-128. Catalog No. 356: Sergeant First Class, Air
Service.   Figure 6-129. Catalog No. 357: Sergeant, Air Service.   Figure
6-130. Catalog No. 358: Corporal, Air Service.

Although chevrons with Catalog Nos. 356, 357, and 358 were
unauthorized, Air Service personnel widely used them in 1918
and 1919.

Figure 6-131. Catalog No. 359: Private First Class, Air Service, 1918–1919.

Instituted in July 1918 and officially authorized for one year
only, this chevron was actually worn by Air Service PFCs well
into 1920.

179

Figure 6-132. Catalog No. 360: Quartermaster Sergeant Senior Grade, Motor Transport Corps, 1918–1920.

The Secretary of War approved this chevron in late September 1918. It was authorized through 1920 and was scheduled to be superseded by Catalog No. 392.

Figure 6-133. Catalog No. 361.

Just as the Tank Corps was authorized master engineers of the senior grade but not of the junior grade, so the Motor Transport Corps was authorized quartermaster sergeants of the senior grade but not of the junior grade. Identified sometimes as a master engineer's or a truckmaster's chevron, this chevron is just another example of the many unauthorized insignia manufactured in the mistaken belief that if some branches have junior and senior grades, then all branches have them.

Left to right: Figure 6-134. Catalog No. 362: Sergeant First Class, Motor Transport Corps. Figure 6-135. Catalog No. 363: Sergeant, Motor Transport Corps. Figure 6-136. Catalog No. 364: Corporal, Motor Transport Corps.

Men in the three grades represented by Catalog Nos. 362, 363, and 364 should actually have worn Nos. 337, 312, and 313, respectively; however, private companies manufactured these Motor Transport Corps chevrons during and after World War I.

Figure 6-137. Catalog No. 365: Private First Class, Motor Transport Corps, 1918–1919.

Authorized on 23 September 1919, this was one of the last PFC insignia authorized for a particular branch. It was officially replaced in July 1919 by a common chevron for all PFCs, although many private firms manufactured chevrons of this design until 1920.

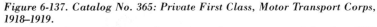

Figure 6-138. Catalog No. 370: Master Engineer Senior Grade, Transportation Corps, 1919–1920.

The winged railway wheel which became part of the Army Transportation Corps insignia in the 1940s was the insignia of this new branch and, as such, became the central motif in this Transport Corps chevron.

Figure 6-139. Catalog No. 371: Master Engineer Junior Grade, Transportation Corps, 1919.

Authorized in January 1919, this was one of the few authorized chevrons that was identical to a senior grade rank but without a star above the branch device.

Left to right: *Figure 6-140. Catalog No. 372: Sergeant First Class, Transportation Corps. Figure 6-141. Catalog No. 373: Sergeant, Transportation Corps. Figure 6-142. Catalog No. 374: Corporal, Transportation Corps.*

It is not known how many soldiers actually wore chevrons cataloged here as Nos. 372, 373, and 374, although no doubt some men of the Transportation Corps did use them. The chevrons were manufactured by at least one private company.

Figure 6-143. Catalog No. 375: Private First Class, Transportation Corps, 1919.

Specified for use only from January until July 1919, this was one of the last branch-oriented PFC chevrons authorized by the War Department.

Chevrons for the Corps of Interpreters and the Intelligence Police Corps

The War Department authorized the following twelve chevrons (Catalog Nos. 380 through 391) for the Corps of Interpreters and for the Intelligence Police soldiers by Change 3 to Special Regulation No. 42. The change, dated 19 February 1918, stated:

> *For organizations not provided with dress chevrons . . . Corps of Interpreters, Corps of Intelligence Police: The same as for corresponding grades in the Medical Department, except that the device of the organization, as prescribed [the letters "INT" and "IP"] . . . will replace the caduceus as issued.*

Special Regulation No. 42 made no further mention of these chevrons and it is doubtful men even wore them. The very next regulation change, published in May, provided for chevrons for "general application," or those common for all branches. Only certain of the Interpreters' and Intelligence Police chevrons would have been replaced in May, while others—such as PFC insignia—should have remained. However, there is no further mention of these insignia in the regulations. Samples sealed in 1919 and detailed clothing specifications written in February 1919 also fail to mention any of these special chevrons.

Catalog No. 380   Catalog No. 381   Catalog No. 382   Catalog No. 383

Catalog No. 384   Catalog No. 385   Catalog No. 386   Catalog No. 387

Catalog No. 388   Catalog No. 389   Catalog No. 390   Catalog No. 391

Figure 6-144. Catalog Nos. 380–391: Special Chevrons for Interpreters and Intelligence Police Corps.

Special 1920 Chevrons

The following four chevrons (Catalog Nos. 396, 397, 398, and 399) were proposed in late 1919 and approved by the Secretary of War on 7 January 1920. Several were made and official samples were sealed in May 1920, but these chevrons were never worn. In addition to Catalog Nos. 396 through 399, Nos. 236, 256, 257, 275, 276, 278, and 279 were also remade at this time. All of these 1920 chevrons can be distinguished by their green wreaths. Also approved and sealed at this same time were Catalog Nos. 209, 210, 212, 213, and 216, which can be distinguished by yellow lyres; Catalog Nos. 270, 273, and 308, which have white lightning bolts; and Catalog No. 282, which was in red.

Left to right: *Figure 6-145. Catalog No. 396: Master Engineer Senior Grade, for Corps of Engineers, Transportation Corps, and Tank Corps, 1920.   Figure 6-146. Catalog No. 397: Master Engineer Junior Grade, for Corps of Engineers and Transportation Corps, 1920.   Figure 6-147. Catalog No. 398: Quartermaster Sergeant Senior Grade, for Quartermaster Corps and Motor Transport Corps, 1920.   Figure 6-148. Catalog No. 399: Quartermaster Sergeant Junior Grade, for Quartermaster Corps and Motor Transport Corps, 1920.*

CHAPTER 7

History of Chevron, Uniform, and Service Stripe Development / Catalog of Post–1920 Chevrons: The Fourth Period

Chevrons and Uniforms

Immediately after the close of the Great War, Congress returned to cost-conscious ways. So massive had been the build up during 1917 and 1918 that Congress began to look at everything connected with Army costs; even the old ways were not sacred. The congressional Reorganization Act, approved 4 June 1920, grouped enlisted soldiers into seven pay grades without any regard to job or specialty, in a break from the historic practice of authorizing each and every position in the Army and listing the pay of each job.

Directly following passage of the act, various sections of the General Staff debated the best way to show the seven pay grades by using the many contemporary chevrons. Many schemes were proposed, but Colonel Robert Wyllie led a campaign to scrap the old job identification concept completely and adopt chevrons that would reflect only pay grades. Ultimately he was successful, and thus established the basic chevron concept still in use today.[1] Only the historical diamond used to designate first sergeants survived as a mark of position. General Order No. 36, 1920, listed which old ranks would be converted to each of the seven pay grades. (An extract of this order is printed in Appendix 2.)

When the War Department adopted the seven chevrons proposed by Colonel Wyllie, the staff sergeant's, sergeant's, and corporal's chevrons retained the previous design, the only change being a switch to a dark blue background. Similarly, the 1920 private first class' chevrons were identical to the 1902–1916 lance corporal's insignia. Initial plans were for soldiers to wear chevrons on the left sleeve only, continuing the 1918 practice conceived to conserve cloth; the Army abandoned this practice in March 1921, however, returning to chevrons on both sleeves.[2]

From 1902 until 1933 the official Army chevrons were made by cutting out the arcs and bars and then sewing them to the background. In 1933 the Army officially adopted *woven* chevrons of the type that had been privately manufactured and bought by the soldiers for several years. The Quartermaster Corps was to replenish stocks with the woven chevrons when the supplies of cut and sewn chevrons were exhausted. In 1936, before the Army actually could procure woven chevrons in quantity, the official sanction against the cut and sewn type was rescinded. The older manufacturing process of sewing cut-out designs to the backing was still considered the best.[3] Because of the Army's reluctance to go to a more modern process, some of these wool designs sewn onto wool backings were still issued well into World War II. During these changes in manufacturing processes for the blue background chevrons, khaki backgrounds came into wide but unofficial use on khaki uniforms. Through the 1920s, 1930s, and 1940s, a variety of uniform manufacturers made embroidered khaki chevrons and many men purchased these insignia.

Wear-Out Period

Because the new 1920 chevrons on blue background were not
immediately available, a lag or wear-out period involving the
World War I rank insignia occurred. The War Department circular announcing the new chevrons stated, "The old-type chevrons now on hand will be issued and worn while serviceable."[4]
The same month in which the Army officially established the
new chevrons, the Quartermaster General personally sent a
memorandum to the War Department General Staff with an
appeal to modify the newly designed rank insignia as far as
background materials were concerned. The Quartermaster
Corps held approximately twelve million old-style chevrons
that could be directly equated to the new designs. Regimental
and battalion sergeant major's chevrons could be issued to
fulfill requisitions for master sergeants and technical sergeants, respectively, while old sergeant first class' chevrons
were exactly the same as the new staff sergeant's insignia, except
for the new background color. Sergeant's, corporal's, and lance
corporal's chevrons likewise were suitable except for the backing.[5]

In Quartermaster stocks were another eleven million chevrons of sixteen different designs that the Army could easily
convert to sergeant's, corporal's, or PFC's insignia by cutting out
a central design. For example, 180,638 mess sergeant's chevrons
were available for conversion to the lower grades simply by
cutting out the cook's cap. A total of 23 million chevrons valued
at $10 million were available, except for the improper back-
ground color.[6] The General Staff directed all of these old
chevrons to be issued and worn before the new rank devices were
made—but this did not come to pass.

Further trouble occurred on 8 January 1921, when Colonel J. R. R. Hannay of the Quartermaster General's Office, testifying before Congress in support of the Army's fiscal requests, left the impression that the $10 million worth of chevrons would be sold for scrap.[7] A furor erupted in several War Department offices as a result, with generals on all sides of the chevron question stating their position and emphasizing that "the others" did not understand the situation.

In the subsequent flurry of memoranda during January and February, the Quartermaster General stressed the problems encountered when trying to issue an item that was scheduled for replacement. "The experience of the Quartermaster Corps has demonstrated that upon the adoption of a new . . . pattern uniform article, it is practically impossible to get rid of existing stocks by issue. Enlisted men will not take the old pattern and prefer, when necessary, even to procure the articles by purchase when not too expensive. This condition exists today and enlisted men are procuring the new pattern chevrons with the blue back."[8]

The Assistant Chief of Staff, replying to the Quartermaster General, wrote, "The chevrons for the Staff Sergeant are simply the old chevron for Sergeant First Class. . . . The chevron for Technical Sergeant is the old chevron for Battalion Sergeant Major. . . . Whenever possible . . . chevrons should be modified by cutting out the insignia of Arm of Service. . . . Thus modified, a wreath without the star is for a Technical Sergeant."[9] To emphasize the point that the old chevrons *would* be issued, an order was sent to the field which prohibited the wearing of the new chevrons so long as any type of old insignia was available for issue.[10] It was to no avail. Most men bought the new chevrons from private sources regardless of the order, while local commanders looked the other way, and the Quartermaster Corps subsequently sold over a ton of chevrons as scrap wool, for less than $60.[11]

Blue denim work clothing continued to be used up to World War II. The War Department stated the artillery denim chevrons used before World War I would again be issued for wear on denim coats until the stocks were depleted and correspondence indicates that issue of denim chevrons continued until at least 1936 for the coast artillery.[12] How many chevrons of pre–1917 manufacture were actually issued during this time is unknown; moreover, certain problems were bound to arise. There was no pre–1917 coast artillery rank represented by the staff sergeant's chevron. The center device from several coast artillery chevrons could have been cut out so the remaining insignia would have represented a staff sergeant, but privately manufactured denim chevrons may also have been made and purchased by soldiers. It is reasonable to assume at least some staff sergeants, and perhaps higher NCOs, did buy and wear denim chevrons made by private firms after 1920.

Figure 7-2. Sergeant Orvill McCombs wore this shirt and chevron in 1923, reflecting the official War Department practice of removing special devices from old chevrons and force-issuing these old chevrons as an economy measure.

The Quartermaster Corps in January 1939 finally declared as obsolete the World War I chevrons of olive drab designs and backgrounds and the surplus denim chevrons.[13] This action officially ended the wear of all but the seven authorized chevrons, Catalog Nos. 400 through 406 (*see* Table 7-3).

Unofficial Chevrons   1920–1942

Almost as soon as the War Department established the new 1920 chevrons, manufacturers began to make the new designs with dark blue backgrounds. Several companies, eager to create a wide market so as to make as much money as possible, made unauthorized chevrons in the belief they would sell. Adding to the confusion was congressional insistence on using the old stock of crossed rifles, crossed cannons, and other chevrons for PFCs previously made on an olive drab background. This mixing of the old and new chevrons caused several problems.

Some manufacturers modified the World War I designs to conform to the seven 1920 pay grades. In these instances, 1918 chevrons had arcs added, or bars cut off, so the authorized pay grade was shown by the proper number of arcs and bars, while the specialty or branch device remained. In this way khaki chevrons of the Motor Transport Corps, as an example, were modified to make a PFC's chevron (one inverted V) with the corps device below. Manufacturers also created unauthorized chevrons by removing a proper World War I device and applying some other device, such as a cook's crescent. In this way some chevrons on olive drab cloth were modified and used into the 1930s.

More common is another invention of the insignia makers, a combination of pre– and post–1920 designs on the navy blue background. The use of branch and specialty chevrons died hard despite the official War Department policy. Private manufacturers, knowing of the change in background colors, made

Figure 7-3. Common types of chevrons of the 1920s (from left to right): a proper sergeant's chevron except for the addition of a medical specialty device, an unauthorized sergeant's chevron with signal specialty device on a khaki background, and two unofficial specialist chevrons.

the old PFC's chevron designs with the new blue backgrounds in the hope of selling them.[14] Since the old PFC designs in the old color were force-issued, the men bought and wore the old designs in the new color. Some of the specialty chevrons such as those for saddlers and wagoners, as well as most NCO devices, were made on the dark blue background in the 1920s and 1930s. Most prevalent of these many chevrons were those worn by Army Air Force members. In World War II a great many Army Air Corps soldiers wore chevrons containing the Air Corps winged propeller.

Chevrons made on the dark blue or the khaki background with specialty or branch devices had evolved from the World War I chevron concept. While these unofficial chevrons were being worn, another set of unauthorized grade insignia were also in use; these, however, had no historical basis. Congress had authorized specialists in the lowest two pay grades in 1920 and given these men extra pay. Various uniform companies began almost immediately to manufacture chevrons for specialists of the sixth grade (PFCs). These chevrons consisted of the one inverted V authorized for PFCs and a series of arcs to designate the special pay grades. The lowest specialty class was designated by one arc, the next class by two arcs, and so forth, up to six arcs for the highest class. A soldier of the sixth grade who was a specialist of the first class was a private first class drawing a base pay of $35.00 a month and $25.00 a month as a specialist. Use of these specialist chevrons varied from unit to unit, depending upon the desires of the company or regimental commanders.

Men wore specialty devices with the specialist chevrons in some units. A cook's cap, a lyre, crossed hammers, or some other device originally used before or during World War I was incorporated in these instances. Again, the use of these chevrons varied from unit to unit. Identifying all of these various unauthorized specialist chevrons with center devices is an impossible task because of the many possible combinations, and therefore no attempt has been made to catalog chevrons of this type.

Throughout the 1920s and 1930s the War Department fought a losing battle against the specialist chevrons. The following excerpt from a letter written in 1935 from the Quartermaster General to the Adjutant General sums up the problem:

> *The specialist's devices were specifically omitted when the first draft of AR 600-35, October 14, 1921, was prepared, and subsequent requests for such devices have been disapproved.*

> *The records of this office do not indicate that the Quartermaster Corps has manufactured or issued specialist's sleeve insignia. It is understood, however, that certain manufacturers have improvised sleeve insignia which have been sold in the Post Exchange. . . .[15]*

*Figure 7-4. A specialist
wearing unauthorized
chevrons is shown at a 1938
National Guard meeting.*

Dress Blue Chevrons

Although the lapel coat began to be phased in during 1926 for
service wear, in 1926 the War Department authorized the high
collar pre–World War I blue uniform on an optional basis.
Chevrons for this uniform were of 1920 design but in branch
colors. For those branches having two colors, the primary color
was shown by the bars and arcs, with the second color chain
stitched around the edges. This uniform was not widely worn
and consequently the branch-colored 1920 series of chevrons
were not widely used.[16]

Olive Drab and Khaki Chevrons

*Figure 7-5. Shown here is a
sergeant first class chevron
made by the Quartermaster
General's Department in the
1930s for wear on the
optional dress blue uniform.*

From 1920 until 1933 the official Army chevrons were made by
cutting out the arcs and bars from olive drab cloth and then
sewing them to a dark blue wool background. From 1933 until
the close of World War II, personnel in the Office of the
Quartermaster General issued various standards and specifications that officially affected the types of chevrons being issued.
Various committees decided to adopt one type of chevron or
another, only to change the decision later on for a variety of
reasons. Wool and cotton backgrounds with embroidered and
cut-out devices and designs came and went and so did woven
chevrons, if the official correspondence is followed. On occasions, the Quartermaster Corps simply bought available chevrons even if these chevrons were not those officially prescribed.

By the start of 1936, the War Department had cotton khaki
bars and arcs on a dark blue cotton background for wear on
khaki uniforms. According to official drawings, the design was
cut out and sewn onto a background, but in practice the men
often wore the design embroidered on the cotton background.
Also, insignia makers began to make chevrons completely of

TABLE 7-1
List of Common Chevrons Made and Worn in the 1940s

Olive drab wool design cut out and sewn to dark blue navy wool background

Khaki or light brown material sewn to dark navy blue background

White or silver bars woven with dark blue or black background

White bars embroidered on dark blue or black backing

Olive drab embroidered on dark blue wool

Khaki embroidered on khaki

Olive drab embroidered on blue cotton

khaki. The resulting chevrons had khaki designs on khaki backgrounds rather than on the official dark blue background. The official stocks of all-wool chevrons were relegated to wear on serge or woolen coats and overcoats, with the more washable chevron for wear on shirts and field clothing.

Woven chevrons also came into being in the 1930s. The Army officially adopted these chevrons as standard for awhile, and in 1942 even bought several thousand woven chevrons in Australia for United States troops stationed in that country.[17] Most often, men purchased these woven insignia from the downtown Army-Navy store, along with other uniform ornaments.

During wartime, with the rapid expansion of armies, troops have often not worn "by the book" uniforms and insignia. The 1920s and 1930s, however, saw the phenomenon of nonregulation insignia come into widespread *peacetime* use. This was especially true during the 1939–1941 expansion of the Army, and is a cause of considerable confusion if someone tries today to classify chevrons by official color and material categories. It is much more realistic to group chevrons by color and material that was widely worn, as has been done in Table 7-1, and then make allowances when a rank device is found that does not precisely fit one of the types listed. Table 7-2 designates catalog numbers for unauthorized chevrons in use during this period.

Men's Chevrons
1939—

Authorized Chevrons 1939–1958
September 1942 saw a new first sergeant's chevron. Because of the rapid growth of the Army during World War II, men who had only a few years service were being promoted to the first grade. To allow experienced men to be promoted to the first grade and simultaneously serve in the key position of first sergeant, this new rank and chevron (Catalog No. 413) was created.[18]

Figure 7-6. Shown here are chevrons of the manufacturing styles of the 1930s and World War II period. The staff sergeant's chevron has a wool olive drab design cut out and sewn to a navy blue wool backing. The private first class's chevron is similar to the staff sergeant's, except the bar is khaki; this indicates the chevron was made for wear on a khaki garment. The first sergeant's insignia has the design embroidered on navy blue wool, while the technician fifth grade's chevron is woven, with the bars appearing silver on a nearly black background. The all-khaki rank chevrons were never officially authorized by the War Department, although men often wore them.

In early 1942 a phase-in period began where various classes of specialists were replaced by three technician grades so specially skilled men could rise to higher grades and have more responsibility. The third, fourth, and fifth grade chevrons for these technicians were the same as for nontechnicians, except that a letter *T* was added.[19] These chevrons are significant since they represent the first time since 1920 that an effort was made to give skilled and technical personnel higher grades rather than just higher pay. Also important was the fact that the War Department directly equated technician grades to noncommissioned officers for the first time since 1920: all specialists were NCOs.

As World War II closed, a major move developed within the offices of the Quartermaster General and the Army Air Force Chief of Staff to reduce the size of most insignia worn on the uniform. The original proposal was to reduce all insignia worn on the sleeves, but only a reduction in chevron size actually occurred. Less material was required for the small chevrons; this would constitute a savings, and it was believed a neater appearance would result. Until 1948 this action was held in abeyance while the stock of World War II chevrons dwindled. Finally the War Department authorized the new smaller 2-inch-wide chevrons in mid–1948.[20] Table 7-3 designates catalog numbers assigned to authorized chevrons of this period.

With the size reduction of chevrons came a color change. The War Department, not satisfied with the technician grades introduced in 1942, instituted two sets of chevrons in an attempt to resolve the problem. There was a distinction between soldiers assigned to combat units and those in noncombat units. Combat personnel wore the small gold chevrons (officially termed "goldenlite") with dark blue designs, and noncombat men wore the opposite: small dark blue chevrons with gold designs. Wear-out of the remaining large pre–1948 chevrons was

Figure 7-7. A World War II technician fourth grade (left), along with a first sergeant and a Signal Corps officer, is shown in Leyte, Philippine Islands, in February 1945. The three technician grades were authorized between 1942 and 1948; their chevrons bear a T.

Figure 7-8. This Army Air Force sergeant first class has stenciled his rank device directly to his coveralls. Such a practice was common in some units during World War II.

TABLE 7-2
Catalog Numbers for Unofficial Chevrons Used 1920–1948

Design	Catalog Number	Rank
	407	Intended for wear by Private First Class, Specialist 1st Class[a]
	408	Intended for wear by Private First Class, Specialist 2d Class[a]
	409	Intended for wear by Private First Class, Specialist 3d Class[a]
	410	Intended for wear by Private First Class, Specialist 4th Class[a]
	411	Intended for wear by Private First Class, Specialist 5th Class[a]
	412	Intended for wear by Private First Class, Specialist 6th Class[a]
	417	Intended for wear by Master Sergeants, Air Corps[b]
	418	Intended for wear by Technical Sergeants, Air Corps[b]
	419	Intended for wear by Staff Sergeants, Air Corps[b]
	420	Intended for wear by Sergeants, Air Corps[b]
	421	Intended for wear by Corporals, Air Corps[b]
	422	Intended for wear by Private First Class, Air Corps[b]

[a] Many of these chevrons were made with a variety of specialty ranks in the center. These specialist grades were replaced by technicians in 1942.

[b] Any specialist device could have been used. Air Corps is the most common.

TABLE 7-3
Catalog Numbers for 1920–1948 Authorized Chevrons[a]

Design	Catalog Number	Dates of Authorization	Rank
	400	1920–1948	Master Sergeant
	401	1920–1948	Technical Sergeant
	402	1920–1942	First Sergeant
	403	1920–1948	Staff Sergeant
	404	1920–1948	Sergeant
	405	1920–1948	Corporal
	406	1920–1948	Private First Class
	413	1942–1948	First Sergeant
	414	1942–1948	Technician 3rd Grade
	415	1942–1948	Technician 4th Grade
	416	1942–1948	Technician 5th Grade

[a] NOTE: Chevrons officially were 3⅛ inches wide, but often vary by ⅛-inch or more.

Figure 7-9. During and after World War II a great many chevrons were made locally overseas for United States soldiers. The three chevrons pictured on the top row were made in India about 1944; the two lower are German made for occupation troops. The German-made technician fifth grade's chevron has the design hand embroidered in silver thread.

earmarked for noncombat troops prior to issue of the new gold on blue design. Additionally, ROTC cadets retained the large chevrons, as the smaller 2-inch-wide insignia were reserved for wear by Army personnel only.[21]

A significant change also occurred when the War Department realigned enlisted grades and titles with the 1948 change. The name *sergeant* was to be reserved for the top three grades so that the title would be indicative of a career soldier. This caused elimination of the three stripes worn by sergeants since 1833. The design of three bars and an arc became that of a sergeant, retitled from the earlier name of staff sergeant. Also, as a result of the title change, the lower pay grades adopted different chevrons. The sixth pay grade, which previously was authorized a single PFC bar, was retitled *private* and given no chevron. Former corporals of the fifth pay grade became PFCs with a single bar, and those men who were in the fourth pay grade began to wear corporal's chevrons.[22] Despite the fact that the historic three bars of a sergeant were rescinded, the small combat and noncombat chevrons for that grade were manufactured before the grade restructure and consequently became surplus.[23]

In February 1951, the Army discarded small chevrons, replacing them with large chevrons of olive drab designs on dark blue twill backgrounds although the new titles associated with each pay grade remained. When the large-size chevrons came back into use in 1951, initially the official width was 3⅛ inches wide, later reduced to 3 inches; actual chevrons varied from 3 to 3¼ inches. After 1951, the 2-inch-wide chevrons became authorized for wear on field jackets.[24] Table 7-4 designates catalog numbers for the 2-inch-wide chevrons.

Figure 7-10. Korea, June 1951, Headquarters Eighth United States Army. This master sergeant wears the 2-inch-wide noncombat insignia of rank.

1958 Grade Restructure

On 1 June 1958, the first basic change in the enlisted grade structure since 1920 occurred. Congress authorized two new "super grades," E-8 and E-9, so rather than seven pay grades there would now be nine. This situation created a need for two new chevrons to be added above the position of master sergeant. However, rather than create two totally new chevrons, the Army decided to add one new NCO chevron to signify the highest grade, and to revive the three inverted V's of a sergeant. The effect of this order was that NCOs would wear one less arc on their chevrons, as shown in Table 7-5. However, some Army officials believed that the immediate removal of an arc for the NCOs in pay grades E-5 through E-7 would adversely affect morale.[25] Because of this concern, the Department of the Army allowed soldiers in pay grades E-5, E-6, and E-7 to continue to wear their pre–1958 chevrons until they were promoted or reduced, at which time the proper chevron would be worn. For example, this phase-in policy allowed an NCO who was a sergeant first class (E-6) before 1 June 1958 to continue wearing his chevron with two arcs until he was promoted to the E-7 pay

TABLE 7-4
Catalog Numbers for Two-Inch-Wide Chevrons (Nonspecialists)

NOTES: Authorized for wear by all personnel, 1948–1951, in two color schemes: gold design on blue, and blue design on gold.

Worn by women, 1948–present, with gold stripes; background colors include taupe, green, white, and blue.

Design	Catalog Number	Dates of Authorization	Rank
	423	1948–present	First Sergeant
	424	1948–present	Master Sergeant
	425	1948–present	Sergeant First Class
	426	1948–1958 1958–present	Sergeant Staff Sergeant
	427	1958–present	Sergeant[a]
	428	1948–present	Corporal
	429[b]	1948–1968 1968–present	Private First Class Private (E-2)
	443	1958–1968 1971–present 1968–1971	Sergeant Major Staff Sergeant Major
	445	1968–present	Command Sergeant Major
	447	1968–present	Private First Class

[a] Two-inch combat and noncombat chevrons (1948–1951) were made prior to the implementation of this chevron scheme, but were not worn owing to a change of grade titles.

[b] For Catalog Nos. 430 *et seq.*, *see* Tables 7-6 and 7-7.

TABLE 7-5
Effect of 1958 NCO Grade Retitlements

Pay Grades	E-4	E-5	E-6	E-7	E-8	E-9
Chevron and Title from 1948 up to 1 June, 1958	Corporal	Sergeant	Sergeant First Class	Master Sergeant		
Chevron and Title after 1 June, 1958	Corporal	Sergeant	Staff Sergeant	Sergeant First Class	Master Sergeant	Sergeant Major

grade. Upon his promotion only his pay would increase, as he was then wearing the proper "new" E-7 NCO chevron. In the interval between 1958 and 1968 confusion existed, since a chevron could reflect an old (pre–1958) lower pay grade or a new (post–1958) higher pay grade. After many delays and false starts, the Department of the Army announced that effective July 1968, all soldiers would wear the chevrons reflecting their current pay grade.[26]

The highest enlisted rank created in 1958 was sergeant major; the first NCOs in this grade were promoted during April 1959.[27] A star in the center of a master sergeant's chevron represented this rank.

After seven years there was a proposal to split those soldiers occupying the E-9 pay grade into sergeants major and chief master sergeants. Sergeants major were to be those E-9's assigned as sergeant major of battalions or higher. Those NCOs in the highest pay grade, but not actually occupying a sergeant major's position, were to continue to wear the chevron with the star, but those actually serving as unit sergeants major added a wreath. The new chevrons were manufactured, but the proposed scheme was not fully put into effect.[28]

The desire to distinguish *unit* sergeants major lingered. The rank device containing only a star was designated for NCOs of the top pay grade who were not serving as unit sergeants major. These men were to be known as staff sergeants major, while the chevron with a wreath and star was brought into use and reserved for those NCOs who served as "Sergeants Major, for units authorized color or standards" (unit flags).[29]

Another chevron revision planned for 1965 was the reintroduction of the title of lance corporal. Since 1948, the two lowest pay grades had no chevron, with the third pay grade being distinguished by the single inverted V of a private first class. The concept was to give the next to lowest pay grade the title and insignia of private first class, with the third grade receiving a new chevron and the title of lance corporal. Though these chevrons were manufactured in the 1960s, just before the plan was to be implemented, the plan itself was canceled. In 1968 this chevron design, consisting of one arc and one inverted V, became authorized for issue to PFCs E-3; the old PFC's insignia of one bar became the chevron for privates E-2.[30]

Specialist Grades

As a part of the continual striving to distinguish between combat leaders and soldiers with special skills, the Army created specialist grades in 1955. Actually, the Army split the top four enlisted grades into two groups: noncommissioned officers and specialists. The NCOs continued to wear the traditional type of chevrons while the new category of specialists—senior enlisted personnel who performed technical or administrative duties—received new insignia. No one received a pay reduction upon conversion to the specialist ranks and no privileges were lessened for the enlisted personnel. In the design of chevrons for these new specialist grades, the national eagle from the Great Seal of the United States was selected for all specialists, with arcs added above the eagle signifying higher pay grades. Specialist chevrons were 2 inches wide, considerably smaller than the NCO stripes. The new grade titles, starting with the highest, were master specialist, specialist first class, specialist second class, and specialist third class.[31]

In anticipation of the issue of green uniforms, the specialist's chevrons introduced in 1955 bore golden designs on a green cotton twill background, the same insignia that was to be worn on the green uniform starting in 1957. When the olive drab wool service uniform was in use after 1955, green and gold specialist's chevrons were worn on it, while the NCO chevrons continued to be the older olive drab on blue.

In 1958, the Department of the Army approved larger specialist's chevrons, 3 inches wide, for wear by male personnel in 1959, reserving the smaller original specialist's insignia for wear only by women. Also in 1958, the Army authorized specialist's chevrons for the two new super grades.[32] When Congress created the grades E-8 and E-9, the Army decided specialists would be included in these new ranks, but since the title of master specialist was in use, and both of the new grades were higher, new names were required. The final decision was to call all of these men specialists and indicate their various ranks by pay grade title.[33] Thus, the uninspired titles of "Specialist (E-4)," "Specialist Five," and the like came into being. Using this method, master specialists became specialists seven, while the two new senior enlisted grades were specialists eight and nine. This shuffling of titles to accommodate the two higher grades notwithstanding, the Army officially declared the chevrons ob-

Figure 7-11. Shown here is a specialist first class in 1957. In anticipation of the introduction of the Army green uniform, specialist's green chevrons with yellow designs were worn on the olive drab uniforms from 1955 until 1961. These narrow chevrons were replaced by wider insignia for men from 1958 to 1961.

solete in 1965, never having used them.[34] Table 7-6 designates catalog numbers for chevrons authorized in this period for specialists.

Dress Uniform Chevrons

The Department of the Army in August 1953 authorized enlisted men to wear on an optional basis dress blue uniforms, including gold color chevrons on a blue background that matched the dress coat.[35] At the end of the 1950s, enlisted men were also authorized to wear the optional white uniform worn by officers for several years. As with the blue uniform, chevron designs were of goldenlite on a background matching the coat.[36] Table 7-7 designates catalog numbers for chevrons for male personnel (nonspecialists).

Sergeant Major of the Army

In 1966 Sergeant Major William Woolridge was appointed to the newly created position of Sergeant Major of the Army, marking the first time since the Mexican War that an enlisted rank was distinguished by other than a chevron. The rank was signified by a collar insignia, the chevrons being those of other sergeants major.

TABLE 7-6
Catalog Numbers for Specialist Chevrons 1955–Present[a]

Design	Catalog Number	Rank	Dates of Authorization
	430	Specialist Third Class Specialist Four	1955–1959[b] 1959–1961[b] 1960–present[c]
	431	Specialist Second Class Specialist Five	1955–1959[b] 1959–1961[b] 1960–present[c]
	432	Specialist First Class Specialist Six	1955–1959[b] 1959–1961[b] 1960–present[c]
	433	Master Specialist Specialist Seven	1955–1959[b] 1959–1961[b] 1960–1978[c]
	434	Specialist Eight	1959–1965[c]
	435	Specialist Nine	1959–1965[c]
	436	Specialist Four	1959–present[d]
	437	Specialist Five	1959–present[d]
	438	Specialist Six	1959–present[d]
	439	Specialist Seven	1959–1978[d]
	440	Specialist Eight	1959–1965[d]
	441	Specialist Nine	1959–1965[d]

[a] NOTE: Catalog Nos. 430 through 435 are 2 inches wide; Catalog Nos. 436 through 441 are 3 inches wide.
[b] All personnel.
[c] Women personnel only.
[d] Men only.

TABLE 7-7
Catalog Numbers for Chevrons for Male Personnel Other Than Specialists 1951–Present[a]

Design	Catalog Number	Dates of Authorization	Rank
	400	1951–present	Master Sergeant
	401	1951–present 1958–present	Sergeant First Class Platoon Sergeant
	403	1951–1958 1958–present	Sergeant Staff Sergeant
	404	1958–present	Sergeant
	405	1951–present	Corporal
	406	1951–1968 1968–present	Private First Class Private (E-2)
	413	1951–present	First Sergeant
	442	1958–1968 1971–present 1968–1971	Sergeant Major Staff Sergeant Major
	444	1968–present	Command Sergeant Major
	446	1968–present	Private First Class
	470	1979–present	Sergeant Major of the Army

[a] Official width is 3 inches; actual widths may vary by ⅛-inch.

Figure 7-12. Collar insignia for the Sergeant Major of the Army.

Figure 7-13. Uniforms, chevrons, and service stripes of senior NCOs in 1981 (from left to right): sergeant major, command sergeant major, and a first sergeant, all wearing the dress blue uniform. The Sergeant Major of the Army, William Connelly, is in the center wearing his unique chevron with two stars, on his white dress uniform. The female first sergeant has the 2-inch-wide chevrons and small service stripes on her dress blue uniform, while the master sergeant (second from the right) wears a green uniform with a white shirt and bow tie for dress occasions.

The collar insignia was made by taking the eagle from the officer's insignia for the Aide to the Chief of Staff and mounting the remaining shield on a standard enlisted brass disk. This insignia was designed in the Office of the Chief of Staff rather than by the Army's Institute of Heraldry, and because of this, the reasoning behind the selection of a collar insignia rather than a special chevron to designate the Sergeant Major of the Army is unknown.[37] In 1979, special chevrons of the Sergeant Major of the Army were authorized.[38]

Although chevrons for females have been made in the grade of Sergeant Major of the Army (Catalog No. 449), a woman has not been appointed to the position (*see* Table 7-7).

Cloth Subdued Chevrons

Shortly after the start of the Vietnam War, the Army recognized a need for subdued insignia. At first, soldiers dyed standard cloth chevrons various shades of black, brown, and green for wear in combat; but by 1966 the Army in Vietnam was issuing chevrons embroidered in black and on an olive drab background. Government-issue cloth subdued chevrons saw only limited use outside Vietnam because of stocks of conventional chevrons in the hands of troops, while in Vietnam locally made chevrons were often worn, as were dyed chevrons or various small metal devices. By early 1968 miniature metal chevrons replaced these embroidered subdued chevrons for wear on fatigue clothing.[39]

Figure 7-14. Shown here are chevrons for the green shirt. Sergeant Major of the Army Connelly (second from the right) *and the two men on Sergeant Major Connelly's right wear the shoulder marks introduced in 1980 for NCOs. Sergeant First Class LeBlanc* (right) *wears the bright brass metal chevrons on the shirt collar. The short sleeve shirt may be worn with or without tie, while a tie is required for the long sleeve shirt.*

Shoulder Marks

In the 1970s, the Army began to experiment with green shirts to replace the current tan shirt and to be more pleasing with the green uniform adopted twenty years earlier. On the green shirt finally adopted, officers showed their grade by using green cloth shoulder loops, embroidered with the rank insignia; enlisted personnel initially wore the bright brass miniature chevrons pinned to the collar of the green shirt. Enlisted personnel expressed dissatisfaction with the pin-on insignia since the frequent removal of the insignia from the lightweight cloth cause the shirt collar to become unsightly.

The Army Uniform Board recommended shoulder marks carrying embroidered miniature chevrons be introduced for noncommissioned officers, and in January 1981 the Chief of Staff approved the recommendation. Enlisted shoulder marks are of black cloth with the appropriate insignia embroidered ⅝-inch from the lower end. Only corporals and ranks above received the shoulder marks; the metal pin-on device remained for wear on the shirt collar by other enlisted personnel. Shoulder marks come in two sizes: 4¼ inches long and 3½ inches long. The size worn depended on the shirt or sweater size:

TABLE 7-8
Catalog Numbers for Enlisted Shoulder Marks
Introduced in 1981

Design	Catalog Number	Rank
	470	Sergeant Major of the Army
	471	Command Sergeant Major
	472	Sergeant Major
	473	First Sergeant
	474	Master Sergeant
	475	Sergeant First Class Platoon Sergeant
	476	Staff Sergeant
	477	Sergeant
	478	Corporal
	479	Specialist E-6
	480	Specialist E-5

NOTE: Only the rank design is shown here. For an example of the full shoulder mark, see Figure 7-14.

smaller garments received the shorter mark and larger garments the larger device.

While the new marks could be worn as soon as the Army Chief of Staff approved the insignia (*see* Figure 7-14) the brass pin-on collar pieces could be worn until 30 September 1983 or until the wearer was promoted. The insignia for privates, privates first class, and specialists E-4 continued to be the brass devices.[40] Table 7-8 designates catalog numbers for the shoulder marks.

Women's Chevrons   Enlisted women became associated with the Army when Congress authorized the WAAC in 1942. [The Women's Army Auxiliary Corps, WAAC, was formed in May 1942, and was the

forerunner of the Women's Army Corps, WAC, which came into
being in September 1943.] Women and men wore the same chevrons until 1944, when a beige off-duty dress was introduced for
women. Chevrons of standard size and design were used but with
a beige background to blend with the uniform. These beige WAC
chevrons were the first official enlisted grade insignia—since
1920—made so that both the design and the background matched
rather than contrasted with the uniform. These beige chevrons,
also known as the "horizon tan" shade chevrons, became standard items for wear with the WAC off-duty dress in 1945.[40a]

The Women's Army Corps introduced a taupe-colored uniform in 1950, and soon special 2-inch-wide brown and gold
chevrons were worn on these uniform coats. Although the Army
reinstituted large 3-inch-wide chevrons in 1951 for male personnel, the distinctive color of WAC uniforms kept the smaller
chevrons for women, and this small size is still solely used on
women's uniforms.[41]

A new optional white uniform was authorized WACs in July 1951. On this white coat, chevrons and service stripes were to be of gold design with a white background.[42] In the summer of 1957 another optional uniform, this one blue, was authorized for enlisted women. In anticipation of the very limited number of people who would need the small gold and blue women's chevrons, the Department of the Army authorized the dress chevrons designed for male personnel to be worn by women when the smaller WAC chevrons were not available.[43]

After a good bit of internal Department of the Army discussion and correspondence concerning the merits of the smaller-size chevron for women *versus* the supply simplification associated with one set of chevrons for all personnel, in 1951 two sizes were prescribed—one for men and one for women. The smaller size for women continued on the justification of the women's smaller sleeve size.[44] From 1959 to 1961 the brown chevrons were phased out and replaced by the 2-inch-wide green and gold chevrons worn today. As the Army developed chevrons for PFCs and sergeants major in the 1960s, 2-inch-wide insignia were made for female personnel.

Metal Pin-On Chevrons

After the end of World War II, a parade ground look began to assert itself. As a consequence of the effort to dress up the uniform, as well as in response to a limited functional need, unauthorized metal chevrons came into wide use. Men wore miniature chevrons on field caps, and soldiers affixed them to helmet liners and scarves. These chevrons varied widely in style and size; some designs were enameled or painted while others were cut out of the metal. The designs, especially the specialist's chevrons of the late 1950s and 1960s, often deviated considerably from any design contemplated by the Department of the Army. Design of the eagles, relative size of the arcs and the chevrons' sides, and width of the bars all fluctuated. Examples of these various insignia are summarized and illustrated in Table 7-9.

The Vietnamese climate caused soldiers to roll up the sleeves of their jungle fatigues. This covered the NCO and specialist stripes and so various small metal chevrons became popular for wear on the shirt pocket flap or the collar to show enlisted ranks. Soldiers wore many of these devices unofficially, but some units required the wear of these insignia. In 1965 the 1st Cavalry Division even published an order requiring a small metal chevron be pinned onto the pocket flap.

In late 1967, the Department of the Army approved a set of small subdued pin-on metal chevrons for wear on various uniforms that eventually included fatigue shirts and jackets, cooks' whites, medical technicians' uniforms, overcoats, and windbreakers. While the black metal chevrons were excellent for combat wear, the use of these chevrons caused a recognition

TABLE 7-9
Collar and Cap Chevrons

Sample Illustrations	Description (Measurements are approximate)
	Bright metal designs cut out, usually ¾ inch wide. Made as early as 1945. Non-issue items are usually with thin recessed posts to hold design together.
	Designs enameled, ¾ inch wide.
	Designs enameled from 1 to 1½ inches wide (usually 1¼ inches wide).
	Painted yellow or subdued on thin metal; made in Vietnam, 1 inch wide.
	Brass and/or paint on thin metal, made in Vietnam, 1 to 1½ inches wide.
	Embroidered cloth for collar; design ¾ inch wide.
	Black metal, cut out, non-issue; ¾ to 1 inch wide.
	Black metal, cut out, issue; ¾ inch wide. White plastic worn behind rank on selected uniforms, 1971–1975.
	Brass cut out, issue; ¾ inch wide.
	Pre–1920 cadet collar insignia[a]; 1 to 1½ inches wide.

---

[a] Some military cadets wore bronze and branch-colored enamel chevrons on shirt and coat collars before 1920.

problem in garrison. To alleviate this situation, in 1971 white plastic backings were placed behind the metal chevrons on some uniforms to aid in identification.[45] As a test, in 1973 the Army issued small bright brass pin-on chevrons for wear on some uniforms. The shiny insignia weere identical to the subdued chevrons in design and size, differing only in the surface finish.[46] A Department of the Army message, sent to the field in February 1975, authorized these bright brass chevrons for wear on the overcoat, raincoat, and windbreaker.[47] Also, in early 1975 embroidered cloth chevrons were authorized to be sewn onto the collars of some field clothing on an optional basis, thus completing the move of cloth chevrons from the sleeve to the collar.[48]

Band Chevrons

Military Academy Band

To keep up tradition, the West Point Band continued to wear blue dress uniforms after World War I. Chevrons on the various blue Military Academy Band uniforms continued to be modeled after the 1903 infantry insignia: white designs on dark blue backgrounds. By the late 1940s manufacturing of these special white and blue chevrons was being accomplished by various uniform makers in New York City. Although the chevron backgrounds were officially to be dark blue, by 1954 manufacturers' invoices showed that black wool was actually being used. On all but extremely close examination, the difference is negligible, with some band members insisting (owing to tradition) that the chevrons were, and still are, on dark blue cloth. Catalog Nos. 400–406, 413, and 442 were all made for the Military Academy Band.[49]

When the Army instituted specialist grades, distinctive specialist's chevrons for the West Point Band were approved for wear and local manufacture. Despite this authorization, band members never wore white and blue specialist's chevrons, as all band members retained their NCO stripes indicative of their pay grade.[50] To harmonize with cadet uniforms, on some occasions band members began to wear a white short sleeve shirt and blue trousers. Special epaulets bearing small metal and enamel chevrons are worn on this uniform. Black wool covers these undress epaulets with a standard Army button worn on the upper end.

The Army Band

While Chief of Staff, General Pershing directed the formation of the United States Army Band. From 1924 until 1943 the Army Band wore gray uniforms trimmed in blue and white, with chevrons of a white design on a blue background.[51] These distinctive uniforms were discarded in North Africa and replaced by slate blue uniforms.[52] On each cuff of this slate-blue uniform was a black disk bearing a white lyre.[53] Although the band

Figure 7-16. A West Point Band member is shown in dress uniform during the 1960s.

Figure 7-17. Shoulder devices are worn on the white short sleeve shirt by West Point Band members.

wore other special uniforms, no more unique chevrons were prescribed until 1968, when a new set of enlisted rank insignia modeled after the large nineteenth-century chevrons were introduced. These 1968 ceremonial chevrons are worn on special high-collar uniforms, both blue and white.[54] In 1974, similar but slightly smaller chevrons were issued to the women in the United States Army Band. Table 7-10 designates catalog numbers for Army Band chevrons.

Other Bands

Besides the Army Band and the West Point Band, other bands also wore special chevrons. One example is the Medical Department Band of the Army Field Service School at Carlisle, Pennsylvania, which was authorized a special uniform in the mid-1930s by the Adjutant General.[55] The gray and white uniform, similar to those worn by high school bands, had oversized chevrons based on the seven enlisted chevrons then authorized.

*Figure 7-18. Special
ceremonial uniforms and
insignia have been worn by
members of the United
States Army Band since
1968.*

**Chevron
Manufacture**

Cloth chevrons, both common (unauthorized) and authorized, may be grouped by type according to material and color. Table 7-11 summarizes this information.

**The Assignment of
Catalog Numbers for
Post-1920 Chevrons**

A summary of authorized and unauthorized chevrons in use in this period is shown in Table 7-12.

Service Stripes

On 17 April 1920, Colonel Robert Wyllie recommended service stripes be instituted for the service uniforms: "The wearing of such stripes is a very old custom in our service, dating back in some form to the Revolution, and there have been numerous requests for their re-establishment. Formerly the stripes were colored according to the arm in which the man served his enlistment, which frequently gave a barber pole effect. A better

TABLE 7-10
Catalog Numbers for Army Band Ceremonial Chevrons

Design	Catalog Number	Rank
	460[a] 465[b]	Sergeant Major
	461[a] 466[b]	Master Sergeant
	462[a] 467[b]	Sergeant First Class
	463[a] 468[b]	Staff Sergeant
	464[a] 469[b]	Sergeant

[a] For male personnel (design 5¾ inches wide)
[b] For female personnel (design 4⅛ inches wide)

appearance will be presented and also a simplification in supply if these stripes are small and made of olive drab placed on a dark blue background so that the blue gives a narrow edging to the striped."[56] In these exact words the enlistment stripe to be used for almost forty years was created. Indeed, the colors specified here proved so pleasing that the Army adopted them for rank chevrons later that year.

The service stripe adopted to signify three years of service was olive drab, 2¼ inches by ⁵⁄₁₆-inch, on a dark blue background forming an ⅛-inch border. Worn on the left sleeve, the first stripe was placed 4 inches above the cuff at a 45-degree angle with subsequent stripes directly above and ¼-inch apart.[57] In December 1920, the Army authorized a second type

Figure 7-19. Members of the Army Medical School Band are pictured in 1935 wearing the chevrons and uniforms approved by the Adjutant General.

of service stripe for men who served a total of three years in the National Guard but not on active duty.[58] In a similar manner gold color service stripes on green were designed in 1958 for male personnel.[59]

Service stripes for the optional 1930s dress uniforms were identical in design to those for the service uniforms. The bars were of branch colors, with the second color piped around the edge when appropriate. For the enlisted men's blue and white uniforms introduced in the 1950s, a ½-inch-wide strip of gold nylon or rayon running across the sleeve was worn.[60]

WAC service stripes, ⅛-inch by 1¼ inch and in the same color as women's chevrons, started with gold on taupe in 1951, continued through the white and blue dress uniforms, and included the green uniform in 1969.[61]

TABLE 7-11
Manufacturing Types of Post–1920 Chevrons[a]

Background Material	Design Material and Color	Dates of Authorization	Remarks
Dark blue wool	Branch colors	1926–1944	Optional dress uniform until World War II; for USMA Band to present
Dark blue wool	Olive drab design cut out and sewn onto backing[b] or embroidered	1920–1948	Worn by some non-combat troops and on field jackets into 1950s
Medium blue wool	White	1924–1943	Army Band dress uniform chevrons
Dark blue cotton	Khaki design	1921–1948	For wear on khaki shirts
Khaki cotton[d]	Olive drab or khaki design cut out and sewn onto backing[b]	1921–1948	For wear on khaki shirts
Black or dark blue	Silver or white	1940–1958	Woven or embroidered
Golden embroidery	Blue embroidery	1948–1951	2-inch-wide combat chevrons
Blue embroidery	Golden embroidery	1948–present[c]	2 inch wide non-combat 1948–1951; current insignia on dress blue uniforms
Taupe embroidery	Golden embroidery	1952–1961	WAC, 2 inches wide
Beige wool or cotton	Beige embroidery	1945–1948	WAC, hospital and off-duty dress
Green wool or cotton	Golden embroidery	1955–present	
White	Golden embroidery	1951–present[c]	
Olive green cotton	Black embroidery	1966–1968	For fatigue uniforms

[a] Types *r* and *s* chevrons from World War I continued to be issued at some posts until 1936.
[b] Some contained unofficial specialty devices from 1920 until 1942.
[c] Includes U.S. Army Band ceremonial chevrons on cotton background.
[d] Not approved by War Department.

214

TABLE 7-12
Summary of Catalog Numbers for Post–1920 Chevrons

Catalog Number	Dates of Authorization[a]	Rank
400	1920–1948	Master Sergeant
	1951–present	Master Sergeant
401	1920–1948	Technical Sergeant
	1951–present	Sergeant First Class
	1958–present	Platoon Sergeant
402	1920–1942	First Sergeant
403	1920–1948	Staff Sergeant
	1951–1958	Sergeant
	1958–present	Staff Sergeant
404	1920–1948	Sergeant
	1958–present	Sergeant
405	1920–1948	Corporal
	1951–present	Corporal
406	1920–1948	Private First Class
	1951–1968	Private First Class
	1968–present	Private (E-2)
407	(1920–1942)	Specialist First Class
408	(1920–1942)	Specialist Second Class
409	(1920–1942)	Specialist Third Class
410	(1920–1942)	Specialist Fourth Class
411	(1920–1942)	Specialist Fifth Class
412	(1920–1942)	Specialist Sixth Class
413	1942–1948	First Sergeant
	1951–present	First Sergeant
414	1942–1948	Technician Third Grade
415	1942–1948	Technician Fourth Grade
416	1942-1948	Technician Fifth Grade
417	(1920–1948)	Master Sergeant (Specialist)
418	(1920–1948)	Technical Sergeant (Specialist)
419	(1920–1948)	Staff Sergeant (Specialist)
420	(1920–1948)	Sergeant (Specialist)
421	(1920–1948)	Corporal (Specialist)
422	(1920–1948)	Private First Class (Specialist)
423	1948–1951	First Sergeant
	1950–present	First Sergeant[b]
424	1948–1951	Master Sergeant
	1950–present	Master Sergeant[b]
425	1948–1951	Sergeant First Class
	1950–present	Sergeant First Class[b]
426	1948–1951	Sergeant
	1950–1958	Sergeant[b]
	1958–present	Staff Sergeant[b]
427	1958–present	Sergeant[b]
428	1948–1951	Corporal
	1950–present	Corporal[b]
429	1948–1951	Private First Class
	1950–1968	Private First Class[b]
	1968–present	Private (E-2)[b]

TABLE 7-12 (Continued)

Catalog Number	Dates of Authorization	Rank
430	1955–1959	Specialist Third Class
	1959–present	Specialist E-4[b]
431	1955–1959	Specialist Second Class
	1959–present	Specialist E-5[b]
432	1955–1959	Specialist First Class
	1959–present	Specialist E-6[b]
433	1955–1959	Master Specialist
	1959–1978	Specialist E-7[b]
434	1959–1965	Specialist E-8[b]
435	1959–1965	Specialist E-9[b]
436	1959–present	Specialist E-4
437	1959–present	Specialist E-5
438	1959–present	Specialist E-6
439	1959–1978	Specialist E-7
440	1959–1965	Specialist E-8
441	1959–1965	Specialist E-9
442	1959–1968	Sergeant Major
	1968–1971	Staff Sergeant Major
	1971–present	Sergeant Major
443	1959–1968	Sergeant Major[b]
	1968–1971	Staff Sergeant Major
	1971–present	Sergeant Major
444	1968–present	Command Sergeant Major
445	1968–present	Command Sergeant Major[b]
446	1968–present	Private First Class
447	1968–present	Private First Class[b]
448	1978–present	Sergeant Major of the Army
449[b]	1979–present	Sergeant Major of the Army
460	1968–present	Sergeant Major, U.S. Army Band
461	1968–present	Master Sergeant, U.S. Army Band
462	1968–present	Sergeant First Class, U.S. Army Band
463	1968–present	Staff Sergeant, U.S. Army Band
464	1968–1970	Sergeant, U.S. Army Band
465	1974–present	Sergeant Major, U.S. Army Band[b]
466	1974–present	Master Sergeant, U.S. Army Band[b]
467	1974–present	Sergeant First Class, U.S. Army Band[b]
468	1974–present	Staff Sergeant, U.S. Army Band[b]
469	c	Sergeant, U.S. Army Band[b]
470	1981–present	Sergeant Major of the Army
471	1981–present	Command Sergeant Major
472	1981–present	Sergeant Major
473	1981–present	First Sergeant
474	1981–present	Master Sergeant
475	1981–present	Sergeant First Class
	1981–present	Platoon Sergeant
476	1981–present	Staff Sergeant

TABLE 7-12 (Continued)

Catalog Number	Dates of Authorization	Rank
477	1981–present	Sergeant
478	1981–present	Corporal
479	1981–present	Specialist E-6
480	1981–present	Specialist E-5

[a] For unauthorized chevrons, dates of use are shown in parentheses.

[b] Chevrons used by women only.

[c] Women joined the U.S. Army Band in 1974 and the rank of sergeant was eliminated in 1970; thus no women wore the chevron. The chevron had been made prior to 1970 in anticipation of women's joining the Band.

CHAPTER 8

History and Catalog of Special Chevrons, Awards, and Insignia

Besides rank and service chevrons, other insignia appeared on the sleeves of enlisted men. The artillery gunner's insignia first appeared in 1896, and because gunners sewed it onto the sleeve near the rank chevron, the Quartermaster Depot classed the insignia as a chevron. In the twentieth century, the coast artillery expanded the number of "rated men," as most of the individuals entitled to these special sleeve insignia came to be called. As the expansion occurred, the rating devices took on even more the general appearance of PFC's chevrons since the backing cloth for ratings *and* for PFC's chevrons were the same size and design.

During World War I, in an effort to save metal, the War Department authorized all of the marksmanship awards to be shown by sleeve disks, which generally appear similar to the many World War I PFC's chevrons. The Quartermaster Corps prepared samples of the marksmanship and artillery insignia along with samples of the rank chevrons and generally treated them all in the same manner. Because of this close relationship of marksmanship and artillery insignia to rank chevrons, the rating and marksmanship chevrons are cataloged in this chapter. Also, special rank chevrons of 1919 and 1920 for the Army Mine Planter Service are cataloged here because of their unique nature. After 1920, enlisted men serving on mine planters wore standard chevrons.

Men of the Army Transport Service and of the Harbor Boat Service were authorized special chevrons. These unique chevrons had little resemblance to other Army rank insignia and are in fact similar to Navy rank insignia, at least for the first thirty-two years. Subsequently, in 1930, the men on Army boats received more Army-like chevrons, even though the rank insignia were still not the same as others used by the Army.

Chevrons cataloged in this chapter are subdivided into groups as follows:

Catalog Number	User
500–529	Artillery Units
530–539	World War I Marksmanship
540–549	Army Mine Planter Service
550–569	Army Transport Service and Army Harbor Boat Service
570–592	Aviation Cadets (Flying Cadets)
595–602	Miscellaneous Units

Artillery Sleeve Insignia

The artillery began to award a red cloth outline of an artillery projectile gunner in September 1896. Artillery gunner's metal badges had been awarded since 1891. The War Department placed a limit on the number of gunner's badges that could be issued, however, although there was no limit on the number of

Figure 8-1. The projectile on the sleeves of these World War I soldiers indicates that they were qualified as gunners.

men who could qualify as gunners. As a result, some men classed as gunners had no distinctive badges because other battery members had achieved higher test scores. To remedy this situation, all gunners were authorized to wear a gunner's insignia on the right sleeve.[1] The red cloth shell was placed on a rectangular backing similar to the 1902–1908 PFC's chevrons.

In 1904, observers, master gunners, and gun commanders also began to wear special insignia, and in 1904 a major expansion to rated positions occurred in the coast artillery. Owing to manufacturing difficulties, however, the Quartermaster Department did not make several rating insignia originally published in 1907 orders; the replacement insignia were first manufactured in 1908.[2]

It is important to note the difference between rated and qualified positions. Chevrons cataloged as Nos. 500, 513, 514, 516, and 522 could be given to most men who qualified for the insignia, as was also the case for Catalog No. 502 before 1908. These insignia indicated *qualification* in a position. Before a man could earn a rating, he first had to qualify as a gunner, for example. Congress strictly limited the number of *rated* positions, however, to a number of men who held certain jobs (such as chief loader or casemate electrician).

Since the place for wearing the qualification chevron and the rating insignia was the same—that is, just below the rank chevron—the rating chevron took precedence and was worn rather than the qualification chevron when a man had earned both. In practice this left the qualification chevrons to be worn by men who were qualified but not rated.[3]

Before World War I, most rating insignia for the dress uniform had a red design in a yellow circle. For undress wear prior to the war and for all wear during World War I, the entire insignia was drab to match the uniform. In 1920, color was reintroduced, with red designs being placed on an olive drab background, except for the casemate electrician who wore five white lightning bolts in a red circle.

The National Defense Act of 1916 changed the 1908 rated positions and various designs came and went from that time until 1941 when the War Department eliminated rating chevrons.[4] Despite this 1941 abolishment of most insignia peculiar to the coast artillery, one sleeve disk, the efficiency "E," remained until 1947.[5]

Figure 8-2. Catalog No. 500: Gunner's Insignia (for First Class Gunners), 1896–1907. Gunner First Class, 1907–1908. Gunner Second Class, 1907–1908. Second Class Gunner, gun or mortar company, CAC, 1908–1921; Second Class Gunner, Field Artillery, 1908–1920.

On 4 September 1896, a new set of target practice rules were established for heavy artillery. Included in these regulations was a provision for a first class gunner's insignia, which was "a piece of scarlet cloth neatly piped and stitched on the outside of the right sleeve halfway between the point of the shoulder and the elbow, below the chevron in a case of a noncommissioned officer. . . ." At this time the insignia was actually a *gunner's insignia* but was often called a first class gunner's insignia.

In 1907, second class gunners were given the chevron cataloged as No. 500 but without the white stitching, the difference in red or white stitching evidently intended to distinguish between first and second class gunners. Almost immediately this was rescinded, and in early 1908 the red projectile became the design used solely by second class gunners. At this same time, first class gunners were given the chevron cataloged as No. 516. Coast artillery second class gunners in mine companies were given No. 514 in 1908, as that insignia was more representative of their qualification than an artillery projectile.

In February 1909, gunner insignia were authorized for wear on both coat sleeves. The design was changed to olive drab and khaki for wear on service uniforms in 1904, with the red projectile reserved for the dress uniform until World War I, when the colored chevrons disappeared completely. In 1920, the device was again authorized with a red projectile on an olive drab disk.

Figure 8-3. Catalog No. 501: Master Gunner, 1903–1908.

This design was to represent qualification beyond first class gunner; for dress uniforms the red shell with white stitching had a yellow wreath added. Men wore this chevron on both sleeves, unlike the gunner's insignia. In 1905 the Army established a school for master gunners at Fort Monroe, and limited attendance to not more than one first class gunner from each coast artillery company. Only those top graduates of the master gunner course qualified for this insignia and standards were high. In May 1907, only thirty-one men in the entire Army were master gunners. This qualified position was changed to a rank in 1907 and the men given the chevron cataloged as No. 276 in January 1908.

Figure 8-4. Catalog No. 502: Observer, 1904–1908; Plotter, 1916–1918.

The red triangle, ¾-inch on a side, was initially worn on both sleeves by those coast artillerymen rated as observers. Because men of many different ranks could wear the rating, there was a variety of rules for wear of this insignia. Privates wore it alone, centered on both sleeves. Gunners who were also rated as observers wore this triangle ½-inch below the gunner's insignia. Master gunners who were rated as observers wore the triangle ¼-inch below the master gunner's wreath. Sergeants and corporals who earned an observer's rating wore the triangle in the angle of their chevron. In 1907, first and second class observers were authorized, and the next year chevrons of Catalog Nos. 511 and 512 came into existence replacing this insignia.

Plotters were given chevrons of Catalog No. 502 in 1916. Thus, for plotters No. 511 replaced No. 502 in 1916, but in 1918 No. 509 was reinstituted as a more appropriate insignia for the duties involved.

Figure 8-5. Catalog No. 503: Gun Commander, 1904–1908.

The Army created an unusual insignia by requiring this device to be worn in the lower angle of the sergeant's chevrons. The scarlet crossed guns had details outlined in black stitching, while olive drab guns had detail stitching in olive drab. Catalog No. 517 replaced this insignia in January 1908.

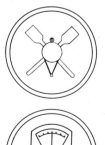

Figure 8-6. Catalog No. 504: Chief Planter, 1907.

The main features are a red ring surrounding a mine and oars. This chevron was replaced by Catalog No. 515.

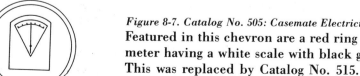

Figure 8-7. Catalog No. 505: Casemate Electrician, 1907.

Featured in this chevron are a red ring and voltmeter, the voltmeter having a white scale with black graduations and needle. This was replaced by Catalog No. 515.

Figure 8-8. Catalog No. 506: Observer First Class, 1907.

A red ring and target with white cross wires characterize this chevron, which was replaced by Catalog No. 511.

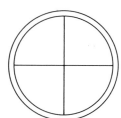

Figure 8-9. Catalog No. 507: Observer Second Class, 1907.

A red ring with white cross wires distinguishes this insignia, which was replaced by Catalog No. 512.

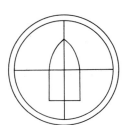

Figure 8-10. Catalog No. 508: Gun Pointer, 1907.

A red ring and projectile with white cross wires show in this chevron, replaced by Catalog No. 518.

Figure 8-11. Catalog No. 509: Plotter, 1907, 1918–1935; Plotter, Chief of Range Section, and Instrument Sergeant, 1935–1941.

A pair of red dividers within a red circle were prescribed in 1907 but this chevron, along with Catalog Nos. 504 through 508, was determined to be too complicated, and No. 511 was selected to replace this proposed insignia. During World War I, the dividers in a circle were prescribed again, but this time the insignia was made and issued.

Figure 8-12. Design No. 510: Chief Loader, 1907, 1912–1941; Chief Planter, 1912–1916.

Described in the 1907 Uniform Regulations but never made at that time, this chevron was reinstituted in 1912 for chief planters and loaders who had worn Catalog No. 515. Chief planters switched back to No. 515 in 1916.

Figure 8-13. Catalog No. 511: Observer First Class, 1908–1941; Plotter, 1908–1916.

Authorized in January 1908 for dress uniforms, this chevron had a red triangle and bar within a yellow circle. Before a soldier could be rated in either position, he had first to qualify as a first class gunner; but the gunner's insignia was not worn by those who earned this rating, as this device has priority for wear. In 1916, first class observers were further restricted to sergeants, corporals, PFCs, and privates.

Figure 8-14. Catalog No. 512: Observer Second Class, 1908–1935; Observer and Chief Binaural Listener, 1935–1941.

The history of this rating insignia is parallel to that cataloged as No. 511.

Figure 8-15. Catalog No. 513: First Class Gunner, mine company, 1908–1921.

This rank was established solely for the few mine companies of the coast artillery; first class gunners who were sergeants, corporals, and privates were authorized to wear this device. While NCO staff members such as supply sergeants and sergeants major could qualify as first class gunners, they could not wear the insignia.

Figure 8-16. Catalog No. 514: Second Class Gunner, mine company, 1908–1921.

The history of this rating device is parallel to that cataloged as No. 513.

Figure 8-17. Catalog No. 515: Casemate Electrician, 1908–1918; Chief Planter, 1908–1912, 1916–1935; Chief Planter and Chief of Planting Section, 1935–1941; Chief Loader, 1905–1912.

This insignia was specified by General Order No. 15, 1908, for three different rated positions: casemate electricians, chief planters, and chief loaders. Catalog No. 510 was instituted in 1912 for chief planters and for chief loaders, leaving this insignia for casemate electricians only. In 1916, chevrons of this design were once again specified for chief planters. Casemate electricians finally were given chevrons of Catalog No. 521 in May 1918 to distinguish them from chief planters.

Figure 8-18. Catalog No. 516: First Class Gunner, gun or mortar company, CAC, 1908–1921; First Class Gunner, Field Artillery, 1908–1921.

This insignia replaced Catalog No. 500 in early 1908 for all but coast artillery mine company first class gunners. While men had to qualify as first class gunners before they could be tested for any rated position, this chevron was worn only by first class gunners who did not wear any rating insignia.

Figure 8-19. Catalog No. 517: Gun Commander, 1908–1935; Gun Commander, Chief of Section, Platoon Sergeant, 1935–1941.

This insignia replaced Catalog No. 503 in January 1908.

Figure 8-20. Catalog No. 518: Gun Pointer, 1908–1941.

Gun pointer ratings were authorized in 1907 and assigned Catalog No. 508 which was never manufactured. This insignia replaced the first design in early 1908.

Figure 8-21. Catalog No. 519: Badge for Excellence in Target Practice, CAC, 1910–1923.

Instituted in mid–1910, this insignia was worn by enlisted men (on the right cuff of the dress coats) of the coast artillery company making the highest gunnery average in each class of heavy gun and mortar competition. Since the troops in Hawaii, the Philippines, and the Panama Canal Zone were not issued the dark blue dress uniforms, this insignia was not worn by these troops until 1916 when it was authorized on an olive drab background. It was replaced by Catalog No. 523 in 1923.

Figure 8-22. Catalog No. 520: Coxswain, 1916–1941.

After Congress authorized coxswains in 1916, the artillery adopted a red ship's wheel in a red circle as the insignia. For service wear during World War I, the chevron was of olive drab on an olive drab background.

Figure 8-23. Catalog No. 521: Casemate Electrician, 1918–1935; Casemate Electrician, Communication Sergeant, and Chief of Casemate Section, 1935–1941.

This rating insignia replaced Catalog No. 515 for casemate electricians, giving these specialists a more appropriate insignia.

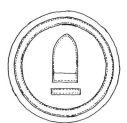

Figure 8-24. Catalog No. 522. Expert Gunner, CAC, 1920–1921.

First prescribed in 1920, this rating insignia consisted of a red shell, bar, and circle on an olive drab disk.

Figure 8-25. Catalog No. 523: Excellence in Coast Artillery Target Practice, 1923–1947.

This insignia with a red embroidered "E" on an olive drab background disk was worn on the coat cuff. The chevron replaced that of Catalog No. 519.

Figure 8-26. Catalog No. 524: Transportation Sergeant, Combat Train Sergeant, Truckmaster, 1935–1941.

Authorized in January 1935 by the Secretary of War, this insignia was not published in regulations.

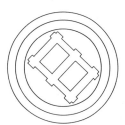

Figure 8-27. Catalog No. 525: Railway Sergeant, 1935–1941.

In January 1935, the Secretary of War authorized a section of railroad track at an angle of 45 degrees to designate railway sergeants rated in the Coast Artillery Corps.

World War I Marksmanship Insignia

From the 1880s on, the Army had awarded various metal marksmanship badges to soldiers. As the United States became involved in the World War, however, War Department officials concluded the metal used in these badges should be conserved. Accordingly, the Quartermaster Corps made a series of cloth sleeve insignia the same size as PFC chevrons to replace the metal badges.[6] Never popular with the troops, these insignia were withdrawn by the Army shortly after the war ended and were replaced by the original badges. Although metal badges were not authorized by regulations, private firms continued to manufacture the original metal insignia throughout the war; consequently, few men actually wore these authorized sleeve devices. Provisions for all of the marksmanship chevrons were from April 1918 until August 1919.[7]

Figure 8-28. Top row, left to right: *Catalog No. 530: Expert Rifleman. Catalog No. 531: Sharpshooter (Rifle). Catalog No. 532: Marksman (Rifle).* Middle row, left to right: *Catalog No. 533: Marksman, Special Course A. Catalog No. 534: Expert Pistol Shot. Catalog No. 535: First Class Pistol Shot.* Bottom row, left to right: *Catalog No. 536: Expert Machine Gunner. Catalog No. 537: Sharpshooter (Machine Gun). Catalog No. 538: Marksman (Machine Gun).*

Army Mine Planter Service Chevrons

Prescribed in January 1919, Army Mine Planter Service regulations were for five scarlet "rating badges" and one "chevron" on dark blue backgrounds. These are cataloged as Nos. 540 through 544; there is also a cook's chevron (Catalog No. 316).[8] The deckhand's chevron was officially replaced by the universal PFC insignia, Catalog No. 336, in late 1919. Circular No. 25, 1920, specifically required only two chevrons peculiar to the Mine Planter Service (Catalog Nos. 544 and 545), although Nos. 280, 316, 336, and 283 could also be worn by men of the Army Mine Planter Service. The 1919 regulations and Circular No. 25 also described two insignia for wear by mine planter warrant officers on the cuffs of their white and olive drab coats. The two officer's insignia are included here because they may be mistaken for World War I PFC chevrons.

Figure 8-29. Top row, left to right: Catalog No. 540: Steward, 1919–1920. Catalog No. 541: Oiler, 1919–1920. Catalog No. 542: Fireman, 1919–1920. Catalog No. 543: Deckhand, 1919. Bottom row, left to right: Catalog No. 544: Assistant Steward, 1919–1920. Catalog No. 545: Steward, 1920. Warrant Officer insignia, 1919–1951. Catalog No. 546 (left): Masters and Mate. Catalog No. 547 (right): Engineers.

Army Transport Service and Harbor Boat Service Chevrons

The Army formed its own "navy," the Army Transport Service (ATS), during the Spanish-American War to transport troops to Cuba and the Philippines and to provide interisland service in the Philippine Islands. A smaller organization, the Harbor Boat Service, operated ferries and small harbor craft, and men in the Harbor Boat Service generally wore the same basic uniform and chevrons as ATS members. Initially, the Army purchased ATS vessels from commercial firms and the contract crew members continued to wear their former civilian work clothing—until September 1899, when uniforms were first prescribed for the new ATS.[9]

Figure 8-30. Top row, left to right: *Catalog No. 550: Third Steward, 1899–1908; Quartermaster, 1899–1930. Third steward's chevrons were embroidered in gray, while quartermaster's were in red.   Catalog No. 551: Fourth Steward, 1899–1908.   Catalog No. 552: Boatswain's Mate, 1899–1930.   Catalog No. 553: Gunner's Mate, 1899–1930.   Second row, left to right: Catalog No. 554: Storekeeper, 1899–1930. Two colors of storekeepers' chevrons were authorized from 1899 until 1908: those for stewards were gray, while all others were red. After 1908 only the red chevrons were used.   Design No. 555: Carpenter's Mate, 1899–1930.   Catalog No. 556: Donkeymen, Oilers, and Watertenders, 1899–1912; Oilers, 1912–1930.   Catalog No. 557: Firemen, 1899–1912; Firemen and Oilers, 1912–1930.   Third row, left to right: Catalog No. 558: Coal Passers, 1899–1930.   Catalog No. 559: Third Steward, 1908–1912. This chevron was embroidered in cadet gray only.   Catalog No. 560: Fourth Steward, 1908–1912. This chevron was embroidered in cadet gray only.   Catalog No. 561: Oiler, ATS, 1930–around 1946.   Fourth row, left to right: Catalog No. 562: Boatswain's Mate, ATS, 1930–around 1946.   Catalog No. 563: Gunner's Mate, ATS, 1930–1942.   Catalog 564: Carpenter's Mate, ATS, 1930–around 1946.   Catalog No. 565: Wheelman, ATS, 1930–around 1946.   Fifth row, left to right: Catalog No. 566; Fireman, ATS, 1930–around 1946; Oiler, HBS, 1942–around 1946.   Catalog 567: Boatswain, HBS, 1930–around 1946.   Catalog No. 568: Coal Passer, ATS, 1930–around 1946; Oiler, HBS, 1933–1942.*

Few chevrons required by these 1899 regulations appear actually to have been worn. Strangely, photos reveal that even though the Army made special efforts to prescribe ATS uniforms from 1899 through 1912, most crewmen did not even wear these uniforms. In one year alone, the Army made over 1,100 ATS chevrons,[10] but what happened to them is unknown. While commenting on the situation in 1920, Colonel Robert Wyllie of the Army Staff wrote, "When the Army required transports for use in the Spanish-American War, they took over vessels with personnel who wore the ordinary uniform of the Merchant Marine. . . . We have simply continued its use in our transport service."[11]

For the first thirteen years, chevrons for stewards (third and fourth stewards and steward storekeepers) were embroidered with cadet gray silk, and all others were worked in scarlet silk. Each leg of the chevron was 1 inch long, the two legs meeting at 120°.[12]

Finally, in 1930, the Army changed to a different type of ATS and HBS chevrons. The Navy influence was finally overcome to an extent, with the new rank insignia more in keeping with the "Army look." These 1930 ATS and HBS chevrons were embroidered in red on a dark blue background.[13]

Chevrons for Aviation Cadets (Flying Cadets)

In 1928 the Air Service designated a special group of enlisted men as flying cadets; the name was changed to aviation cadets during World War II. Cadets wore special slate blue uniforms, with chevrons of black material on a slate blue background. Examples of these uniforms are in Figure 8-63 showing cadets in radio training. The cadet first sergeant is in the center, his position indicated by the traditional diamond below his sergeant's chevron. Regulations called for cadet corporals to wear one bar, sergeants two bars, lieutenants three bars, and captains

Figure 8-31. Flying cadets at Randolph Field, 1940, wearing their special slate blue uniforms. The cadet first sergeant in the center is wearing his unique chevrons.

Figure 8-32. Flying cadet corporals wore one bar and cadet sergeants wore two bars. These overcoat chevrons lasted until they were replaced in 1940 by chevrons similar to those worn by West Point cadets.

four bars, although the Quartermaster Corps also made and issued first sergeant's chevrons. Overcoat chevrons were of similar design but larger, covering the upper sleeve.[14]

The large and small chevrons were of similar design until May 1940, when the Air Corps added additional flying cadet chevrons. At the same time, the large chevrons were modified more along the lines of those used by West Point cadets. Overcoat chevrons were given steeper sides, and a vertical tie was added at the ends of those chevrons having two or more bars.[15] Initially, both the large and small 1940 flying cadet chevrons continued to be made with the design in black felt sewn onto a back of slate blue melton. Owing to the increase in the number of cadets, the uniforms soon came to be the khaki and olive drab issued to all enlisted men. Consequently, chevron colors came to be the same as those used by enlisted personnel: olive drab on navy blue background.[16] Thereafter aviation cadet corporals wore the standard PFC chevrons on shirts; cadet sergeants wore normal corporal stripes, and aviation cadet lieutenants wore the regular chevrons of a sergeant. Supply of some of the special chevrons became a problem; in January 1943, Army Air Force Headquarters directed local commanders to improvise those aviation cadet chevrons which were not on hand for issue by the Quartermaster General. Some of the chevrons thus produced were of the wrong colors, such as a black or dark blue design on an olive drab background for the overcoat. More important, and in line with the intent of the directive, this gave commanders the

Figure 8-33. The post–May 1940 practice of wearing standard enlisted uniforms is shown, with the cadet captain distinguished by the four bars and his saber. Cadet corporals and sergeants are among the men being inspected in this photograph.

authority to make and issue other chevrons for wing and group commanders and staff officers, as was done at some training centers.[17]

The termination date of aviation cadet chevrons has not been precisely determined, since chevrons were in use in 1946, but 1947 photographs show the cadets wearing shoulder boards or armbands to designate rank. Termination date therefore is noted for cataloging purposes as "around 1946."

Figure 8-34. Left to right: *Catalog No. 570: Flying Cadet Captain, 1928–1940 (overcoat).   Catalog No. 571: Flying Cadet Lieutenant, 1928–1940 (overcoat).   Catalog No. 572: Flying Cadet sergeant, 1928–1940 (overcoat).   Catalog No. 573: Flying Cadet Corporal, 1928–1940 (overcoat).*

Figure 8-35. Catalog No. 574: Flying Cadet First Sergeant, 1928–1940 (overcoat).

Not specifically authorized by the Quartermaster General, this chevron nevertheless is called for in some official documents and certainly was made and issued by 1938.

Figure 8-36. Left to right: *Catalog No. 575: Flying Cadet Captain (coat), 1928–1940; Aviation Cadet Company Commander (shirt), 1940–1946. Catalog No. 404: Flying Cadet Lieutenant (coat), 1928–1940; (shirt) 1940–1946.   Catalog No. 405: Flying Cadet Sergeant (coat), 1928–1940; (shirt) 1940–1946.   Catalog No. 406: Flying Cadet Corporal (coat), 1928–1940; (shirt) 1940–1946.*

Figure 8-37. Design No. 576: Flying Cadet First Sergeant (coat), 1928–1940; (shirt) 1940–1946.

This chevron was not officially authorized until 1941. This appears to have been an oversight in regulations because letters of the 1930 era mention this chevron, and pre–1941 use of the chevron is known (*see* Figure 8-31).

Figure 8-38. Left to right: *Catalog No. 577: Aviation Cadet Battalion Commander (shirt), 1940–1946.   Catalog No. 578: Aviation Cadet Battalion Adjutant (shirt), 1940–1946.   Catalog No. 579: Aviation Cadet Battalion Sergeant Major (shirt), 1940–1946.   Catalog No. 580: Aviation Cadet Supply Sergeant (shirt), 1940–1946.*

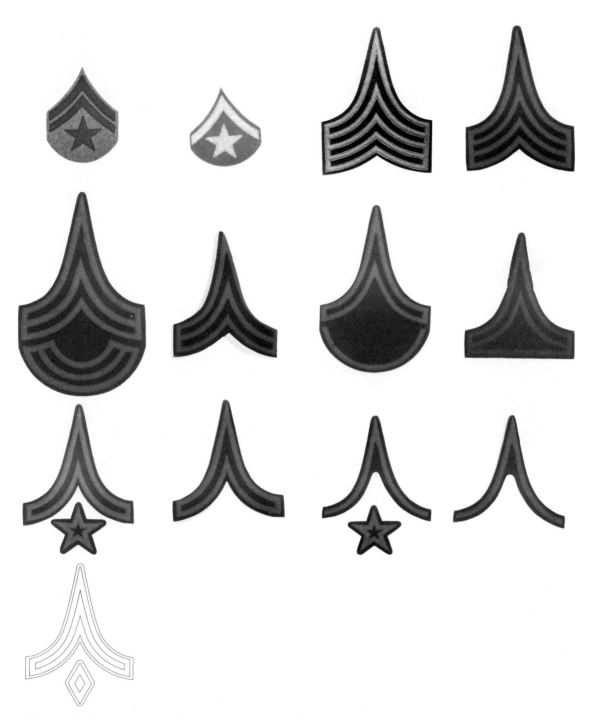

Figure 8-39. Top row, left to right: *Catalog No. 581: Aviation Cadet Color Sergeant (shirt),*
1940–1946. *Catalog No. 582: Aviation Cadet Color Corporal (shirt), 1940–1946.* *Catalog No. 583: Aviation*
Cadet Battalion Commander (overcoat), 1940–1946. *Catalog No. 584: Aviation Cadet Company*
Commander (overcoat), 1940–1946. Second row, left to right: *Catalog No. 585: Aviation Cadet Battalion*
Adjutant (overcoat), 1940–1946. *Catalog No. 586: Aviation Cadet Lieutenant (overcoat),*
1940–1946. *Catalog No. 587: Aviation Cadet Battalion Sergeant Major (overcoat), 1940–1946.* *Catalog No.*
588: Aviation Cadet Supply Sergeant (overcoat), 1940–1946. Third row, left to right: *Catalog No. 589:*
Aviation Cadet Color Sergeant (overcoat), 1940–1946. *Catalog No. 590: Aviation Cadet Sergeant (overcoat),*
1940–1946. *Catalog No. 591: Aviation Cadet Color Corporal (overcoat), 1940–1946.* *Catalog No. 592:*
Aviation Cadet Corporal (overcoat), 1940–1946. Fourth row: *Catalog No. 593: Aviation Cadet*
First Sergeant (overcoat), 1940–1946.

Figure 8-40. Aviation cadets are shown raising the flag in 1941. The center cadet is a color sergeant.

Miscellaneous Insignia (Music School, Training Camps, Postal Agency)

Figure 8-41. Catalog No. 595: Army Music School, 1921–1934; 1943–1945.

From 1921 until 1934, the insignia was worn by privates of the Army Music School in the same place on their uniforms as for chevrons. PFCs, corporals, and sergeants wore the disk immediately below the standard chevrons for those grades. For three years, starting in 1943, this design was made with a black embroidered background and a white lyre for wear by the United States Army Band on the cuff of the dress coat.

For a staff sergeant of the Army Music School, the insignia was prescribed to be worn "between the chevrons and the arc." The chevron thus prescribed was a revision of Catalog No. 211, but made in the post–1920 color scheme.

Figure 8-42. Catalog No. 596: United States Training Camps.

This is not a rank chevron but an identification patch. Because of its size and construction, it may be confused with some World War I PFC chevrons.

Figure 8-43. Catalog No. 597: Postal Employees, AEF, 1918–1919.

Worn on a standard Army uniform, this gray chevron with a red border and red letters signified that the wearer belonged to the United States Postal Agency in the AEF.

Chevrons for Telephone Operators

During the 1918 AEF buildup, Signal Corps officials decided that women would go to France as telephone operators. Called "Hello Girls," these women wore uniforms and shoulder patches, and earned medals and ranks similar to soldiers. Women served as operators in three grades, all distinguished by chevrons. The chief operator's chevron consisted of a mouthpiece inclosed in a wreath with five sparks above, while supervisors wore a chevron showing a mouthpiece in a wreath. Some chevrons also carried a horizontal or V-shaped bar below the wreath. The chevron for operators showed only the mouthpiece and was worn on the left sleeve.

Figure 8-44. Left to right: Catalog No. 600: Chief Operator, 1918–1919. Catalog No. 601: Telephone operator's supervisor, 1918–1919. Catalog No. 602: Telephone operator's chevrons in the National Collection at the Smithsonian Institution. Catalog No. 603: Telephone operator's chevron worn in 1918 (from the Signal Corps Museum).

TABLE 8-1
Manufacturing Code Letters for Special Chevrons

Background Material	Design Material and Color	Dates of Authorization	Remarks	Code Letter
Dark blue wool	Red[a]	1902–1917	Artillery and Mine Planting Service	k
Dark blue wool	Red	1926–1941	Coast Artillery Corps dress uniforms	k
Olive drab wool	Red[a]	1902–1917	Artillery and Mine Planting Service	l
Olive drab	Red	1920–1941[b]	Coast Artillery Corps ratings	l
Khaki cotton	Red[a]	1902–1904	Artillery	m
Khaki cotton	Red	1920–1941	Coast Artillery Corps ratings	m
White duck	Red[a]	1902–1904	Artillery	n
Khaki cotton	Flannel	1904–1911	Artillery	q
Khaki cotton	Flannel or embroidery	1918–1919	Marksmanship awards	q
Olive drab wool	Olive drab wool, flannel, or embroidery	1904–1920	Artillery and Marksmanship awards	r
Olive drab wool	Olive drab embroidery	1920–1951	Catalog Nos. 545 and 546	r
White duck	White embroidery	1920–1951	Catalog Nos. 545 and 546	w
Blue	Gray silk	1899–1912	Army Transport Service	ax
Blue	Red silk	1899–c.1917	Army Transport Service	ay
Blue	Red wool or embroidery	c.1917–1947	Army Transport Service	ay
Slate blue	Black wool	1928–1940	Flying Cadet	az
Navy blue	Olive drab wool	1940–1947	Aviation Cadet	aa

[a] Wreath for Catalog No. 501 was yellow; circles for artillery rating devices prior to World War I were yellow. For pre–World War I men assigned to school troops at the Coast Artillery School, the device was green.
[b] Catalog No. 523 authorized until November 1947.

APPENDIXES

Appendix 1

TABLE 9A-1
Summary of Manufacturing Code Letters

Background	Design	Dates of General Use	Remarks	Code Letter
The coat itself	Various colors	1821–1850s[a]	Chevron bars sewn directly to coat sleeves	*a*
Wool	Branch-colored worsted binding	1850s[a]–1872	Normally 8 to 10 inches wide	*b*
Wool	Branch-colored silk binding	1850s[a]–1872	Normally 8 to 10 inches wide	*c*
Branch-colored wool	Made by chain stitching	1872–1902	Any insert will be on blue wool with a quarter-circle-shaped top. Normally 9 to 10 inches wide	*d*
Blue wool rectangle 5½ × 9 inches	Branch colored wool	1872–1902	For specialty marks	*d**
Blue wool square 3½ × 3½ inches	Signal flags hospital device	1864–1891 1901–1902		*d*
Branch-colored wool	Made by chain stitching	1872–1880s[b]	Insert will fill entire angle of chevron, as in Figure 3-13	*e*
Branch-colored wool	Made by chain stitching	1880s–1890s[c]	Unofficial; see Figure 3-14	*f*
Branch-colored wool	Gold lace	1884–1905[d]		*g*
Cotton or light wool, branch-colored	Made by chain stitching	1898–1902	Inserts are khaki	*h*
Khaki rectangle	Branch-colored cotton	1898–1902		*h*
Khaki square 3½ × 3½ inches	Colored medical device	1901–1902		*h*
Dark blue wool	Branch-colored wool	1902	Official type chevrons for the blue shirt. Only chevrons with pre–1902 colors or with inserts requiring the chevron to go point down should be in this code. Many shirt chevrons also fit code *k* and were worn on coats for many years	*i*
Varies	Branch colors	1898–1905[c]	Unofficial shirt chevrons for blue shirts. Usually 2½ to 5 inches wide	*j*
Dark blue wool	Branch colors	1902–1917		*k*
Dark blue wool	Branch colors	1926–1944		*k*
Dark blue wool	white	1903–present	Worn by U.S. Military Academy Band. Originally started as use of infantry chevrons on the dress blue uniform	*k*
Olive drab wool	Branch colors	1902–1904		*l*
Khaki cotton	Branch colors	1902–1904		*m*
White duck	Branch colors	1902–1904		*n*
Rust color cotton	Tan or brown	1902–1908	Authorized wearout through 1910	*o*
White duck	Olive drab	1904–1918	Medical and recruiting only after 1907	*p*

TABLE 9A-1 (Continued)

Background	Design	Dates of General Use	Remarks	Code Letter
Khaki cotton	Medium khaki or flannel bars; hand-embroidered weaths and specialty marks	1904–1911	Remaining stocks issued through 1916	q
Olive drab wool	Olive drab	1904–1920	Chevrons about 2½ to 3 inches wide	r
Khaki or olive drab cotton	See remarks	1911–1920	Design in medium khaki, or for WW I privately made chevrons, in dark browns, greens, and other subdued colors. These were for the summer-weight uniform	s
Blue denim	Outlined in branch-colored chain stitching	1910–1918		t
White duck	Outlined in buff chain stitching	1913–1918	Used by Quartermaster Corps cooks and bakers only	u
Olive drab felt	Olive drab bars with green wreaths, yellow lyres, or white lightning	1920	Authorized but not issued	v
White duck	White embroidery	1920–1951	Warrant-officers of the Mine Planter Service only	w
Dark blue wool	Cut out of olive drab cloth	1920–1943	3 to 3½ inches wide; nominal width of 3⅛ inches	aa
Medium blue wool	White bars	1924–1943	U.S. Army Band	ab
Dark blue	Olive drab embroidery	1925–1948	Nominal width 3⅛ inches	ac
Dark blue	Khaki, cut out and sewn to background	1936–1948		ad
Khaki	Khaki, cut out and sewn to background	1930–1943		ae
Khaki	Khaki embroidery	1930–1948		af
Black or dark blue	Silver	1940–1948	Woven into one piece of material	ag
Black or dark blue cotton	White or silver embroidery	1936–1948		ah
Golden yellow	Blue embroidery	1948–1951	2 inches wide, for combat troops	ai
Blue	Golden yellow embroidery	1953–present	Male dress blue uniform	aj
Blue	Golden yellow embroidery	1948–present	Initially for noncombat troops; for women's dress uniforms after 1951; 2 inches wide	ak
Blue twill	Embroidered olive drab	1951–1959	3 inches wide	al
Black cotton	Golden yellow embroidery	1968–present	U.S. Army Band ceremonial chevrons, male personnel	am

TABLE 9A-1 (Continued)

Background	Design	Dates of General Use	Remarks	Code Letter
Black cotton	Golden yellow embroidery	1974–present	U.S. Army Band ceremonial chevrons, female personnel	*an*
Taupe	Golden yellow embroidery	1951–1961	For women only, 2 inches wide	*ao*
Beige wool	Beige embroidery	1944–1951	For women's winter uniforms of beige, chevron 3 inches wide	*ap*
Beige cotton	Light beige embroidery	1944–1951	For women's summer uniforms of beige, chevrons 3 inches wide	*aq*
Green	Yellow embroidery	1958–present	For men, 3 inches wide	*ar*
Green	Yellow embroidery	1955–present	Initially for specialists, later for women; 2 inches wide	*as*
White	Yellow embroidery	1958–present	3 inches wide	*at*
White	Yellow embroidery	1951–present	For women; 2 inches wide	*au*
White	Yellow embroidery	1968–present	U.S. Army Band ceremonial chevrons, male personnel	*av*
White	Yellow embroidery	1974–present	U.S. Army Band ceremonial chevrons, female personnel	*aw*
Dark blue	Gray silk	1899–1912	Used by the Army Transport Service	*ax*
Dark blue	Red	1899–1947	Used by the Army Transport Service	*ay*
Slate blue	Black	1928–1940	Used by Flying Cadets	*az*
Olive drab	Black embroidery	1966–1968	For fatigue uniforms	*ba*
Black shoulder mark	Gold embroidery	1981–present	Long length	*bb*
Black shoulder mark	Gold embroidery	1981–present	Short length	*bc*

[a] Exact dates of transition are not known.
[b] Official chevrons should all have been type *d*, but the Army is known to have issued some type *e* during the 1870s.
[c] Not authorized by the War Department. General dates of use are shown.
[d] Ending date of 1911 for Coast Artillery Corps. First replaced in 1902.
*NOTE: Code letters are repeated when a manufacturing style is applicable to more than one rank. A group of chevrons produced by the same manufacturing process constitute a set; the same code letter is applicable to all chevrons in a given set.

TABLE 9A-2
Alphabetical Listing of Pre–1872 Rank Titles with
Corresponding Catalog Numbers

Rank	Catalog Number
Company Quartermaster Sergeant	17
Corporal	1, 4, 9
First Sergeant	7, 12
Hospital Steward	14
Ordnance Sergeant	13
Pioneer	15
Principal Musician	2
Quartermaster Sergeant	1, 2, 6, 11
Regimental Commissary Sergeant	18
Regimental Hospital Steward	19
Senior Musician	1
Sergeant	1, 3, 8
Sergeant Major	1, 2, 5, 10
Signal Service	16

TABLE 9A-3
Alphabetical Listing of 1872–1902 Rank Titles with Corresponding Catalog Numbers

Rank	Catalog Number
Acting Hospital Steward	112, 113
Artificer	136
Battalion Color Sergeant	123
Battalion Quartermaster Sergeant	104, 105
Battalion Sergeant Major	103
Battery Quartermaster Sergeant	105
Chief Musician	106
Chief Trumpeter	107
Color Sergeant	121, 123
Commissary Sergeant	124
Company Quartermaster Sergeant	105
Cook	134
Corporal	132
Corporal, Signal Corps	118
Drum Major	126
Electrician Sergeant	138
Farrier	135
First Class Private, Signal Corps	120
First Sergeant	130
Hospital Steward	109, 110, 111
Lance Acting Hospital Steward	114
Lance Corporal	133
Lance Corporal, Signal Corps	119
Mechanic and Artificer	136
Ordnance Sergeant	121, 122
Pioneer	151
Post Commissary Sergeant	124
Post Quartermaster Sergeant	125
Principal Musician	108
Private, Hospital Corps	115
Quartermaster Sergeant	101
Regimental Color Sergeant	123
Regimental Commissary Sergeant	102
Regimental Quartermaster Sergeant	101
Regimental Sergeant Major	100
Saddler	137
Saddler Sergeant	127
Sergeant	131
Sergeant First Class, Signal Corps	116
Sergeant Major	100
Sergeant Major Junior Grade	103
Sergeant Major Senior Grade	100
Sergeant Second Class, Signal Corps	117
Signal Service	16
Squadron Sergeant Major	103
Stable Sergeant	129
Troop Quartermaster Sergeant	105
Veterinary Sergeant of Field Artillery	128

TABLE 9A-4
Alphabetical Listing of 1902–1920 Rank Titles with Corresponding Catalog Numbers

Rank	Catalog Number
Acting Hospital Steward	252
Artificer	318
Assistant Band Leader	200, 204, 210
Assistant Chauffeur	327
Assistant Engineer	279
Band Corporal	213
Band Leader	202, 208, 209
Band Sergeant	212
Battalion of Engineers, Quartermaster Sergeant	304
Battalion Quartermaster Sergeant	304
Battalion Sergeant Major	303
Battalion Supply Sergeant	304
Battery Quartermaster Sergeant	306
Bugler	207
Bugler First Class	206
Chauffeur	326
Chauffeur, First Class	325
Chief Mechanic	319, 320
Chief Musician	202
Chief Trumpeter	203
Color Sergeant	309
Company Quartermaster Sergeant	306
Cook	316
Corporal	313
Corporal, Air Service	353
Corporal, Bugler	205
Corporal, C.W.S.	292
Corporal, Corps of Engineers	264
Corporal, Hospital Corps	253
Corporal, Intelligence Police	390
Corporal, Interpreter Corps	384
Corporal, Motor Transport Corps	364
Corporal, Ordnance	232
Corporal, Quartermaster Corps	227
Corporal, Signal Corps	242
Corporal, Tank Corps	348
Corporal, Transportation Corps	374
Deckhand	336
Drum Major	214, 215
Electrician Sergeant	270
Electrician Sergeant, First Class	271, 273, 308
Electrician Sergeant, Second Class	270, 272, 308
Engineer	278
Farrier	315, 317
Fireman	280, 281, 282
First Sergeant (Drum Major)	215
First Sergeant	311
First Class Private (*see* Private First Class)	

TABLE 9A-4 (Continued)

Rank	Catalog Number
Horseshoer	317
Hospital Sergeant	250, 257, 277
Hospital Steward	251
Intelligence Police Sergeant	387
Interpreter Sergeant	381
Lance Acting Hospital Steward	254
Lance Corporal	314
Lance Corporal, Hospital Corps	254
Lance Corporal of Ordnance	233
Lance Corporal, Signal Corps	244
Lance Corporal, Quartermaster Corps	229
Master Chemical Sergeant	295
Master Electrician	274, 276, 308
Master Electrician, Quartermaster Corps	225
Master Engineer, Junior Grade	261, 397
Master Engineer, Junior Grade, Transport Corps	371, 397
Master Engineer, Senior Grade	260, 396
Master Engineer, Senior Grade, Tank Corps	396, 340, 342, 344
Master Engineer, Senior Grade, Transport Corps	370, 396
Master Gunner	275
Master Hospital Sergeant	256
Master Intelligence Police Sergeant	386
Master Interpreter Sergeant	380
Master Signal Electrician	243, 308
Master Signal Electrician, Air Service	350
Mechanic	318
Mechanic-Saddler	321
Mess Sergeant	328
Motor Sergeant	324
Musician, First, Second, and Third Class	216
Oiler, Mine Planter Service	279
Ordnance Sergeant	230, 235, 236
Principal Musician	204
Private First Class	336
Private First Class (all arms)	336
Private First Class, Air Service	354
Private First Class, Artillery	331
Private First Class, Cavalry	330
Private First Class, C.W.S.	293
Private First Class, Engineers	265
Private First Class, Gas Service	294
Private First Class, General Headquarters	334
Private First Class, General Recruiting Service	333
Private First Class, Hospital Corps	255
Private First Class, Infantry	329
Private First Class, Intelligence Police	391
Private First Class, Interpreter Corps	385
Private First Class, Motor Transport	365
Private First Class, Ordnance	234

TABLE 9A-4 (Continued)

Rank	Catalog Number
Private First Class, Provost Marshal General's Dept.	335
Private First Class, Quartermaster Corps	228
Private First Class, Service Schools	332
Private First Class, Signal Corps	247
Private First Class, Tank Corps	341, 343, 345
Private First Class, Transportation Corps	375
Private, Hospital Corps	255
Post Commissary Sergeant	220
Post Quartermaster Sergeant	221
Quartermaster Sergeant	223, 224
Quartermaster Sergeant, Junior Grade	399
Quartermaster Sergeant, Junior Grade, Motor Transport	399
Quartermaster Sergeant, Quartermaster Corps	221
Quartermaster Sergeant, Senior Grade	226, 398
Quartermaster Sergeant, Senior Grade, Motor Transport	360, 398
Radio Sergeant	270, 308
Regimental Commissary Sergeant	302
Regimental Quartermaster Sergeant	301
Regimental Sergeant Major	300
Regimental Supply Sergeant	301
Saddler	321
Sergeant	312
Sergeant, Air Service	353
Sergeant, Bugler	203, 204, 211
Sergeant, First Class	337
Sergeant First Class, Air Service	351
Sergeant First Class, C.W.S.	290
Sergeant First Class, Engineers	262
Sergeant First Class, Hospital Corps	251
Sergeant First Class, Intelligence Police	388
Sergeant First Class, Interpreter Corps	382
Sergeant First Class, Motor Transport	362
Sergeant First Class, Ordnance Department	237
Sergeant First Class, Quartermaster Corps	222
Sergeant First Class, Signal Corps	240
Sergeant First Class, Tank Corps	346
Sergeant First Class, Transportation Corps	372
Sergeant, Intelligence Police	389
Sergeant Interpreter Corps	383
Sergeant Major, Junior Grade	303
Sergeant Major, Senior Grade	300
Sergeant, Motor Transport	363
Sergeant of Band and Assistant Leader, USMA	200
Sergeant of Corps of Engineers	263
Sergeant of C.W.S.	291
Sergeant of Field Music, USMA	201, 204
Sergeant of Hospital Corps	252
Sergeant of Ordnance	231
Sergeant of Quartermaster Corps	221
Sergeant of Signal Corps	241

TABLE 9A-4 (Continued)

Rank	Catalog Number
Sergeant, Tank Corps	347
Sergeant, Transportation Corps	373
Squadron Sergeant Major	303
Squadron Supply Sergeant	304
Stable Sergeant	310
Supply Sergeant	306
Troop Quartermaster Sergeant	306
Wagoner	322

TABLE 9A-5

Alphabetical Listing of Post–1920 Rank Titles with
Corresponding Catalog Numbers

Rank	Catalog Number
Command Sergeant Major	444, 445, 471
Corporal	405, 428, 478
Corporal (Specialist)	421
First Sergeant	402, 413, 423, 473
Master Sergeant	400, 424, 461, 466, 474
Master Sergeant (Specialist)	417
Master Specialist	433
Platoon Sergeant	401
Private (E-2)	429
Private First Class	406, 429, 446, 447
Private First Class (Specialist)	422
Sergeant	403, 404, 426, 427, 464, 469, 477
Sergeant (Specialist)	420
Sergeant Major	442, 443, 460, 465, 472
Sergeant Major of the Army	448, 449, 470
Sergeant First Class	401, 425, 462, 467, 475
Specialist E-4	430, 436
Specialist E-5	431, 437, 480
Specialist E-6	432, 438, 479
Specialist E-7	433, 439
Specialist E-8	434, 440
Specialist E-9	435, 441
Specialist First Class	407, 432
Specialist Second Class	408, 431
Specialist Third Class	409, 430
Specialist Fourth Class	410
Specialist Fifth Class	411
Specialist Sixth Class	412
Staff Sergeant	403, 426, 463, 468, 476
Staff Sergeant (Specialist)	419
Staff Sergeant Major	442, 443
Technical Sergeant	401
Technical Sergeant (Specialist)	418
Technician Fifth Grade	416
Technician Fourth Grade	415
Technician Third Grade	414

Appendix 2

Conversion to 1920 Grades

War Department General Order No. 36, 19 June 1920, specified which men would be transferred to each of the seven pay grades created by Congress on 4 June 1920. The following designations, effective 1 July 1920, are from that order:

1. Enlisted men of the first grade (master sergeants) included:

Regimental sergeants major
Sergeants major senior grade
Quartermaster sergeants senior grade
Master hospital sergeants
Master engineers senior grade
Master electricians
Master signal electricians
Engineers, C.A.C.
Regimental supply sergeants
25 percent of ordnance sergeants authorized
50 percent of master gunners authorized for C.A.C.
Band sergeant and assistant leader, USMA Band
Enlisted band leaders until selection and appointment of band leaders as warrant officers have been made

2. The second grade (technical sergeants) included:

Hospital sergeants
Master engineers junior grade
75 percent of ordnance sergeants authorized
Electrician sergeants first class
Assistant engineers, C.A.C.
Quartermaster sergeants
Electrician sergeant, Artillery School Detachment, USMA

3. The second grade (first sergeants) included all NCOs designated as first sergeants.

4. The third grade (staff sergeants) included:

Squadron and battalion sergeants major
Sergeants major junior grade
Battalion supply sergeants
Sergeants first class
50 percent of master gunners authorized for C.A.C.
Master gunners, Artillery School Detachment, USMA
Assistant band leaders (except in USMA bands)
Sergeant buglers
Electrician sergeants second class
Radio sergeants
Color sergeants
Sergeant field musician, USMA

5. The fourth grade (sergeants) included:

Band sergeants
Stable sergeants
Mess sergeants
Company supply sergeants
All sergeants not specifically designated specialists fourth class

6. The fifth grade (corporals) included:

Band corporals
Corporal buglers
All corporals not specifically designated as specialists fifth class

7. The sixth grade (privates first class) included:

PFCs
Some privates drawing extra pay

Specialists could be appointed from either privates first class or privates. Enlisted men who were drawing some extra duty pay or who had special skills, such as surgical assistants, were appointed to various specialist ratings. Also, some of the pre–1920 grades were converted to various specialist ratings. The initial rating of specialist was:

1. Specialists first class were musicians first class, USMA Band.

2. Specialists second class were oilers, Army Mine Planter Service.

3. Specialists third class were appointed from:

Stewards, Army Mine Planter Service
Firemen, C.A.C., and Army Mine Planter Service
Musicians first class (except in USMA Band)
Musicians second class, USMA Band

4. Specialists fourth class were appointed from:

Chief mechanics
Horseshoers
Cooks
Musicians second class (except in USMA Band)
Musicians third class, USMA Band
Sergeants previously authorized for duty as bakers, blacksmiths, clerks, harnessmakers, laundry workers, storekeepers, warehousemen, wheelwrights, checkers, painters, plumbers, carpenters, horseshoers, and chauffeurs

5. Specialists fifth class were appointed from:

Chauffeurs, first class, Signal Corps
Chauffeurs, Signal Corps
Musicians third class (except in USMA Band)
Saddlers
Assistant stewards, Army Mine Planter Service
Deck hands, Army Mine Planter Service
Mechanics
Wagoners
Corporals previously authorized for duty as bakers, black-smiths, clerks, harnessmakers, laundry workers, storekeepers, warehousemen, wheelwrights, checkers, painters, plumbers, carpenters, horseshoers, and chauffeurs

6. Specialist sixth class were appointed from:

Buglers first class
Buglers

Pay and Relative Strength of Enlisted Grades as Provided in 1920 by Act of Congress

On and after 1 July 1920, the grades of enlisted men shall be such as the President may from time to time direct, with monthly base pay at the rate of $74.00 for the first grade, $53.00 for the second grade, $45.00 for the third grade, $45.00 for the fourth grade, $37.00 for the fifth grade, $35.00 for the sixth grade, and $30.00 for the seventh grade. Of the total authorized number of enlisted men, those in the first grade shall not exceed 0.6 per centum, those in the second grade 1.8 per centum, those in the third grade 2 per centum, those in the fourth grade 9.5 per centum, those in the fifth grade 9.5 per centum, those in the sixth grade 25 per centum. . . .

Existing laws providing for continuous service pay are repealed to take effect 1 July 1920, and thereafter enlisted men shall receive an increase of 10 per centum of their base pay for each five years of service in the Army, or service which by existing law is held to be the equivalent of Army service, such increases not to exceed 40 per centum.

Under such regulations as the Secretary of War may prescribe, enlisted men of the sixth and seventh grades may be rated as specialists, and receive extra pay therefore per month, as follows: First class, $25; second class, $20; third class, $15; fourth class, $12; fifth class, $8; sixth class, $3. Of the total authorized number of enlisted men in the sixth and seventh grades, those rated as specialists of the first class shall not exceed 0.7 per centum; of the second class, 1.4 per centum; of the third class, 1.9 per centum; of the fourth class, 4.7 per centum; of the fifth class, 5 per centum; of the sixth class, 15.2 per centum.

UNITED STATES PATENT OFFICE.

FRANCIS S. JOHNSTON, OF PHILADELPHIA, PENNSYLVANIA, ASSIGNOR TO GEORGE SPENCER JONES, OF SAME PLACE.

IMPROVEMENT IN CHEVRONS.

Specification forming part of Letters Patent No. **135,124**, dated January 21, 1873.

To all whom it may concern:

Be it known that I, FRANCIS S. JOHNSTON, of Philadelphia, in the county of Philadelphia and State of Pennsylvania, have invented a new and valuable Improvement in Chevrons and method of making the same; and I do hereby declare that the following is a full, clear, and exact description of the construction and operation of the same, reference being had to the annexed drawing, making a part of this specification, and to the letters and figures of reference marked thereon.

Figure 1 of the drawing represents a corporal's chevron. Fig. 2 indicates a sergeant's chevron; Fig. 3, a sergeant-major's chevron; Fig. 4, a quartermaster-sergeant's chevron; Fig. 5, an ordnance-sergeant's chevron. Fig. 6 shows the back of an ordnance-sergeant's chevron. Fig. 7 shows a hospital-steward's chevron; Fig. 8, a service-stripe; Fig. 9, a common stripe; Fig 10, an orderly-sergeant's chevron; Fig. 11, a piece of cloth from which the curved top pieces are cut, as indicated in dotted lines; Fig. 12, a piece of cloth from which the chevrons are cut; Fig. 13, a piece of cloth from which the straight top pieces are cut.

My invention has reference to the uniform of soldiers, and particularly to the insignia of rank worn by non-commissioned officers. It consists in an improved method of making and attaching the chevron, combining at once greater elegance of appearance, cheapness, and durability.

Heretofore chevrons were made and attached substantially in the following manner: The stripes or other device upon the arm were made of silk or worsted braid, which was sewed to a piece of cloth, which in turn was sewed to the cloth or material composing the coat or blouse; and besides the broad stripe, which formed the usual basis of the design, a second narrow strip of different color was laid on. The essential idea of this method is the sewing on of braid, and its defects are many.

In the first place, the expense was great when compared with that of my improvement. The first cost of the braid alone was heavy, and also the outlay for the piece of cloth on which it was sewed. It was also an expensive matter to have the braid sewed into the device desired. Then, too, it was found very difficult, if not wholly impossible, to have the work neatly done. Where the design, for instance, was composed in part of a star, which, to look well, must be sharp at all its points and symmetrical throughout, an artistic piece of work could never be obtained; and even when the execution was as good as the faulty method permitted, the result was not admirable. Braid is never rich-looking as compared with cloth, owing to the coarseness of texture of the former.

My improvement obviates these several defects, and commends itself at once on the score of greater beauty, cheapness, and durability.

Instead of employing braid, which has to be sewed upon the piece of cloth, as already described, for attachment to arm of the coat to form the chevron, I use cloth, which is cut by any suitable means, to form the basis of the design required, using also a thread, run preferably by machine, for the purpose of indicating a division-line, as hereinafter fully described.

In the drawing, Fig. 12 represents a piece of cloth of any necessary length and of suitable width. The dotted lines represent the manner in which it is cut in V-shaped pieces, whereby all the material except the fragments at each end of the piece is directly utilized without any waste whatever. Fig. 1 shows a chevron, *a*, composed of the V-shaped strip of cloth with a line or lines, *b*, as required, made by a machine-stitch, using by preference silk thread for that purpose. In Figs. 3 and 4 are shown chevrons worn by officers of different grades. These are made with a V-shaped portion similar to that of Fig. 1, and an upper cross-piece, straight, as shown at *c* in Fig. 3, and curved, as at *d* in Fig. 4. The upper strip *c* may be cut straight from the cloth, incurring no waste whatever, while the strip *d* is a portion of a circle or ring cut from the cloth, in manner similar to that shown in Fig. 13.

Fig. 5 shows a chevron worn by an ordnance-sergeant, which is made in the following manner: I first take a piece of cloth, which forms the basis, and this I cut into the shape shown at *e*, having its lower portion V-shaped, and above this parallel sides and a curved top. At the point indicated at *f* I cut out a star-shaped portion, and back of this I

Figure 9A-1. Shown here is a photograph of the initial page of the patent document. The text is given in full, as are all illustrations that accompanied the original document.

UNITED STATES
PATENT OFFICE

FRANCIS S. JOHNSTON, OF PHILADELPHIA, PENNSYLVANIA, ASSIGNOR TO GEORGE SPENCER JONES, OF SAME PLACE.

IMPROVEMENT IN CHEVRONS.

Specification forming part of Letters Patent No. **135,124,** dated January 21, 1873:

To all whom it may concern:

Be it known that I, FRANCIS S. JOHNSTON, of Philadelphia, in the county of Philadelphia and State of Pennsylvania, have invented a new and valuable Improvement in Chevrons and method of making the same; and I do hereby declare that the following is a full, clear, and exact description of the construction and operation of the same, reference being had to the annexed drawing, making a part of this specification, and to the letters and figures of reference marked thereon.

Figure 1 of the drawing represents a corporal's chevron. Fig. 2 indicates a sergeant's chevron; Fig. 3, a sergeant-major's chevron; Fig. 4, a quartermaster-sergeant's chevron; Fig. 5, an ordnance-sergeant's chevron. Fig. 6 shows the back of an ordnance-sergeant's chevron. Fig. 7 shows a hospital-steward's chevron; Fig. 8, a service-stripe; Fig. 9, a common stripe; Fig. 10, an orderly-sergeant's chevron; Fig. 11, a piece of cloth from which the curved top pieces are cut, as indicated in dotted lines; Fig. 12, a piece of cloth from which the chevrons are cut; Fig. 13, a piece of cloth from which the straight top pieces are cut.

My invention has reference to the uniform of soldiers, and particularly to the insignia of rank worn by non-commissioned officers. It consists in an improved method of making and attaching the chevron, combining at once greater elegance of appearance, cheapness, and durability.

Heretofore chevrons were made and attached substantially in the following manner: The stripes or other device upon the arm were made of silk or worsted braid, which was sewed to a piece of cloth, which in turn was sewed to the cloth or material composing the coat or blouse; and besides the broad stripe, which formed the usual basis of the design, a second narrow strip of different color was laid on. The essential idea of this method is the sewing on of braid, and its defects are many.

In the first place, the expense was great when compared with that of my improvement. The first cost of the braid alone was heavy, and also the outlay for the piece of cloth on which it was sewed. It was also an expensive matter to have the braid sewed into the device desired. Then, too, it was found very difficult, if not wholly impossible, to have the work neatly done. Where the design, for instance, was composed in part of a star, which, to look well, must be sharp at all its points and symmetrical throughout, an artistic piece of work could never be obtained; and even when the execution was as good as the faulty method permitted, the result was not admirable. Braid is never rich-looking as compared with cloth, owing to the coarseness of texture of the former.

My improvement obviates these several defects, and commends itself at once on the score of greater beauty, cheapness, and durability.

Instead of employing braid, which has to be sewed upon the piece of cloth, as already described, for attachment to arm of the coat to form the chevron, I use cloth, which is cut by any suitable means, to form the basis of the design required, using also a thread, run preferably by machine, for the purpose of indicating a division-line, as hereinafter fully described.

In the drawing, Fig. 12 represents a piece of cloth of any necessary length and of suitable width. The dotted lines represent the manner in which it is cut in V-shaped pieces, whereby all the material except the fragments at each end of the piece is directly utilized without any waste whatever. Fig. 1 shows a chevron, a, composed of the V-shaped strip of cloth with a line or lines, b, as required, made by a machine-stitch, using by preference silk thread for that purpose. In Figs. 3 and 4 are shown chevrons worn by officers of different grades. These are made with a V-shaped portion similar to that of Fig. 1, and an upper cross-piece, straight, as shown at e in Fig. 3, and curved, as at d in Fig. 4. The upper strip e may be cut straight from the cloth, incurring no waste whatever, while the strip d in a portion of a circle or ring cut from the cloth, in manner similar to that shown in Fig. 13.

Fig. 5 shows a chevron worn by an ordnance-sergeant, which is made in the following manner: I first take a piece of cloth, which forms the basis, and this I cut into the shape shown at e, having its lower portion V-shaped, and above this parallel sides and a curved top. At the point indicated at f I cut out a star-shaped portion, and back of this I stitch a piece of blue cloth, made by preference in the shape of a star, and of larger dimensions than the opening. I then take another piece of blue cloth, shown at g, which I cut in the manner plainly indicated in the drawing—namely, with its lower portion V-shaped, having a curved upper portion and a large star cut in its center, permitting the cloth, which forms the basis of the chevron, with its central star backed with blue cloth, to show through. The piece of cloth which is cut from the outside, of blue, I use to form the backing of the smaller star cut in the basepiece, diminishing it somewhat, but yet leaving it larger than the small star opening in the base-piece. I also from the necessary lines b by means of the stitch, as already described. The lower stitch b, when formed, may be some distance—say a quarter of an inch—from the edge of the cloth. To make it form an edging, I cut a straight slit in the base cloth extending from the apex of the same to the apex of the V formed by the lower line of the stitching *b*, and turn down the edge, uniting it by sewing at the apex and at the other extremities.

The chevron worn by a hospital-steward is shown at Fig. 7. The former method of constructing this was as follows: A piece of blue cloth of the requisite dimensions—say eight inches in length and two in breadth—was first taken. Upon this was laid a piece of green cloth of the same length, but about half an inch narrower, so as to leave a border or margin of blue cloth a quarter of an inch wide on each side. Upon this piece of green cloth was worked with yellow silk or floss a caduceus of the same pattern as that shown in the drawing, and upon the blue-cloth border a fancy stitch was made with the same thread. This was a cumbrous, costly, and roundabout manner of producing a design which by my method is produced with ease and elegance and at slight expense. In the first place, the piece of blue cloth, which was a heavy expense, was unnecessary, and gave a bulky appearance to that which was intended to be ornamental; the needle-work upon the caduceus and stripe was difficult of execution; and, lastly, the floss came off and adhered to other portions of the coat. According to my improvement this chevron is made of a single piece of green cloth; the caduceus is cut out by a knife made for the work, and the opening is backed with a piece of yellow cloth, a stripe or line being also run with yellow thread near the edge of the green cloth, in the manner already described.

Fig. 10 shows a chevron of the pattern allowed first sergeants, which is made in the same way as that described in Fig. 5, the design being varied by substituting a diamond for the star, and by making the top straight instead of rounded.

Fig. 8 shows the "service" stripe, which heretofore was made in the following manner: A piece of blue cloth of, say, the following dimensions was taken, namely, about eight inches in length and two inches in breadth. Upon this was laid a piece of braid about half an inch wide and of the same length as the cloth to which it was sewed, leaving a margin of cloth on each side—say three-quarters of an inch in width. On each margin, and about an eighth of an inch distant from the braid already mentioned, was sewed a strip of narrow braid of color adapted to the particular branch of the service. Instead of this method I take simply a piece of blue cloth, of the dimensions mentioned—say eight inches by two—and upon this I run, in the manner already described, two lines of stitching, distant about half an inch from each other, and using different-colored thread, according to the branch of the service for which the chevron is intended—yellow for cavalry, red for artillery, &c.

It will thus be seen that I effect a great saving in cloth, diminish the expense of making, and obtain a far more durable and ornamental chevron than that made in the former style. I

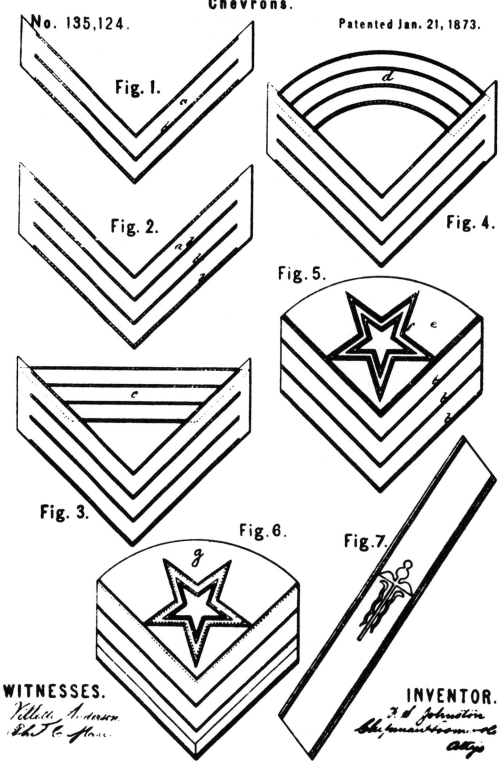

F. S. JOHNSTON.
Chevrons.

2 Sheets--Sheet 1.

No. 135,124.

Patented Jan. 21, 1873.

Fig. 1.

Fig. 2.

Fig. 4.

Fig. 5.

Fig. 3.

Fig. 6.

Fig. 7.

WITNESSES.

INVENTOR.

F. S. JOHNSTON.
Chevrons.

No. 135,124.

Patented Jan. 21, 1873.

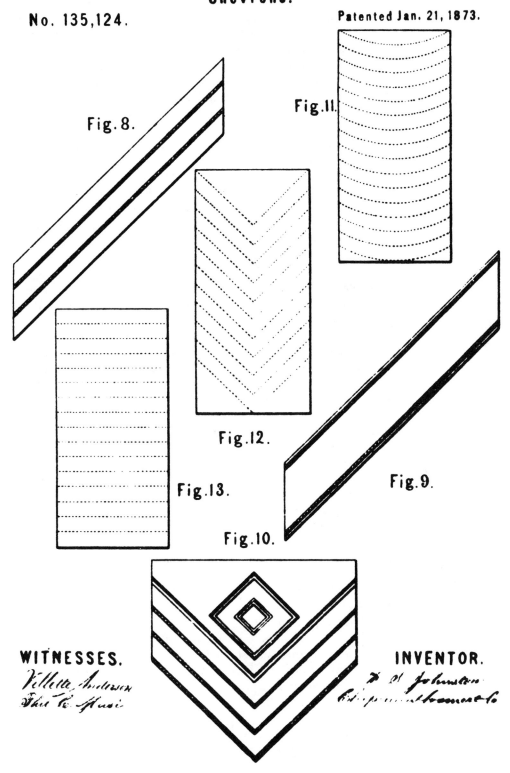

Fig. 8.

Fig. 11.

Fig. 12.

Fig. 13.

Fig. 9.

Fig. 10.

WITNESSES.

INVENTOR.

use less base cloth, as by my method of cutting (as is best illustrated in the V-shaped portions) the central portion of the base cloth, which was retained under the old method, is cut out and utilized or forms part of a second chevron. Then I dispense wholly with the costly and cumbrous system of braiding, one of the defects of which was that it was often difficult to match the braid with the trimming of the coat designed to be of the same shade and color. According to my method the trimmings and chevrons may be cut from the same piece of goods, thus obtaining exact uniformity. Another advantage of my method is as follows: In case of promotion—say from corporal to sergeant— a new chevron is furnished the officer thus advanced. This chevron is substituted for the old one, which is removed to make place for the new. Now, under the old method the stripes were sewed onto a piece of blue cloth, which, being new, showed to disadvantage on an old coat; but according to my method a sergeant, for instance, is supplied with a chevron which is made of cloth of a single color—as, for instance, yellow in the cavalry arm. This, when sewed directly to the arm of the coat or blouse, offers no disagreeable contrast of old and new blue cloth.

It will, of course, be understood that the color of the materials employed will be varied according to the branch of the service in which the chevron is used—light blue for infantry, yellow for cavalry, red for artillery, and Solferino for ordnance. The chevrons of corporals and sergeants require, therefore, only one color of cloth, the stripes being indicated by black thread, as already described, as is also the case with quartermaster-sergeants and sergeants-major. First sergeants and ordnance-sergeants, having, respectively, a diamond and a star, require also blue cloth, (dark,) which is cut and attached to the striped portion, as already described. Hospital-stewards wear green cloth, the caduceus being backed by the color appropriate to their branch, the thread forming the stripe being of the same color.

The chevrons may, if desired, be made with raw edges; but I prefer to make them bound, the method being that already described in reference to the chevron of ordnance sergeant.

What I claim as my invention, and desire to secure by Letters Patent, is—

The improved article of manufacture herein described, consisting of a chevron cut from cloth in any desired pattern, with stitched lines, as set forth.

In testimony that I claim the above I have hereunto subscribed my name in the presence of two witnesses.

FRANCIS S. JOHNSTON.

Witnesses:
WILLIAM H. LEE,
M. DANL. CONNOLLY.

NOTES AND ABBREVIATIONS

Abbreviations

AG	Adjutant General
AGO	Adjutant General's Office
ANR	*Army Navy Register*
AR	Army Regulation
A. RPT.	Annual Report
C	Change Number
CIRC	Circular
C/S	Chief of Staff
DA	Department of the Army
GO	General Order
GPO	Government Printing Office
HQA	Headquarters of the Army
LR	Letters Received File, National Archives Records
LS	Letters Sent File, National Archives Records
OCMH	Office of the Chief of Military History, U.S. Army
QMC	Quartermaster General
RG	Record Group, National Archives Records
SEC. WAR	Secretary of War
SPC	Clothing and Equipage Specification
SR	Special Regulations
TAG	The Adjutant General
TIOH	The Institute of Heraldry
UR	Uniform Regulations
U. SPC.	Uniform Specifications
WD	War Department

Chapter 2

1. Archives de la Sabretache, Paris, serie EE; Archives des Colonies, serie A, vol. 17, nos. 2 and 15; Archives des Colonies, serie A, vol. 11, no. 41; Archives de la Marine, serie A1, vol. 110, no. 38.
2. *Order of the King*, 8 August 1775. / Letter from Rene Chartrand, Canadian Parks and Sites Branch, to author, January 1981.
3. Dawnay, N. P., *The Badges of Warrant and Non-Commissioned Rank in the British Army*, The Society for Army Historical Research, Gale & Polden Ltd., London and Aldershot, 1949. / Lefferts, Charles M., *Uniforms of the American, British, French, and German Armies in the War of the American Revolution*, edited by Alexander Wall, WE Inc., Old Greenwich, Conn., n.d.
4. Conversation with Mr. Detmar Finke, OCMH: this letter from Winfield Scott to C. Irvine, 31 January 1815, was used in the preparation of an OCMH study on the enlisted rank structure. The letter has since been lost. The author located a letter to the Quartermaster General from the Baltimore Board, dated 16 February, 1815, discussing sample artillery coats with chevrons for sergeants and corporals.
5. USMA Archives, Post Order Book, Battalion Orders of 28 September 1817; Battalion Orders, 4 November 1818. / Todd, Frederick, P., *Cadet Gray*, Bonanza Books, New York, 1955, p. 110.
6. Peterson, Mendel L., "American Epaulettes 1775–1820," *Military Collector & Historian*, vol. II, no. 2, and "American Army Epaulettes 1814–1872," *Military Collector & Historian*, vol. III, no. 1.
7. RG 94, "General and Special Orders, Adjutants' and Inspector Generals' Office," vol. 2 (no. 4), p. 249.
8. *General Regulations for the Army*, WD, printed by M. Carey and Sons, Philadelphia, 1821, Article 65.
9. RG 94, Cox-Irvine LR, box 85, letter of 3 April 1829, from John Brown to Irvine.
10. *General Regulations for the Army*, 1821, and *General Regulations for the Army*, 1825, Article 65, paras. 837–48.
11. Ibid.
12. RG 94, box 85; *see above*, note 9.
13. GO 38, AGO, 2 May 1833. / RG 92, Irvine LR, Box 51, Clothing Estimates, 7 Dec. 1833.
14. RG 94, Register of LR, Office of C & E, file Q1409, 30 May 1848, and letter from Jessup to Col. Stanton, 30 May 1848. / Also see *Military Collector and Historian*, vol. V, no. 1, March 1953, p. 18, "Duncan's Light Battery, Company A, 2nd U.S. Artillery, 1847" by Colonel Harry Larter, for additional information and notes on Horse and Light Artillery uniforms.
15. GO 18, AGO, 4 June 1846.
16. *General Regulations* (see note 18, *below*), p. 212; also *Regulations* (note 20, *below*).
17. GO 18, AGO, 4 June 1846.
18. *General Regulations for the Army of the United States*, War Department, Washington, 1847, pp. 186–215.
19. A. Rpt. AG, 1849, Display A: "Organization of the Army of the United States, 1849."
20. *Regulations for the Uniform and Dress of the Army of the United States, June 1851*, Philadelphia, William Horstmann and Sons, 1851.
21. RG 92, Uniform Board Proceeding, 22 January 1851.
22. RG 94, 12-U-1851, 28 April 1851.
23. Heitman, Francis B., *Historical Register and Dictionary of the United States Army*, vol. 1, Washington: GPO, 1903, p. 395.
24. RG 94, LR, E-36-1851, 2 May 1851.

25. WD, *Regulations for the Army of the United States, 1861*, New York, Harper & Brother, pp. 439–440 (para. 1400).
26. RG 94, LR, 12-U-1851; RG 94, LR, E-36-1851.
27. GO 4, AGO, 26 March 1855.
28. GO 55, AGO, 10 August 1861.
29. Rodenbough, Theodore E., *From Everglade to Canon*, New York, Van Nostrand, 1875, pp. 237–38.
30. Heitman, Francis B., *Historical Register and Dictionary of the United States Army*, vol. 2, Washington: GPO, 1903, pp. 600–601, 604–605. / *Uniform Regulations for the Army of the United States 1861*, Smithsonian Institution, Washington, 1961, pp. 19, 20, 57. It is now known these photographs were taken in 1867.
31. A. Rpt. QMG, 1868, 1871 price lists, show each type of chevron by branch. No chevrons are listed for engineer troops. It must be assumed, however, cavalry chevrons were issued.
32. LS June 1864 to May 1865, Office of the Signal Officer of the Army, vol. 3, pp. 114–15. Additional material in this paragraph of text is referenced to pp. 161–62.
33. Myer Papers, Signal Corps Museum: *Legislation and Orders . . . 1860 to 1873*, p. 20. / LR, XX, Office Chief Signal Officer, 28 September 1868, no. 47.
34. A. Rpt. QMG, 1868, p. 82.
35. RG 92, "Uniforms" file, April and June 1867. / A. Rpt. QMG, 1868, pp. 81–82.
36. A. Rpt. QMG, 1868, 1871.
37. GO 92, AGO, 22 July 1879. / A. Rpt. QMG, 1871, 1872.
38. John Paterson, colonel of a Massachusetts regiment, April to December 1775; colonel 15th Continental Infantry, 1 January 1776; brigadier general Continental Army, 21 February 1777 to close of war; brevet major general, 30 September 1783; died 1808. See Heitman, op. cit., vol. 1, p. 773.
39. *Uniforms of the Army of the United States Illustrated 1774–1889*, published by QMG, n.d. This book contains the uniform plates by Henry A. Odgen, in addition to historical uniform orders. / Quoted portions of the 1782 order that follow in the text are also from this source.
40. GO 50, AGO, 11 June 1832, p. 27.
41. *General Regulations for the Army*, 1847, p. 211.
42. Instituted by GO 2, AGO, 13 February 1850. Revoked by GO 25, AGO, 23 August 1850.
43. UR 1851, 1857, 1861.

Chapter 3

1. GO 92, 26 October 1872. / A. Rpt. QMG, 1873, p. 24.
2. Surgeon General CIRC No. 8, 1875, p. 1.
3. GO 92, AGO, 26 October 1872.
4. SPC 131, 5 March 1885.
5. A. Rpt. QMG, 1912, p. 18.
6. ANR, 2 July 1898, vol. 24, p. 11. GO 39, 51, and 112, HQA, 1898.
7. A. Rpt. QMG, 1900, p. 101.
8. LR 240, 1883, Office QMG, 5 March 1883.
9. RG 92, various letters and memos, Office QMG and Philadelphia Depot.
10. RG 92, Consolidated Correspondence Files 209 and 211, "Chevrons." / GO 107, AGO 12 September 1884.
11. A. Rpt. Sec. War, 1886, p. 332.
12. A. Rpt. Sec. War, 1887, p. 512, and 1888, p. 522.
13. CIRC 26, WD, 25 July 1898.
14. RG 92, Letters and Endorsements no. 112724, March–July 1900.

15. Ibid., 11th Endorsement, 18 July 1900, by the QMG. / Letter 163446, from the QMG to TAG, 15 March 1901.
16. Ibid. / RG 92, Bimonthly Philadelphia Inventories, no. 153403, 1900, 1901.
17. Virtually all photographs examined of actual specialists wearing these chevrons show that the excess material was trimmed, as shown with Design No. 135. / On the identification of the gunnery expert mentioned in the text paragraph below, under the heading Other Devices, *see* GO 41, AGO, 4 September 1896, Section VIII.
18. A. Rpt. QMG, p. 214.
19. UR 1872, p. 18.
20. GO 18, HQA, 16 February 1889.
21. GO 74, HQA, 20 August 1891, pp. 2–3.
22. GO 81, HQA, 17 July 1902, paras. 62, 78.
23. GO 21, AGO, 20 March 1876.
24. A. Rpt. QMG, 1883, pp. 56–57. / GO 92, AGO, 9 August 1882.
25. GO 2, AGO, 6 January 1900, para. II.
26. GO 168, AGO, 14 September 1899.
27. Photocopy of handwritten letter from Lt. Casey to the Secretary of War, dated 30 June 1890, on file at TIOH.
28. RG 92, Bimonthly Philadelphia Inventories, no. 153403, 1900, 1901.
29. GO 126, AGO, 4 October 1900.
30. Samples of 1872–1876 chevrons are held in the national collections at the Smithsonian Institution.
31. A. Rpt. QMG, 1901, p. 69.
32. SPC 126, 28 January 1885. / GO 56, AGO, 11 August 1887. / SPC 196 and 197, 27 January 1888.
33. A. Rpt. Sec. War, 1896, p. 403.
34. A. Rpt. QMG, 1901, p. 68.
35. GO 15, AGO, 13 February 1901, GO 56, AGO, 17 June 1902.
36. A. Rpt. AG, 1872, General Returns of Actual Strengths.
37. A. Rpt. AG, 1902, General Returns of Actual Strengths.
38. GO 144, AGO, 7 November 1901. / GO 28, AGO, 12 March 1903. / GO 62, AGO, 28 April 1903.
39. Army Organization Act of 2 February 1901.
40. RG 92, Clothing Reports no. 153403, for 1900 and 1901.
41. W. A. Raymold Catalogue No. 302, April 1899, pp. 38–39.
42. UR 1872, 1881, 1886, 1898, 1902.
43. Photocopy of unnumbered brief, AGO, December 1882, on file at TIOH.
44. RG 94, Brief no. 1154, AGO 1883, dated 12 April 1883.
45. GO 103, AGO, 29 November 1879. / AR of 1881, para. 2746.
46. GO 107, AGO, 12 September 1884.
47. GO 45, AGO, October 17, 1896. / *Regulations and Decisions Pertaining to the Uniform of the Army*, 11 May 1897, 28.
48. GO 56, AGO, 6 June 1874.
49. GO 37, AGO, 13 August 1896.
50. GO 3, AGO, January 1897. / *Regulations and Decisions* (*see* note 47, above), p. 29.
51. GO 92, AGO, 9 August 1882.
52. Photocopy of unnumbered brief, AGO, December 1882, on file at TIOH. / GO 38, AGO, 6 June 1883.
53. GO 107, AGO, 12 September 1884. / *Uniform of the Army of the United States, as amended to up December 1886*, para. 2730. / GO 81, AGO, 17 July 1902, p. 28.
54. A. Rpt. Sec. War, 1885, pp. 223–24.
55. *Regulations for the Army of the United States*, Harper and Bros., New York, 1861, p. 1.

Chapter 4

1. RG 92, letter of 5 March 1883, letter from Asst. QMG, Philadelphia Depot, with 8 endorsements; clothing and equipage letter no. 553.
2. WD, AGO, CIRC No. 12, 4 June 1897.
3. WD, AGO, CIRC No. 11, 31 December 1898.

Chapter 5

1. RG 92, various letters, no. 163446, March–May 1901, and no. 178141, 1902.
2. RG 94, no. 423890, 16 July 1902. / ANR, 6 December 1902, p. 323. / Letter from Maj. Gen. Young to TAG, 24 December 1902, copy on file at TIOH.
3. RG 92, no. 178141 with endorsements, 28 July 1902, 4 August 1902, and 12 September 1902.
4. A. Rpt. QMG, 1903, p. 6.
5. A. Rpt. QMG, 1904, pp. 4–5. / GO 202, WD, 4 December 1905. / RG 94, no. 1263561, 26 July 1907; and GO 161, WD, 1 August 1907. / Memorandum Report to Acting C/S from First Division, G.S., no. 1055766, 25 November 1905.
6. RG 94, no. 1367424, 30 April 1908.
7. GO 117, WD, 15 June 1909. / A. Rpt. QMG, 1912, p. 18.
8. RG 92, no. 163446, 1 and 15 March 1901 and 27 May 1901. RG 94, no. 368585, 15 March 1901.
9. RG 92, no. 163446, 8 March 1901, Uniform Board minutes. / A. Rpt. QMG, 1901, p. 70.
10. GO 81, AGO, 17 July 1902, para. 78. / GO 197, WD, 31 December 1904, para. 89.
11. Letter to Asst. Sec. War from QMG, 15 June 1904, copy on file at TIOH.
12. Letter to QMG from TAG, 4 January 1904, copy on file at TIOH.
13. A. Rpt. QMG, 1904, p. 5.
14. RG 111, box 10, RB no. 4786, and others in this series.
15. GO 81, AGO, 17 July 1902, para. 99. / GO 132, AGO, 31 December 1902, para. 104. / GO 197, WD, 31 December 1904, para. 81. / GO 169, WD, 14 August 1907, para. 106. / Memo for Asst. Sec. War from Asst. C/S, 13 April 1908, copy on file at TIOH.
16. GO 197, WD, 31 December 1904.
17. Memo for Asst. Sec. War from Asst. C/S, 29 April 1907, copy on file at TIOH.
18. RG 92, no. 234560, 4 April 1908.
19. GO 140, WD, 25 June 1907.
20. CIRC 27, WD, 7 April 1908.
21. C5, UR 1912, 12 March 1914.
22. RG 92, no. 234560, 23 July 1908.
23. GO 221, WD, 4 November 1909. / RG 92, no. 234560, 13 January 1910.
24. Annual price lists, 1911–1916.
25. C2, UR 1912, 13 March 1913.
16. Letter from CO, 1st Aero Squadron to TAG, 9 July 1914, with 16 Endorsements; O.C.S.O. no. 35787; AGO no. 2186669.
27. Minutes of the Uniform Board, 2 March 1916, copy on file at TIOH.
28. GO 63, WD, 15 May 1917. / GO 86, WD, 3 July 1919.
29. Memo for TAG from Asst. C/S, 7 June 1918, on file at TIOH.
30. Memo, Office C/S, 8859–29, 19 April 1918.
31. Two different War Plans Division Memos, both 8647–106, 25 April 1918.
32. Memo for C/S, Equipment Branch, no. 6136, 9 August 1919, on file at TIOH. / Memo to Director of Purchases from Chief, Clothing and Equipage Division, 13 August 1919, on file at TIOH.
33. Letter from Clothing & Equipage Division to C/S Equipment Branch, 28 August 1919, with incls. on file at TIOH.

34. Memo to Director of Purchases from Chief, Clothing and Equipage Division, 13 August 1919, on file at TIOH.
35. Memo for QMG from Purchase, Storage, and Traffic Division, 30 August 1919, on file at TIOH.
36. Letter from Clothing and Equipage Division to Zone Supply Officer, Philadelphia, 29 November 1919, on file at TIOH.
37. A sealed sample book of this type is in the possession of the author.
38. Memo for TAG; with comments, 15 June 1920, copy on file at TIOH. / Memo for the C/S from Chief, Equipage Branch, 30 July 1920, on file at TIOH.
39. WD drawing CE 15, 27 March 1920.
40. A. Rpt. QMG, 1903, pp. 5–6 / Marginal notes, Bimonthly Inventories, Philadelphia RG 92, no. 153403.
41. Letter from Asst. Sec. War to QMG, 23 June 1904, copy on file at TIOH. / GO 122, WD, 13 July 1904. / Annual price lists, 1911–1916.
42. GO 60, WD, 10 December 1903.
43. GO 15, WD, 18 January 1908.
44. GO 11, WD, 22 January 1909.
45. C6, U. Spc. 1915, 12 October 1916.
46. Examples include band musicians of various grades, established by C1, SR42, 31 December 1917, and chauffeur grades established by C4, SR42, May 1918.
47. RG 92, no. 234560, 23 July 1908.
48. Letter from Asst. Surgeon Reynolds to Surgeon General, 14 June 1902, with endorsements to TAG, on file at TIOH.
49. RG 92, endorsement on no. 178141, 28 July 1902.
50. GO 132, AGO, 31 December 1902.
51. RG 92, no. 178141, 28 July 1902, 12 September 1902.
52. GO 118, WD 15 June 1909. / Memo for Asst. Sec. War from Acting C/S, 9 August 1909, copy on file at TIOH. / Ibid., 3 September 1909. / GO 39, WD, 10 March 1910.
53. See above, notes 50 and 52 as regards documentation for 9 August and 3 September 1909. / GO 169, WD, 14 August 1907.
54. See above, note 52 as regards documentation for 1909.
55. See above, note 32 as regards documentation for 9 August 1919.
56. Uniforms of the United States Army, plates by Henry A. Ogden, text by Marvin Pakula; Thomas Yoseleff, New York, 1960, Introduction.
57. Sealed samples, May 1920, are in the author's collection.
58. Various interoffice memos in RG 92 reflect this practice.
59. These photos are in RG 111, RB 4786, box 10; RG 111, RB 4706, box 8; and additionally in RG 111.
60. GO 66, AGO, 13 May 1911.
61. GO 24, WD, 2 February 1907.
62. ANR, 7 December 1907, p. 10. / No. 3670/53d O.C.A., 6 January 1908, copy on file at TIOH.
63. GO 15, WD, 18 January 1908.
64. GO 125, WD, 25 June 1909.
65. GO 40, WD, 25 October 1912.
66. 4th Indorsement, J.A.G.O. to QMG, 25 August 1916, to letter 421.6-113-CE (Genl.), QMG to TAG, 3 July 1916.
67. GO 169, WD, 14 August 1907, para. 90.
68. CIRC 83, WD, 29 November 1907.
69. GO 109, WD, 13 June 1910.
70. GO 109, WD, 13 June 1910. / General Staff Report no. 3868, 31 March 1909, copy on file at TIOH.
71. CIRC 206, WD, 7 June 1920.
72. Memo for C/S from Chief, Equipage Branch, 30 July 1919, on file at TIOH.
73. A. Rpt. Sec. War, 1907, p. 111. / GO 24, WD, 2 February 1907.

Chapter 7

1. Memo for TAG from B. Gen. Henry Jervey, 15 June 1920, with 8 added comments, subject: rank insignia for noncommissioned officers, copy on file at TIOH.
2. CIRC 72, WD, 16 March 1921.
3. Minutes of the QM Technical Committee, 4 August 1933, copy on file at TIOH. / Minutes of the QM Technical Committee, 13 December 1935, copy on file at TIOH. / 4th Ind. for AGO to QMG, 11 January 1936, to letter dated 30 July 1935, copy on file at TIOH.
4. CIRC 72, WD, 16 March 1921, para. 9b.
5. Letter from TAG to QMG, subject: Insignia of grades for enlisted men, 15 January 1921, with indorsements and cited correspondence on file at TIOH. / Memo #2329 for QMG from Asst. C/S, 12 February 1921.
6. Memo no. 2329, *see above*, note 5.
7. *Hearing Before Subcommittee of House Committee on Appropriations . . . for 1922*, pp. 716–18.
8. 1st Ind., Minutes . . . 4 August 1933; *see above*, note 3.
9. Letter dated 15 January 1921; *see above*, note 5.
10. CIRC 72, WD, 16 March 1921, para. 9b.
11. *Hearings Before Subcommittee of House Committee on Appropriations . . . for 1923*, pp. 429–30.
12. Minutes . . . 13 December 1935; *see above*, note 3.
13. Minutes . . . 13 December 1935; *see above*, note 3. 4th Ind. for AGO to QMG, 11 January 1936; *see note 3, above*.
14. Dusenbury & Schab Inc., Catalog, copyright dated 1925.
15. 3d Ind. from QMG to TAG, 27 June 1936, on file at TIOH.
16. CIRC 5, WD, 26 January 1929. / AR 30-3000, 1 July 1937.
17. Samples are in the national collections at the Smithsonian Institution.
18. C3, AR 600-35, 22 November 1942.
19. CIRC 264, WD, 19 December 1941.
20. DF from Deputy, Mil. Pers. Svc. GP to QMG, subject: Reduction of size of sleeve insignia and badges, 5 September 1946, copy on file Mil. Hist. Research Collection. / CIRC 202, DA, 7 July 1948.
21. Military Specification MIL-I-3477, 25 April 1951. / 2d comment, DF from Chief, Mil. Pers. Mgmt. GP, to QMG, subject: Insignia, 11 May 1948, copy on file Mil. Hist. Research Collection.
22. *Army Information Digest*, August 1948, p. 24. / CIRC 202, DA, 7 July 1948.
23. Samples on file at TIOH. / *Army Information Digest*, July 1948, pp. 70–71.
24. SR 600-60-1, 26 October 1951, para. 7.
25. *Army*, April 1965, pp. 28–30.
26. DA message no. 865848, 28 May 1968.
27. *Army Information Digest*, May 1966, p. 34.
28. *Army Information Digest*, April 1965, pp. 40–41. / *Army Information Digest*, September 1965, p. 2.
29. DA message no. 856258, 21 March 1968.
30. DA message no. 865848, 28 May 1968.
31. *Army Information Digest*, August 1954, pp. 8–16. / AR 615-15, 2 July 1954. / C1 AR 615-15, 26 April 1955.
32. Samples of chevrons sealed 27 June 1958 and 16 June 1959 are on file at TIOH.
33. AR 670-5, September 1959, p. 79.
34. *See above*, note 32.
35. C1 SR 600-32-10, 7 August 1953.
36. AR 670-5, September 1959.
37. DF from C.O., TIOH to TAG, subject: Comments on the insignia of the Sergeant Major of the Army, AGAH-C, dated 20 July 1966.
38. AR 670-1, 15 February 1975.

39. DA message no. 292128Z, December 1967.

40. AR 670-1, 1 November 1981, para. 4-10, fig. 4-6. / DA message no. 060100Z, January 1981, subject: Arcost Uniform Issues, from Army Uniform Board (DAPE-HRL-U).

40a. Erna Risch, *A Wardrobe for the Women in the Army: QMC Hospital Studies 12*, October 1945, pp. 56–57. / Memo for QMG from Director of Plans and Operations, ASF, subject: Insignia, sleeve, chevron for WAC Hospital dress, 2 June 1945, copy on file Mil. Hist. Research Collection. / AR 600-39, 4 August 1944, para. 10b.

41. *Army Information Digest*, October 1965, p. 52. / SR 600-37-2, 17 July 1951.

42. SR 600-37-2, 17 July 1951.

43. C7, SR 600-37-2, 13 July 1957.

44. AR 670-32, 29 January 1960, p. 4. / Intra Office Reference Sheet, from Heraldry Branch to C & TM Division, subject: Insignia of Service, WAC: 24 October 1958, with one additional comment.

45. Samples sealed 3 June 1968 under 29 December 1967 authority are on file at TIOH. / AR 670-5, 8 January 1971, para. 14-10, c.

46. *Army Times*, 22 August 1973, p. 1.

47. DA message no. 212019, February 1975.

48. Letter from Secretary, Army Uniform Board, to author, 22 August 1973, with samples of cloth collar insignia. / DA message no. 241315Z February 1975, subject: Subdued insignia.

49. Assorted invoices on file at USMA Band. / Conversations and letters between USMA Band and members USMA Band and author, 1970–1971.

50. Letter, subject: Distinctive Specialist Chevrons for USMA Band, from HQ USMA to QMG, 21 June 1955, with attached memo, copy on file at TIOH.

51. *Military Collector & Historian*, fall 1972, p. 93.

52. Conversation with Master Sergeant Charles Kline, former Supply Sergeant of the Army Band.

53. *Military Collector & Historian*, fall 1972, p. 90.

54. Samples sealed 15 December 1967 are on file at TIOH and were first worn at the 1968 Inauguration.

55. *Recruiting News*, 15 June 1936, back cover.

56. Memorandum for the C/S, 17 April 1920, file "Equip. 7642," on file at TIOH.

57. CIRC 206, WD, 4 June 1920.

58. Memo for TAG from Director, OPNS DIV, G.S., subject: Service stripes for enlisted men, 30 November 1920. / CIRC 408, WD, 14 December 1920.

59. OQMG Drawing A-11-5, 18 November 1958.

60. AR 670-5, September 1959, para. 36b (5).

61. SR 600-37-2, 17 July 1951. / AR 670-32, 29 January 1960.

Chapter 8

1. "The US Army Artillery Badges," *The Medal Collector*, October 1972, pp. 4-29.

2. ANR, 7 December 1907, p. 10. / GO 15, WD, 18 January 1908.

3. GO 89, WD, 22 May 1908. / *Regulations for the Uniform of the United States*, 26 December 1911, para. 84e.

4. CIRC 103, WD, 23 May 1941.

5. C9, AR600-35, 24 November 1947.

6. Memorandum for the C/S, subject: Insignia for marksmanship qualifications, from chairman, Equipment Branch, 16 April 1918, on file at TIOH.

7. GO 41, WD, 24 April 1918. / GO 106, WD, 28 August 1919.

8. *Regulations Governing the Uniform in the Army Mine Planter Service*, 14 January 1919.

9. *Regulations Prescribing Uniforms of the United States Army Transport Service*, 28 September 1899.
10. A. Rpt. QMG, 1901, p. 54.
11. Memo for QMG, subject: Uniforms for the ATS, from Chief, Equipment Branch, 13 August 1920, on file at TIOH.
12. *Regulations* . . . 28 September 1899 (note 9, *above*). / SPC 968, 10 June 1908.
13. AR 30-1180, 1 October 1930.
14. AR 30-3000, 1 July 1937. / *Insignia and Decorations of the US and Armed Forces*, National Geographic Society, 1 December 1944, p. 40.
15. CIRC 52, WD, 22 May 1940. / WD drawing 5-2-17, 21 June 1934. / WD Drawing 5-2-17, 15 May 1940. / WD Drawing 5-2-22, 21 May 1940. / Copies of these drawings on file Mil. Hist. Research Collection.
16. *Insignia and Decorations* (note 14, *above*), p. 81.
17. Series of interoffice memos and a memorandum for record, all dated in January 1943, between G-1 and A-1, on file Mil. Hist. Research Collection.

PHOTOGRAPH AND ILLUSTRATION CREDITS

Sources are listed below, with permission having been granted to the author for use in this volume. Prefixes used to abbreviate collection names are shown hereunder. All unattributed photographs are from the collection of the author, and all unattributed drawings were made by the author.

AC = Author's collection (attribution stated only when such objects are shown with other objects)

DAVA = Defense Audio-Visual Agency

KU = University of Kansas, Pennell Collection

LC = Library of Congress

NA = National Archives

SI = Smithsonian Institution

USA = United States Army

Chapter 1

Figure 1-1	NA 111-B-293
Figure 1-2	J. N. Jacobsen
Figure 1-3	William Christen
Figure 1-4	USA SC 130535
Figure 1-5	J. N. Jacobsen

Chapter 2

Figure 2-1	Courtesy of Richard W. Riley, Governor of South Carolina
Figure 2-7	SI 41684-10
Figure 2-11	LC B817-7296
Figure 2-12	J. N. Jacobsen
Figure 2-13	J. N. Jacobsen
Figure 2-14	SI 15
Figure 2-15	Drawn by Chester Yatsak
Figure 2-16	Drawn by Chester Yatsak
Figure 2-18	SI 55

Chapter 3

Figure 3-1	National Park Service
Figure 3-2	KU
Figure 3-3	KU 1762C
Figure 3-4	NA 92-UF-3-6-21
Figure 3-5	NA 92-UF-3-6-11
Figure 3-6	NA 77-F-131-26-6
Figure 3-10	NA 111 SC 98441
Figure 3-11	SI 40
Figure 3-12	Arizona Historical Society Library
Figure 3-14	NA 92-PS-2-8
Figure 3-16	SI 14
Figure 3-17	SI Library, W. A. Raymold Catalog No. 300, for 1897
Figure 3-19	SI 72-5172

INDEX

Computer-Generated Finding List to the Text, Illustrations, and Tables